THAT'S REVOLTING!

THAT'S REVOLTING! QUEER STRATEGIES FOR RESISTING ASSIMILATION

EDITED BY MATTILDA, AKA MATT BERNSTEIN SYCAMORE

Cover photograph by Chris Hammett

Book and cover design by Nick Stone

Published by Soft Skull Press
71 Bond Street, Brooklyn, NY 11217

Distributed by Publishers Group West
www.pgw.com | 800.788.3123

Printed in Canada

Library of Congress Cataloging-in-Publication Data

That's revolting! : queer strategies for resisting assimilation / edited by
Mattilda, aka Matt Bernstein Sycamore.
      p. cm.
  Includes bibliographical references.
  ISBN 1-932360-56-5 (alk. paper)
 1. Gay liberation movement—United States. 2. Gays—United States—Identity.
3. Assimilation (Sociology) I. Sycamore, Matt Bernstein.

HQ76.8.U5T47 2004
306.76'6'0973—dc22
                              2004019806

CONTENTS

CHILDREN, THE TRUCKS, CHAINMAIL, TIME, THE BORDER, SKIN PROBLEMS, THE FEDS, AND THE URBAN ECO-VILLAGE OF YOUR DREAMS

PISS, TRANSNATIONAL CAPITAL, LICE REMOVER, THE PIERS, MARY, STUFFED-UP TURKEYS, AND RICKI LAKE

For JoAnne (1974–1995)

For David Wojnarowicz (1955–1992)

BREAKING GLASS: AN INTRODUCTION

I've been lucky enough never to live with a TV in my "adult" life. Though I generally struggle to stay as far as possible from the little glowing box, occasionally there is something I just *must* watch—something educational, of course. In 2000, on HBO's *If These Walls Could Talk 2*, I learned that in the 1950s, lesbians struggled with grief and alienation; in the 1970s, lesbians were pretty political; but by 2000, lesbians just needed sperm. The final scene, where lesbian role models Ellen DeGeneres and Anne Heche(!) frantically pursue every avenue for getting sperm (while seated on white sofas), truly captured the contemporary lesbian experience.

Most of my TV education/exposure comes from a TV left on as background noise during your average pay-for-play sex session (I'm getting paid). At the very first "live/work" luxury loft I visited in San Francisco (the ceilings were so high!), my trick had switched from porn to *Queer As Folk* when I got out of the shower. I couldn't figure out which was more real, those blond boys humping each other in soft focus on TV, or this trick, a leather guy on the (leather) sofa, framed by black-and-white photos of nude muscleboys on exposed brick walls. The guy had black towels and sheets because he was rough—*he* must have been more real.

I glimpsed my only segment of *Queer Eye for the Straight Guy* flickering in the background of a sterile Ritz Carlton hotel room that looked like it had been seriously downsized since the glory days. That segment involved moving some sort of pillar into the middle of someone's bathroom, or maybe I was looking at it from the wrong angle. The trick was straight, and he was enthralled—I could tell by his dreamy eyes that his wife would never let him put a pillar in the middle of *their* bathroom.

I never expected to watch Showtime's *The L Word*, but one night, at a friend's house, I caught a glimpse of a documentary on the making of this groundbreaking series. I was so excited by the hairstyles—every lesbian had a professionally coiffed, windswept salon style!—that I stayed at my friend's house to watch TV while they went out. In this documentary, I learned that there are no lesbians playing lead roles in *The L Word* because straight actresses are better at playing lesbians. "It's been almost ten years since *Go Fish*," the 1994 breakthrough lesbian hit, someone (the producer? the director? a lesbian?) tells us, and, "It's about time."

It was about time for straight actresses, several of whom are neighbors (in L.A.!) to tell us how great it feels to play a lesbian. Moving from Blaxploitation to Lesploitation (les is more!), Pam Grier gets the best line, "*The L Word* is about living the life you love . . . and loving the life you live." It was about time for lesbians to be seen carrying Chanel shopping bags (luxurious product placement!).

On my way to finally get a glimpse of lesbian drama TV-style, I had my own drama when I missed the bus and couldn't deal with the idea of paying ten dollars to catch a cab to *The L Word*. What I later learned is that, in the show, the straight guy, who looks like he's visiting from *Queer As Folk*, fucks his tiny bicurious girlfriend (she has bangs and straight hair 'cause she's innocent). We get to watch the bicurious bangs bobbing up and down on *Queer As Folk*'s straight piece. Jennifer Beals, last seen giving us Danskin in 1983's *Flashdance*, plays Pam Grier's high-rolling half-sister (she's the one with the Chanel shopping bag, what a *fee* . . . ling!). Jennifer Beals (post-nose job) and her blonde girlfriend are planning to have a power baby, so Jennifer wants to enlist the help of a friend with sperm. But her girlfriend is aghast—he's so big and . . . black! The person working at the clinic says the big guy will probably fill a whole cup with sperm, and girlfriend might need a c-section because the baby will be so . . . big!

But there's more. In episode two, Jennifer Beals's girlfriend has a breakthrough. She says, "There's no reason on earth I wouldn't want to make a baby with you using a donor who was black." A friend quips, "You're really cutting-edge—lesbian moms, biracial child." These *less*-bians are so full of wisdom, especially Jennifer Beals, who says, "Monogamy isn't just hypothetical, some people practice it." Though a straight guy gets some action too. He tells the closeted tennis player, struggling at the country club to win a Subaru advertising sponsorship, to wear the shorts because they show off her . . . tennis playing. Later, though, after she gets the contract, he tells her, "Subaru is interested in more than your ass."

But why am I torturing you with all this crap? Well . . . there's nothing like the real thing . . . *baby*. I wanted to give you, dear reader, a glimpse of how assimilation robs queer identity of anything meaningful, relevant, or challenging—and calls this progress. Twenty years (or even ten years) ago, one might not have imagined the largest national gay rights lobbying group (Human Rights Campaign) endorsing a right-wing Republican Senatorial candidate (Al D'Amato in New York, 1998), or the San Francisco Pride parade adopting the Budweiser advertising slogan as its official theme (2002). The gay mainstream presents a sanitized, straight-friendly version of gay identity, which makes it safe for David Geffen, Rosie O'Donnell, or Richard Chamberlain to come out and still rake in the bucks. By the twisted priorities of this gay mainstream, it's okay to oppose a queer youth shelter because it might interfere with "community" property values, or to enact neighborhood "beautification" programs that require the wholesale arrest of homeless people, transgendered people, sex workers, youth, people of color, and anyone else who might get in the way of a whitewashed gayborhood.

As an assimilationist gay mainstream wields increasing power, the focus of gay struggle has become limited to the holy trinity of marriage, military service, and adoption. Speaking of the holy trinity, don't forget ordination into the priesthood! Even when the "gay rights" agenda does include real issues, it does it in a way that prioritizes the most privileged while consistently fucking over everyone else. This agenda fights for an end to discrimination in housing, but not for the provision of housing; domestic partner health coverage but not universal health coverage. Even with the most obviously "gay" issue, that of anti-queer violence, the gay rights agenda fights for tougher hate crimes laws, instead of fighting the racism, classism, transphobia (and homophobia) intrinsic to the criminal "justice" system.

As the gay mainstream prioritizes the attainment of straight privilege over all else, what gets left behind is any critique of the dominant culture, whatsoever. Take *The L Word*, for example. It's okay to add a black person (or even a mixed-race baby!) for a little color, as long as the characters can still use racist and misogynist jokes as punch lines. All this furthers the creation of a hybrid less-being who behaves more like a tacky fag than any dyke outside the straight male imaginary. Did I mention the scene where the soon-to-be-mothers cradle a vial of sperm like it's a cocktail (one L even has a martini glass in hand), and for a few seconds you really wonder if they're going to drink that . . . *luscious libation*.

But doesn't the creation of a world where it's safe for gay Republicans, gay realtors, and gay action figures to come out of the closet and live full, healthy, happy lives—doesn't this create more options for all of us? No—it creates more options for gay Republicans to support a warmongering, bigoted agenda, more options for gay realtors to sell luxury property, and more options for gay action figures to . . . be plastic.

Speaking of plastic (and *Queer As Folk*), I remember when I first moved to San Francisco in 1992 and was completely terrified by the conformity, hyper-masculinity, and blind consumerism of the legendary gay Castro district. I knew instantly that it could never be my "community," and always assumed that it wasn't anyone else's, either. Then one day, just recently, I was walking through the Castro with a friend of mine, whose social group includes a number of gay white men in their fifties, and everywhere guys were smiling at him and reaching out with great big hugs. I realized, then, that the Castro was *somebody's* community, and this was, for a moment, a revelation.

What is sad about the Castro (and similar gay ghettos across the country and world), and indicative of what gay people do with even a little bit of power, is that these same smiling gay men have failed to build community for queers (or anyone) outside their social group. Many gay men (even in the Castro) still remain on the fringes, either by choice or lack of opportunity. But as the most "successful" gays (and their allies) have moved from outsider status to insider clout, they have consistently fought misogynist, racist, classist, and ageist battles to ensure that their neighborhood remain a community only for the rich, male, and white (or at least those who pass). They've succeeded in clamping down on the defiance, anger, flamboyance, and subversion, once thriving in gay subcultures, in order to promote a vapid consume-or-die, we're just like you mentality. Of course, this serves the interests of gays with power, but what is heartbreaking (and infuriating) is that so many others follow along like zombies. Homo now stands more for homogenous than any type of sexuality aside from *buy Diesel jeans/Gap khakis/Abercrombie cargo shorts*.

I can't tell you how many times I've been presented with the argument that fighting assimilation takes attention away from the "real" battle, which is fighting anti-gay violence. This false dichotomy hides the fact that assimilation *is* violence, not just the violence of cultural erasure, but the violence of stepping on anyone more vulnerable than you in order to get ahead. Gay landlords evict people with AIDS to increase property values; gay bar owners arrest homeless queers so they don't get in the way of business; and gay political consultants ensure the election of pro-development, anti-poor candidates who ensure that the ruling class not only remains in power but systematically sucks the poor dry.

Nowhere is the tyranny of assimilation more evident than in the ways that the borders are policed. In February of 2003, I attended a demonstration outside the LGBT Center in San Francisco. We arrived at "our" Center to protest pre-election pandering by Gavin Newsom, a wealthy, conservative (and straight) politician, who orchestrated a fundraiser in order to buy the powerful "gay vote."

As soon as the police (called by the center) escorted Newsom inside, they were free to take care of us with their batons. I was thrown face first into oncoming traffic; a police officer bloodied one protester, shattering her tooth; several of us were arrested; one person was put into a chokehold by police until he passed out. Center staff watched, and did nothing. Their immediate statement, faced with the spectacle of queers getting bashed on their doorstep, was to voice their dismay that we were protesting a Center fundraiser. Gay liberation began as a struggle against police control of our bodies and lives, and here we were—thirty-five years after Stonewall, in San Francisco, arguably the gayest of overpriced American cities—getting bashed by police with the tacit approval of gay "leaders." Now *that's* progress.

Against the nightmare backdrop of assimilation, queers striving to live outside conventional norms become increasingly marginalized. A ravenous gay mainstream seeks control, not only of our bodies and minds, but of the very ways we represent our own identities. Assimilation means erasure; any queers that call attention to this tyranny risk ostracism, imprisonment, or worse.

Of course we're enraged and depressed (and sometimes driven to suicide) by the ways in which mainstream gay people steadily assimilate into the dominant culture that we despise. The radical potential of queer identity lies in remaining *outside*—in challenging and seeking to dismantle the sickening culture that surrounds us.

That's Revolting is a radical queer intervention in the culture wars. This anthology presents activist writing that uses queer identity as a starting point from which to reframe, reclaim, and reshape the world. It challenges the commercialized, commodified, and hyper-objectified view of gay/queer identity projected by the (gay and straight) mainstream media. *That's Revolting* presents queer struggles to transform gender, revolutionize sexuality, build community/family outside of traditional models, and dismantle hierarchies of race, class, gender, sexuality, and ability.

This anthology consists of personal histories, rants, interviews, conversations, activist struggles, political analysis, practical advice, and glamour. Contributors include early gay liberation activists, counterculture demons, fringe artistes, renegade academics, the dispossessed, the obsessed, and various other enemy combatants—in other words, it's a book by a bunch of freaks, fruits, perverts, and whores. *That's Revolting* explores and critiques specific struggles to challenge the monster of assimilation and proposes new ways to oppose homogenization, globalization, and all the other evils of this ravaging world. Pick it up and smash something.

CHURCH, STATE, DR. LAURA, THE MERRY-GO-ROUND, PATRIOTS, THE CONSPIRACY, AND DIAPERS

DR. LAURA, SIT ON MY FACE

ROCKO BULLDAGGER

I'm serious! Where have you gone? You haven't been quieted by a few little boycotts, have you? I miss hearing your condemnation, your excited and flushed, righteous indignation. Come back, no one can dirty-talk me like you did!

Dr. Laura, I want to pay homage to you and all you have done for queers like me. You understand me better than anyone else in the media. You know that queer people are not merely seeking acceptance and a marketable identity. You know we have a radical agenda. While the Human Rights Campaign and the Gay and Lesbian Alliance Against Defamation are out there presenting a sweet and innocuous picture of homosexuality, you know the truth. A homo is not the boy or girl next door. In fact, a homo might be neither boy nor girl. Queers are a bunch of sadomasochistic perverts out to destroy family life as you know it. We don't just want gay marriage, we want sexual liberation where every single person can choose who, when, and how they fuck. We want that choice to be meaningful and informed. Queers like me want everyone, including straight folks, to feel the effects of our liberation. We're out to create a world where lovers can cut, brand, fist, bleed, shit, and piss on each other, love each other our very own way, and do all the terrible things I know you are thinking of, Dr. Laura, and getting wet as you imagine them.

Yes, that's right, I know how to get you off. I know that when you see that rainbow flag, visions of whips, chains, and anal sex dance seductively through your head. You're right, Dr. Laura, the respectable faces of military service and same-sex partner benefits are just a thin veneer harboring our radical queer transgender pro-sex agenda.

Our worlds are not so different, we could show each other a few things about depravity. What really lurks in your mind, Dr. Laura, when you think about homosexuals? Our decadent, debauched lifestyle? Our nonchalant attitude toward sex? Our efforts to shake off centuries of sexual shame? Our willingness to sacrifice traditional morality for our own love and pleasure? Do you envy us? I'm glad you are stirring up fear of homosexuals. It reminds me of what I want out of being queer in the first place. It makes me feel dangerous, and gives me a lot to live up to.

Dr. Laura, you can sit on my face any time, because I owe you. Without you, people might forget about perverted dykes like me and think all lesbians are cozy, bland, and asexual like Ellen or Rosie. Please hurry, get on that radio and remind the world that I am depraved; remind them that I am part of a sexual revolution designed to deconstruct the social state as we know it, that I am going to turn their culture upside down, sleep with their daughters, turn their sons into sissies, distribute porn to their local elementary school, condoms to their teenagers, and just about spoil all their cock-sure (phalogocentric) fun.

Yes, a few people come out of the closet and you act like it's the end of Western Civilization. Well honey, maybe it is. Keep talking it up and I won't have to worry so much about my voice not reaching anyone. Who would have heard of my kind of queers if it weren't for you? There is no such thing as bad publicity. I don't mind the distortion. Just think, no one as far outside of the queer community as your listeners would even know there existed female-to-male transsexuals if you had not gone out of your way to condemn them back in 1999. How many budding transsexuals received their first introduction to the possibility of surgical transition through the self-righteous condemnation of folks like you? When I was a kid, I was confronted with the most homophobic depictions of queerness, yet all that hysteria was a clear sign that I wasn't alone, even if all I had to look forward to was a lifetime of trips to the emergency room with gerbils up my ass.

Dr. Laura, I hope you never shut up. You see my sinister grin? That's because I get off on our dynamic too. In a way, you created me. Being a threat is sexy, and I have risen to the evil queer identity your discourse helps create and perpetuate. You need me too, honey. Don't pretend you wouldn't have imagined me if I did not exist. You go on dreaming of me, obsessing over my evil ways. Dr. Laura, don't deny it. You and I share so many of the same sexually intense, perverse thoughts and fantasies. We have more in common than our friends would ever suspect. So sit on my face and tell me all about depravity, please, just one more time, Doctor!

IT'S ALL ABOUT CLASS

TOMMI AVICOLLI MECCA

I'll never forget that picket in Philadelphia in the fall of 1972.

It was raining like crazy—and cold—the kind of chill that stayed with you for hours after you found refuge in a nice warm place.

I wasn't wearing gloves, something I regretted every moment we circled that bar on Delancey Street in Philadelphia's gay ghetto. I wasn't wearing a raincoat either, so my pants and shoes were soaked. I had an umbrella, but it didn't help, the rain was hitting us on all sides. I continued walking in that circle, picking up the pace, trying to generate heat in my body. Around and around we went, about fifteen of us, black and white men, handing out flyers to patrons heading into the bar, and chanting for an end to racist carding policies at one of the city's most popular gay hangouts.

The white patrons who rushed past us didn't particularly care what we were doing. As I remember it, they just wanted to get into the bar. They wanted to find a body for the night or dish with their friends or maybe even play pool. They certainly didn't want to hear that their favorite watering hole carded blacks. Many of them probably didn't care.

The queer community has never been a monolithic entity. There've always been divisions along racial, gender, age, and class lines. As far back as I can remember—and I came out in April 1971—there were gays who lived in mansions and those who lived in the streets, gays who worked for Wall Street and those who sold their bodies to pay the rent. There were gays of all colors, but black gays hung out in one section of the city and whites in another. There were gay Republicans and gay Socialists, though they seldom sat in the same room together.

The post-Stonewall gay liberation movement was aware of these differences and tried to address them. It understood the connections between struggles against racism, sexism, classism, ageism, and homophobia. The Stonewall Riots were born from the fires lit in the '60s by the civil rights and anti-Vietnam War movements. Many of the early pioneers of post-Stonewall gay organizations had put their bodies on the line against desegregation in the South, and taken to the streets to end the unjust war in Southeast Asia. Contrary to popular opinion, not all were white. And contrary to popular opinion, it was not singer Judy Garland's death that prompted queens to fight back that night in late June 1969 outside the Stonewall, but the upheaval of a generation of young people saying no to racism and war.

A couple weeks after Stonewall, Kiyoshi Kuromiya, a Japanese-American who was born in a WWII detention camp and who marched in the mid-'60s at the yearly July 4 gay pickets at Independence Hall, started the Philadelphia Gay Liberation Front (GLF), taking the lead from the newly formed New York GLF. I came out at a GLF coffee hour at Temple University a year-and-a-half later.

I had already been aware of civil rights and peace issues, having marched since I was sixteen in civil-rights and antiwar marches. I was kicked off my Catholic high school student newspaper for submitting articles against the war and against the school haircut rule (hair could not touch the back collar of your shirt or the vice principal took you into his office and cut it himself). I had a reputation for being a hippie. At sixteen, I smoked my first joint behind the corner store run by a friend's parents and became involved with a boy in my English class. Rebellion seemed to be part of my soul. Little did I know at the time that southern Italians had a history of anarchism and that two of my *paesani*, Sacco and Vanzetti, were executed unjustly for being poor and ethnic. During their trial, Judge Thayer called them "dagos," making the proceeding all the more about getting rid of what society saw as members of a separate and inferior Southern European race.

GLF was a good place to come out. It embraced the struggles of all oppressed peoples, declaring in its mission statement that for queers to be free, all people must be free. So one week we might be marching for affordable housing with poor black mothers, another week we might be demanding the passage of the Equal Rights Amendment with middle-class white women. GLF had a substantial black membership and leadership, unlike most of the other gay organizations. By 1973, GLF was swallowed up by the one-issue-oriented Gay Activists Alliance. Despite its primary focus on "gay rights," Philadelphia GAA did at times embrace other concerns, particularly race, gender, and class issues.

In the early '70s, I helped organize the GAA pickets against gay bars that discriminated against blacks and women. Strict carding policies (as well as dress codes) determined who got into those establishments, many of which had no fire exits or violated other safety and/or health codes. On any given night the rules could be changed to keep out those whom bar owners considered undesirable. For example, there might be a rule against open-toed shoes (commonly worn by women and drag queens), or a requirement for two or more pieces of "valid ID," which of course was only required of blacks.

As we picketed night after night, I remember being asked more than a few times, "Why're you doing this? You should be supporting OUR bars." My response was, "But they don't support US." Obviously I held a more inclusive definition of who "we" were.

Our nightly pickets did not stop the racist and sexist carding policies. Over a decade later, while I was editor of the *Philadelphia Gay News*, a racist ad was submitted by a chic gay club under investigation by the city's Human Rights Commission for discriminatory carding policies against blacks. The ad for "Congo Night" featured a giant King Kong and plugged an act called the "slave boy" dancers. Lorrie Kim, Local News Editor, and myself talked the publisher out of running it.

In the '70s, GAA often organized opposition to efforts to stop late-night gay male cruising in a certain area of downtown Philadelphia. Known as the "merry-go-round," it was a four-block square that sat in the heart of a rather well-to-do section of our gay ghetto, a district that ran the entire Western (and a part of the Eastern) length of Spruce Street. In fact, mention Spruce Street to someone back then and they immediately started smirking and making derogatory remarks about "those people." Everyone knew who lived on Spruce Street.

The merry-go-round ran from Twentieth to Twenty-first on Spruce Street, down Twenty-first to Delancey, down Delancey to Twentieth and up Twentieth back to Spruce. It was a neighborhood that included the historic Pearl S. Buck house. Neighbors there, many of them gay monied types, objected to the "noise" created by the cruising and the cars circling 'round and 'round (thus the nickname "merry-go-round"). They also objected to some of those who frequented the neighborhood.

The denizens of the merry-go-round were mostly young and working-class or thirty-something and middle-class. They poured out of the bars at two a.m. and headed to the merry-go-round hoping to get lucky and score a trick from a passing car or a fellow cruiser on foot. Others, including young, loud, and proud drag queens (some of them black and Latino), never made it into the bars because of the aforementioned carding policies. These working-class queers were, I always believed, the real objects of the distrust and hatred of the monied gays.

The merry-go-round wasn't just for cruising. I remember my first sexual experience there. Though certainly I had been groped and fondled many times and done my share of the same, one night a man led me into a darkened alley near the back of the Buck house and went down on me. Standing there getting blown was an incredibly liberating, yet frightening, experience. Liberating because it felt primordial—sex under the stars and in the open—yet frightening because I was breaking the law. I was, at that moment, a criminal, an outlaw in the eyes of heterosexual society. In fact, my first sex ever with a man was in a dark alley in South Philly when a friend and I stole a copy of *Playboy* from the neighborhood drugstore, went into an alley to read it, and he wound up with his pants down and my mouth on his cock.

Becoming one of the monied gays, living in a posh apartment or house on Delancey Street, was never my aspiration. A working-class kid from the southern Italian immigrant streets of South Philly, I knew that to those who lived in the expensive real estate of Delancey Street, I was still a "greaseball," an uncouth and uncultured WOP. At that point in time, Italians had never been elected to public office in Philadelphia. We were still marginal whites, a little too ethnic for the silver-spoon crowd. Even Archie Bunker referred to us as "dagos" and put us in a class with Jews and "Polacks."

Standing there in that alley getting a blowjob became an act of extreme rebellion for me. I knew I had crossed a line. I was forever marked as an outsider.

The battle over this cruising area waged on for years. Police were called in to harass and arrest folks who hung out there. Despite all of the efforts of GAA, only temporary resolutions could ever be worked out with neighbors and police. We flyered the area, asking cruisers to respect the neighborhood and keep their voices down; we met with police; we formed patrols to watch the area and report on police activities. Meanwhile, I continued to cruise those streets, hanging out with friends and playing a cat-and-mouse game with the cops. I learned all the tricks of the trade: how to spot a police car from far off, what alleyways would lead to safety, how to warn others of the encroaching "Alice" (our code name for the police). Cruisers in this area had our own language—and it served to protect us from arrest. For instance, "Neshinew" was a straight guy prone to violence. You could spread the word about some straight thug who frequented the place without incurring his wrath because he didn't know what you were saying about him.

The struggle for control of the "merry-go-round" was my first encounter with the issue of the right to public space. It was a battle that would re-emerge time and again. In the late '80s, police began cracking down on a park cruising area near the Schuykill River not far from the merry-go-round. The park, nicknamed "Judy Garland Park" by cruisers, surrounded on three sides by fairly expensive houses and apartments, was a traditional site for gay male outdoor sex. The actual area where sex happened was along the river, hidden by bushes and trees, though neighbors claimed men were having sex on their front steps as well. With the help of a progressive gay lawyer, I mobilized a patrol of the area on weekend nights, leafletting men who came to cruise to warn them of the undercover police presence. The police were not pleased, but they did not stop us. We also attended neighborhood meetings to talk to residents about the situation. Our efforts managed to quiet things down and neighbors and cruisers settled down to a peaceful co-existence—for the time being.

Twenty years after my time in the Gay Activist Alliance, I was again engaged in a battle over class issues, only this time it was in San Francisco's famed Castro district and the players were middle-class (almost exclusively white) neighbors and homeless queer youth.

I moved to San Francisco in October 1991. I left a job as the managing editor of the *Philadelphia Gay News* to come to work at A Different Light, a queer bookstore in the Castro. I needed a change. Many of my close friends had died of AIDS. In 1990, both of my parents died within the course of nine months. I had just put my beloved fourteen-year-old cat to sleep because she was full of cancer. Philadelphia seemed like a graveyard.

San Francisco was the place to go. It was political and radical. It was home to the Castro, the center of the queer universe. To walk down the same streets as Harvey Milk and Sylvester was inspiring.

My first political battle, in 1995, was over Proposition 187, a statewide measure to stop undocumented immigrants from obtaining social services, including emergency-room care. I formed a group called Queers United Against 187. We held a two-night benefit to raise much-needed funds at Josie's Cabaret and Juice Joint, then the Castro's only performance space. I had done a month-long stint there in March 1992, performing my one-man show, *All in All I'd Rather Be Having Sex*, a look at the sexual misadventures of a certain Italian/American queer.

I continued organizing over the years, working at A Different Light and living in the Castro. There was no lack of battles: Proposition 209, a statewide measure to outlaw affirmative action; Proposition E, a citywide attempt to get rid of rent control on two and four-unit buildings; and Proposition G, a measure to strengthen tenant protections against owner move-in evictions. Being at the bookstore gave me an advantage: I was in the heartland of queerdom every day. I had my finger on the pulse of things. So when merchants began a campaign against the homeless in the Castro, I knew I had to do something.

Lack of affordable housing was a longtime problem in the Castro. When queers first migrated to Eureka Valley, as it was then called, in the late '60s and early '70s, rent was cheap. It wasn't until the late '70s, after queers had given the neighborhood a worldwide reputation and renamed it the Castro, that the real-estate speculators and profiteers did what they do best: kick out the poor and bring in the rich. In the last year of his life, Harvey Milk himself was forced out of his apartment and camera store on Castro Street when his rent was tripled. There was no rent control at the time. It was the beginning of the gentrification of the neighborhood. Since that time, the neighborhood has been a high-rent—and therefore more exclusive—district, always with its share of homeless and poor queers.

Homelessness suddenly became a concern to merchants in the Castro around the same time as the dot-com boom was beginning. Hordes of highly paid workers from Silicon Valley were rushing into the city to rent everything in sight. They would line up at open houses and outbid each other—and the desperate lower-income folks—for apartments. The vacancy rate dropped. Apartment prices went up and up. Landlords, desperate to get rid of long-term tenants benefiting from rent control, tried everything they could think of—intimidation, threats, illegal evictions. Owner move-in evictions skyrocketed. Long-term tenants with AIDS, survivors from the '70s, were pushed out. Commercial rents began to climb.

Queer kids who fled to San Francisco from all parts of the world to seek relief from homophobic towns and families were unable to afford to live there, even with jobs. The traditional method of survival, piling into flats and turning every room into a bedroom, didn't work anymore. Rents on flats jumped from about $1,200 per month to $2,000 to $3,000. Even with four or five people in a flat, rent could be as high as $600 per person. A minimum-wage job could not support that kind of rent.

Many kids started living on the streets of the Castro and panhandling to make a few bucks to eat. Merchants didn't like it. They thought the kids were hurting their businesses, that they would drive away tourists, the mainstay of the Castro economy. There was only one thing to do: remove the problem.

The first attack was through a "Create Change, Don't Give It Out" poster campaign in 1998. The Castro merchants' group, MUMC (Merchants of Upper Market and Castro), went around to all the shops along Castro, Market, and Eighteenth streets asking them to put the signs in their windows. A Different Light refused. Objecting to the sign, I organized a series of meetings of merchants, neighbors, and activists. Our small core group included Jim Mitulski, pastor of the Metropolitan Community Church (MCC); Sandra Ruiz, aide to out queer Supervisor Tom Ammiano; and others. We eventually hatched a plan for an emergency queer youth shelter.

To say that the idea was controversial is an understatement. It shook the neighborhood like a 9.5 earthquake. Neighbors went ballistic. They accused us of lowering their property values. They said that roving bands of druglords would rule the streets, that their children wouldn't be safe and their homes would be robbed. They brought up the very same concerns I'd heard a decade before in Philadelphia from straight neighbors objecting to AIDS hospices.

The first shelter was at the Eureka Valley Recreation Center, a block north of Castro on Eighteenth Street. It remained open for only three months. The second was in a church building that MCC owned in Noe Valley, a liberal community near Castro where many lesbians traditionally lived, which had become a very exclusive white middle-class enclave. The shelter was only for the rainy months, which in San Francisco extend from the beginning of November to the end of March. When that shelter closed, Mitulski moved it temporarily to the main MCC church in the Castro. Always there was controversy, neighbors yelling about property values, and fears of drug-crazed kids trashing the neighborhood.

After the MCC shelter closed, I brought together a community group in the Castro to discuss setting up a more permanent space. We were gaining consensus on the idea of a shelter when queer Supervisor Mark Leno announced he had found a space at Castro and Market—at a former gym, now boarded up. The ensuing battle to establish the facility at Castro and Market was year-long and pitted neighbor against neighbor, business against business. I was part of the Community Advisory Committee formed by Leno to come up with a master plan for the shelter. Again, I listened to neighbors accusing homeless kids of every crime imaginable. One lesbian mother feared for her children's safety walking home from school, and another lesbian swore her child would get "cooties" from these kids, while straights talked of disease-carrying homeless youth spoiling their lily-white neighborhoods.

Interestingly enough, at one of the meetings a homeless youth stood up and talked about how at least one of the gay men who objected to the shelter habitually tried to pick him up in the early morning hours. He accused this man, and others, of wanting access to homeless kids late at night when he was horny, yet not wanting to provide the kids with shelter or services.

After a year, the majority of the committee members voted against the plan for a shelter, which we had painstakingly prepared. This was a major betrayal of the process, but to his credit, Leno went ahead with the plan anyway. What's perhaps saddest about the fight for the queer youth facility is that queer organizations and leaders, for the most part, remained silent. Few weighed in on the controversy. Fewer still jumped in and supported us. I guess they were afraid of alienating the business interests, especially the real estate companies that gave them money.

That homeless queer youth facility exists even as I write this article, and it has been a major success, despite the gloom-and-doom predictions of its opponents. Though its lease is running out after two years of operation, it was just extended for a few months while Arc of Refuge, which runs it, readies another location outside the Castro (rents inside the Castro are prohibitive). The extension on the lease was done with full neighborhood approval. A lot has changed in two years. Neighbors saw that their dire warnings about drugs and violence were unfounded.

It didn't teach them any real lessons. A year after a facility opened, some of the same folks who opposed it were campaigning for an antihomeless measure put on the ballot by an ambitious supervisor, Gavin Newsom, a so-called pretty-boy type who grew up with a silver spoon in his mouth and wanted desperately to be mayor. That Newsom had done nothing to address homelessness in his nearly eight years on the Board of Supervisors didn't matter to his supporters. He was suddenly their champion.

What he proposed to do was take away general assistance (GA) checks from the homeless and instead give them housing, food, etc. The problem was that the housing and services didn't exist. Though folks urged Newsom to put the housing and services in place before proceeding with the measure, he ran with it anyway. Despite the flaws in his plan, it passed overwhelmingly, in the Castro and city-wide. After its passage, Newsom and his allies scrambled to find housing. A court gutted the measure, saying it was the purview of the Board to take away GA checks. Then a battle began to get the Board to pass the measure. It went down in defeat a couple months later when the Board failed to approve it. Those who supported Newsom and his antihomeless measures have not gone away.

December 2003: a heated mayoral runoff in San Francisco. In one corner, the champion of downtown business interests, the aforementioned Gavin Newsom. In the other, a newcomer to San Francisco politics, a Democrat-turned-Green, Matt Gonzalez. A standard David and Goliath story. Thirty years ago, there would be no question as to who would win the gay vote. Today, there is a split, a huge split, in the queer community between those who ally themselves with the ruling class, big money, and the Chamber of Commerce, and those who see themselves in coalition with the poor and working class, who see class issues as a vital part of our movement.

In other words, those who opposed the queer youth shelters tend to support Newsom, those who supported the shelters, Gonzalez.

That Newsom would have a sizable chunk of gay votes exposes our failure to make class issues an integral part of our movement. That all but one gay elected official would fall behind Newsom in a show of party loyalty as Democrats, while ignoring the class issues inherent in this candidate's attacks on the poor and homeless, is indicative of the disregard the ruling gay establishment in San Francisco feels for poor and working-class people. No amount of party loyalty should deter a leader with class consciousness from speaking out against poor-bashing, no matter what the price is to his/her political career.

The outcome of this particular race is important. What is more important, however, is whether the queer movement will continue to court the rich and powerful as a way of obtaining influence and power while refusing to address issues affecting the poorest among us.

SITES OF RESISTANCE OR SITES OF RACISM?

PRIYANK JINDAL

THE GAY WHITE NATION

Racism is articulated over and over again by the LGBT movement, especially in this time of increased Amerikan militarization. After September 11, there was a very clear response from the gay "community": gay bars suddenly discovered what fabulous fashion patriotism makes, drag shows suddenly had an infusion of patriotic themes, and Amerikan pride and gay pride flags were found flying proudly side by side. The front page of the *Philadelphia Gay News* captured this post 9-11 gay patriotism with the image of an Amerikan flag with a pink handprint emblazoned on it. Gay press ran constant coverage of the many gay and lesbian people affected by the "terrorists." In this coverage, the discussion of "terrorism" as a racist ideology remained unquestioned, and in fact was perpetuated; the big bad brown person was just as scary to gays and lesbians as to straight people.

The gay "community" focused on lesbian and gay people who died in the Towers, the bravery of gay firefighters and cops, and of course the "heroics" of Mark Bingham, the gay "hero" who died on the third plane. Lesbian and gay individuals and organizations set forth a blatant pro-war agenda. The gay "community" organized benefits for the September 11 fund and embraced New York Mayor Rudolph Giuliani without any interrogation of how his racist policies have affected people of color and sex workers in New York, as if to make it clear: 9-11 affected everyone the same; terrorists do not discriminate.

The response of the mainstream gay community to 9-11 was to focus on how "we" were affected just like the rest of white Amerika, and to prove that "we" would respond in the same way: to stand behind the war on terrorism. This essentially means standing behind the killing and terrorizing of brown people inside and outside Amerikan borders. The gay community's emphasis on the similarities in experience between (white) heterosexuality and lesbian and gay homosexuality, through a shared racism against brown folk, has helped white gays and lesbians to assimilate and become part of the white heterosexual nation.

That the project of gay assimilation was desired and accomplished through white supremacy is not surprising, considering that the mainstream gay and lesbian community countered Jerry Falwell's homophobia by contrasting his actions with that of the "hero" Mark Bingham. 9-11 created a space for the privileged gay community to talk about their rights vis à vis the terrorists. Who is worse, the white middle-class gay person next door who wants to see Amerika "succeed" just as much as any heterosexual, or the terrorists? This strategy seems to be working: for the first time in seven years, New York Governor Pataki has been willing to meet with the white upper/middle–class gay community, and even President Bush has denounced Falwell's comments. Bush has yet to apologize for the "war on drugs," otherwise known as Operation Lock Up the Brown People. The tactics used to publicize the issue of "equal" rights (which, according to the white gay community, people of color already gained through legislative acts such as integration) is best summed up by Judy Weider, editor-in-chief of *The Advocate*, "When you ask what difference does it make if the heroes were gay, I say I agree with you. That's precisely our point. They were just like everybody else. So we ask, why is it that when they died, they were equal to everyone, but had they lived they would not have the same equality as heterosexuals?"

The discussion of gay rights shaped by this ideology centers around providing assistance to gay partners; fighting for gay marriage, gay adoption, and Social Security benefits; and fighting against the don't ask/don't tell policy. Needless to say, these are not the most pressing issues amongst working-class, poor, and transgendered people of color whose race, documentation, class status, or gender identity often prevent them from receiving the wide array of social benefits afforded to white, middle-class gays and lesbians. For many of us whose family members are heavily recruited into the military—as of 1999, 37 percent of the Amerikan military was made up of people of color, and the number has been steadily increasing—fighting for our right to be used as cannon fodder in the racist Amerikan dream is not our biggest concern.

We are fighting against Amerikan recruitment policies that target working-class youth of color, and fighting to end Amerikan militarization and imperialism, which threaten our safety and the safety of our loved ones inside and outside Amerikan borders. We are fighting to end the oppression of transpeople of color who face state violence even, and sometimes especially, because of our ability to pass, and fighting to end the gentrification and subsequent displacement of working-class youth of color, which is often led by the white gay community. We are fighting to end the police brutality that singles out queer youth of color, and fighting to create our own spaces, or even spaces where we can safely exist. These are our battles. But once again, my experience as a transgendered person of color, and more so the experiences of working-class and poor queer people of color, are not only marginalized and silenced but also trampled on in the name of gay "rights." My resistance to the mainstream gay movement is based on my need for survival. It is based on the need to make queer liberation synonymous with anti-imperialism, not gay inclusion into Amerika's blood-stained genocidal dreams.

SITES OF RESISTANCE, SITES OF RACISM

So far, this discussion has used the example of 9-11 to examine ways in which the white mainstream gay community benefits from racist ideologies in order to produce a public forum to talk about white gay rights. But what about "alternative" sites of resistance that are supposedly created in opposition to the white gay mainstream?

Most spaces identified as radical queer spaces, unless they are explicitly for people of color, generally lack any significant attention to or inclusion of issues or struggles not specifically queer. In this context, unfortunately, those spaces are not radical alternatives to gay identity, but a continuation of the legitimization of white identity that exists in gay mainstream culture. This has led to deep-rooted forms of racism in alternative sites of resistance. Organizers of these spaces may give lip service to an antiracist agenda, but in practice their actions maintain the status quo.

I have tried over and over again to be a part of these radical spaces but, unless they are specifically for people of color, I am generally the only brown face in the bunch.

There are alternative sites of resistance where white queers participate in movements that are not specifically queer, like Philly Queers Against the War. These could be spaces where the white supremacy inherent in mainstream gay culture is challenged, but these groups are generally all white. Thus these spaces offer little potential for queers of color to address the ways in which homophobia exists in our own communities, and to bring to light the ways in which issues generally associated only with racism are also intimately tied to the institution of heterosexuality. It seems that the underlying belief represented through these groups is that queers are only white; the political agenda of queers of color is once again left out of the picture.

Standing as allies to "other" liberation movements is a vitally important act for white queer folks to do, but it must be done with the consciousness that the issues white queers are standing in solidarity with *are* queer issues in a very real way, especially and very specifically for queers of color. When this doesn't happen, which unfortunately is quite often, when other liberation movements are always placed outside the realm of queerness, queer is once again associated with whiteness, racism is once again a straight issue, and queers of color are once again marginalized, silenced and trampled on, this time by queer radicals.

Why do sites of radical queer resistance consistently fail to effectively resist racist ideology? The answer is that these sites have been created from and organized around the lived experiences and political agendas of white people. It is easy to recognize the blatant classism, racism, and transphobia in the agenda of mainstream gay culture, especially in its use of 9-11 as a strategy for assimilation. It is not always as easy to locate the racism and classism inherent in the agendas of radical queer spaces.

For example, while the mainstream gay movement fights for gay marriage, an institution rooted in white middle-class heterosexual privilege, anti-assimilationist queers throw radical sex parties. But fighting Dworkinism and other forms of sexual conservative politics with a sex-positive agenda can also reproduce the racism inherent in the mainstream gay movement. The queer sex-positive political agenda claims a woman's right to fuck who she wants to fuck, reclaims the word "slut," challenges the idea that a woman has to remain pure or untouched, and fights against the idea that she can never have agency in a sexual situation. It is also based in transgressing the ideals of *white* womanhood.

I wholeheartedly support queer women's desires to fuck without shame or stigma, and this is very much a part of the political agenda for queer people of color. But reclaiming the word "slut" and fighting to not be considered pure don't work as well when historically women of color have been on the receiving end of state violence in a way that has constructed us as always being sexually open; women of color can't be raped because we've been considered sexually accessible throughout Amerika's history of slavery and genocide. The current sex tourism industry, where white straight men go to find "exotic" women of color and white gay men go to find "exotic" men of color, and the frequent socially sanctioned sexual assault of women, men, and transgendered folks of color in prison and detention centers are two very obvious examples of the ways in which the historically racist and violent sexualization of people of color continues today.

White women, on the other hand, have historically been constructed as inherently pure, and the perceived threats to that purity were created to maintain and construct racist perceptions of black men and to justify their subsequent lynching or, more currently, imprisonment. While white women's bodies were always sexualized as virginal and appropriate, the bodies of women of color have been constructed as oversexualized and out of control in the creation of the white Amerikan nation, as is obvious by the methods of national containment; the racist myth of the welfare queen or the forced sterilization of over 200,000 black women in Amerika in the 1970s are just two of many examples. Our struggle as women and queer people of color is to fight for sexual agency, but to do it with a consciousness about how our oppression has functioned through the racialization of our sexualities.

The sex-positive movement does not address the interconnectedness of sexuality and racism or pivotal differences in power between white queers and queers of color. A few years ago, I went to a sex party in NYC for queer women and trans allies. I was looking for a space to play that didn't police desire in the ways I'm normally subjected to. What I found was just the opposite. I was one of two people of color there. Doing S/M play in an all-white environment where power relations regarding race are not explicitly dealt with, talked about, or even recognized is not creating radical alternatives to the racism in the mainstream gay movement. This, rather, is indicative of the racism that permeates the sex-positive movement.

Play parties and other noncommunity-based queer venues are frequently located in low-income communities of color. Oftentimes these venues place themselves in these communities without any consciousness about the racism and classism inherent in their actions. About a year-and-a-half ago there was a play-party venue located in Philly, in a working-class people-of-color neighborhood, that got raided by the cops. The white S/M community tried to fight stereotypes hurled at them through racist and classist ways of talking about the disinvestment of neighborhoods of color, and by essentially reproducing a lot of the arguments that are used to justify gentrification. They tried to counter stereotypes about the S/M community by discussing how happy the mostly family-based neighborhood was to have the S/M space. They actually talked about how white S/M sex spaces were bringing property values up, and how they kept their area clean and it stood out compared to the rest of the neighborhood.

An e-mail sent out by one of the people involved said, "The city should be kissing our butts 'cause there aren't that many people wishing to live here and invest in the community." The implication here was that the people who ran the S/M space should not be the targets of police brutality because they're helping the city deal with its unsightly elements; apparently police brutality should only be levied against more deserving communities. There was no discussion about how this was reproducing racist and classist arguments that were pro-gentrification, such as the perception of brown folk as "needing" white people for "revitalization." The implication that white people can bring up brown folks' property rates, not because of racism, but because, as the owners of this particular establishment put it, they take care of their property, was left uninterrogated; apparently years of racist city disinvestment leading to blight and gentrification was not the root cause, it was simply that white people take care of their things better.

Instead of discussing how queer desire in this country is literally and figuratively policed, and making links to communities of color and our daily lived experiences of police brutality, the customers and owners of the play party reproduced the racist and classist actions hurled against working-class communities of color. And, as a way to top it all off and make their political stance crystal clear, the venue put out gay pride flags, leather pride flags, and, of course, Amerikan flags. This is a tactic we've seen before in the mainstream gay "community." Without understanding or addressing the ways white supremacist ideology informs and is intimately tied to our ideas of gender and sexuality, the "radical" queer sex-positive agenda cannot be a site of meaningful resistance and will continue to reproduce the same racism and white privilege that exist in the fight for gay marriage and the gay rights movement in general.

We see this pattern again in "radical" drag king shows where performers generally fail to interrogate the role of racism in their performance of gender. I have been to performances where I am one of the few brown faces in the crowd, and all the performers are white but not all the performances are of white masculinity. There are many instances where white queers perform masculinities of color and do not recognize this as a very racist act. Just because it's queer blackface doesn't make it any less racist. I've also been to several drag king shows and have not been entertained by the positive sexualization of cops on stage. In a context where racialized and gendered state violence results in the incarceration of over two million people of color, sexualizing the racist, classist, homophobic, and transphobic brutality of cops is not a radical act. By sexualizing male cops with handcuffs and batons, white queers do not disrupt the racism inherent in the actions of police, and in fact positively sexualize this police brutality on communities of color. I go to drag king performances because they have the incredible possibility of decentering and challenging the naturalization of masculinity and the racism inherent in that process, but in the context of blackface and the eroticization of racist desires, the radical transformative possibilities of these performances are crushed in favor of a racist and classist queer political agenda.

Creating truly radical sites of resistance requires not just alternative queer spaces that espouse a different politic than the one in the mainstream gay movement; it requires that the creators of those spaces pay diligent attention to who is leading the construction of those spaces to ensure that the new spaces do not reproduce the same white supremacist ideology as the mainstream.

RADICAL SITES OF RESISTANCE

Throughout this essay I have examined the ways in which gay mainstream culture and radical sites of queer resistance are based in white supremacist ideology, but I have not talked about radical sites and acts of resistance for queer people of color. Resistance takes place when like-minded queer people of color come together to talk, reflect, and take action on issues that are pertinent to our lives, without having to cut off parts of our experiences as oppressed people. Resistance happens when people of color challenge homophobia in our own communities, while also challenging white stereotypes that people of color are inherently homophobic. Resistance happens when queer people of color in NYC come out to protest a racist drag show performance where a white gay man does blackface of a woman with eight kids on welfare. It happens when working-class queer and transgendered youth of color organize to fight against the gentrification of the piers in NYC. It happens when queers of color challenge prison activists to examine alternative ways to provide safety for marginalized members of our communities, and simultaneously fight against the prison industrial complex.

We resist both the mainstream gay culture and the still white, still racist alternatives because, as queer people of color, our resistance is not necessarily about choice, it is about survival.

FIGHTING TO WIN

DEAN SPADE

In August of 2002, I founded the Sylvia Rivera Law Project, a nonprofit organization providing free legal services to low-income transgender, transsexual, intersex, and gender-variant people. That same year, the Sexual Orientation Non-Discrimination Act (SONDA) passed in the New York State Legislature. To understand the significance of SONDA's passage, it's helpful to give a brief reminder about queer activism in New York State, and in particular to call to mind the event that some credit with sparking the current LGBT rights movement, the Stonewall rebellion. The Stonewall rebellion was an explosion of gorgeous resistance one night in 1969—when the sexual and gender outsiders of the time, tired of being abused by cops, arrested for cross-dressing, and beaten and raped just for gathering in bars and clubs, struck back against the police with bottles and high heels and whatever else they could find. The Stonewall rebellion was instigated by low-income people, people of color, trans people like Sylvia Rivera, and other sex/gender outsiders who were the most common and easiest targets (like they still are) for homophobic and transphobic cops. It was those people, not people who were comfortably closeted in well-paying jobs, who got kicked around to the point where they wouldn't take it anymore. They shocked and inspired the whole world with their bravery and defiance, changing the meaning of sex and gender politics forever.

Fast-forward thirty years, to SONDA: a culminating moment, no doubt, in the struggle that those queer and trans rebels—street workers, outlawed for the clothes they wore and the people they fucked—kicked up a notch that night in 1969. But, in a sadly typical turn of events, SONDA turned out to be as much a defeat as a victory because, despite persistent lobbying and activism from trans communities in New York State to the gay rights organization pushing the legislation, SONDA excluded gender identity discrimination protection, covering only sexual orientation. At the same time, in the very neighborhood where the Stonewall Inn is located, a coalition of gay and straight high-income renters and home owners have teamed up to rid their streets (their group is literally called RID, or Residents In Distress) of the queer and trans youth of color who have found each other and formed community in the public spaces of that neighborhood for years. The residents engage in vigilantism and have pressured politicians to increase police presence in the area, resulting in extensive harassment and false arrests (particularly against trans youth of color), as well as police brutality against the youth. For homeless and marginally housed teens, this environment typically turns into warrants for arrest and eventual time in the juvenile and adult criminal justice systems.

What happened to the alliance that existed between queer and trans people, between people fighting street harassment by cops and people fighting employment discrimination for being gay, that seems to have existed at least in some format during the Stonewall era? What does it mean for activists that we see wealthy gay and lesbian people setting an agenda that excludes and/or harms low-income queers, trans people, and queers of color? Emergent trans movements are in some ways mainstreaming for the first time, with funding available for new trans organizations and the beginnings of legal and legislative victories for trans communities. What kind of analysis do we need to make sure that we don't replicate the mistakes of the gay and lesbian rights movement? As a trans activist who survived my youth on public benefits systems that have now been all but destroyed, I'm dead set on seeking an analysis and praxis for trans activism that starts with those facing the most severe consequences of the gender binary: the people who are also struggling against white supremacy, xenophobia, ageism, ableism, and the criminalization of poverty.

What I would like to see most is trans activism and trans analysis that reflects the most urgent issues in trans life and that creates dynamic responses and ideas that move us to think in new ways about the systems and institutions we're dismantling, and the alliances we're building to create the world we want to live in. In order to talk about the urgency of a trans analysis and activism root-ed in fighting racism and poverty, I want to give a little bit of a big picture about how trans and gender-variant people are overrepresented in punitive systems whose punitive measures are driv-en by racist and anti-poor cultural understandings.

Trans people face enormous, and mostly unaddressed, discrimination in education, employ-ment, health care, and public benefits. Many trans people start out their lives with the obstacle of abuse or harassment at home, or are kicked out of their homes by their parents on the basis of their gender identity or expression. Some turn to foster care, but often end up homeless when they experience harassment and violence at the hands of staff and other residents in foster care facili-ties. The adult homeless shelter system is, similarly, inaccessible to them due to the fact that most facilities are gender-segregated and will either turn down a trans person outright or refuse to house them according to their lived gender identity. Similarly, harassment and violence against trans and gender-different students is rampant in schools, and many drop out before finishing or are kicked out. Many trans people also do not pursue higher education due to fears of applying to schools and being required to reveal their birth name and birth sex, having not been able to change these on their documents. Furthermore, trans people face severe discrimination in the job market and are routinely fired for transitioning on the job or when their gender identity or expression comes to their supervisor's attention. In most of the U.S., this kind of discrimination is still not explicitly illegal.

Trans people also have a difficult time accessing the entitlements that exist, though in a reduced and diminished form, to support poor people. Discrimination on the basis of gender identity is common in welfare offices, on workfare job sites, in Medicaid offices, and in Administrative Law Hearings for welfare, Medicaid, and Social Security Disability benefits. These benefit programs have been decimated in the last ten years and are generally operated with a punitive approach that includes frequent illegal termination of benefits and the failure to pro-vide people with their entitlements. For most people seeking to access these programs consistent-ly during a time of need, the availability of an attorney or advocate to help navigate the hearings process has been essential to maintaining benefits. Unfortunately, most poverty attorneys and advocacy organizations are still severely lacking in basic information about serving trans clients and may reject cases on the basis of a person's gender identity or create such an unwelcoming environment that a trans client will not return for services. Based on community awareness of this problem, many trans people will not even seek these services, expecting to be subjected to humiliating and unhelpful treatment. The resulting lack of access to even the remaining shreds of the welfare system leaves a disproportionate number of trans people in severe poverty and engaging in criminalized work such as prostitution or the drug economy in order to survive. This, in turn, results in large numbers of trans people becoming entangled in the juvenile and adult criminal justice systems, where they are subjected to extreme harassment and violence.

We all interact with gender-segregated facilities and institutions, like bathrooms and locker rooms, but many of us haven't thought about what it means that almost every institution designed to house, exploit the labor of, and control low-income people and people of color is gender-segregated. In all of these locations gender binaries are enforced by means of humiliation, assault, and rape. We are aware that the prison industry is sustained by false discourses of crime and safety ND that the cutbacks in welfare are justified by an entrenched and racist belief that poverty stems from personal irresponsibility rather than structural market forces. We are aware that the drug war, responsible for mass incarceration of people of color in the U.S. for nonviolent crimes as well as for U.S. military violence abroad in places like Colombia, is similarly fueled by racism and anti-poor sentiment. However, in part because a white liberal civil rights discourse has framed the LGBfakeT rights movement, the vital importance of these issues to the lives of most trans people has often remained underdocumented, underanalyzed, and insufficiently acted upon by our emergent movements.

Further, the connections between opposition to the consolidation of global capital and domestic queer and trans activism remain underdiscussed. In part, this is because "globalization" is frequently conceived of as only a "third world" (or two-thirds world, as I've heard one activist call it) issue. Many U.S. activists still fail to make connections between the domestic oppression, to which many of us contribute and from which many of us benefit, and the manifestations of the consolidation of global capital in poorer countries. Too many people still find it easier to examine and oppose oppression elsewhere than to examine privilege and oppression in their own city, state, or country. Prisoners, immigrants denied the right to wage or safety protections, people working in criminalized economies like sex and drug work, and others make up the growing population of people inside and outside the U.S. upon whom the operation of our economy is utterly dependent, but who are blamed and vilified for their position at the bottom of the economy. Trans people, of course, are a part of this bottom layer, excluded from much educational and economic participation, and from most poverty programs, by our failures to comply with gender prerequisites for participation. This, in my view, is where our analysis, our creative efforts toward change, and our power should stem from. If we understand ourselves as a population struggling against increasingly vicious forces of capitalism, which do their harm through vectors of race, gender, immigration status, ability, and age, how can we begin to envision a strategy that actually engages our struggle?

I think it's time we question our alliances—where do we fit in the current mainstream LGBfakeT movement? This movement has become focused on inclusion in institutions like private property, marriage, the military, Boy Scouts, etc. Mainstream LGBfakeT organizations choose to fight for homos to be able to pass our apartments on to each other, rather than for tenants' rights or low-income housing. They fight for people who are employed to be able to get their partners on their private health coverage, but take no stand on Medicaid and do nothing to promote universal healthcare. They rally around passing hate crimes laws, which put more punishment power in the hands of an overtly racist criminal system, but do little or nothing for the countless trans and queer people incarcerated in the adult and juvenile justice systems.

A good example of the priorities of the LGBfakeT movement was the fight over Props 21 and 22 in California in 2000. Prop 21 called for a new law that would make it easier to punish juvenile offenders as adults and would change and expand the definition of "gang" activities to make it easier to target low-income youth of color and give them harsher sentences. Prop 22 was an anti-gay marriage law. Student activists in many of California's public schools worked on amazing cross-issue campaigns, opposing Props 21 and 22 with coalitions of queer people, people of color, and low-income people. The GLBT center in L.A. rallied around Prop 22, but made no statements about Prop 21. They conceptualized this utterly symbolic struggle about whether or not same-sex marriages would be recognized in California *if* they ever become legal somewhere else as vital to GLBT politics, but did not see the creation of real policy that targets low-income youth and youth of color as a "gay" issue.

We see similarly skewed priorities when groups like the Human Rights Campaign or Empire State Pride Agenda endorse conservative politicians like Al D'Amato and George Pataki, who are enemies of public education and promoters of the criminal injustice system. These are the same groups that back pieces of legislation like ENDA and SONDA, which don't include trans rights. This is representative of the single-issue politics that has emerged as a certain sector of well-funded groups and individuals have narrowed the focus of what was, at its inception, a more broad-sweeping fight for the rights of queer and trans freaks, to a struggle for the rights of a few race-and-money-privileged people to be able to access their birthright piece of the capitalist pie. With every passing year, I feel more alienated from that struggle and more invested in finding and building alliances with groups that are working on the issues that pose the most serious obstacles to trans people's ability to live with dignity and self-determination. More and more I'm interested in making alliances and connections to the methods of analysis used by other people whose bodies are labeled wrong—disabled people, fat people, for example—who've pioneered methods of examining rights discourses and medico-legal governance that have vital crossovers with trans experience.

Ultimately, I know we are fighting battles for our lives, and the lives of those we love, and to win we'll have to use every strategy in our arsenal—including litigation, mass protest, graffiti, zines, media activism, filmmaking, one-on-one and group consciousness-raising, vandalism, theft, and God knows what else. This includes, in my work, sometimes making alliances with groups who've formerly taken positions that I think suck—because they have some access or power that can be useful to help a trans person in need right now. But I want us to have a strategy and analysis that is not just about begging the LGBfakeT organizations to finally include and notice us, when they've been notoriously unconcerned with the struggles of people fighting the kinds of systems in which trans people are embroiled.

I want us to reach out to find new coalitions, merge our analysis in new ways with people who are already prioritizing the rights of low-income people, people of color, people with disabilities, HIV-positive people, old people, and youth. I think the circumstances we're living in, locally and globally, are overwhelming—and we have to remember that there are more of us suffering under capitalism and imperialism than benefiting. It can be easy to drop out of these struggles or to choose to ignore these issues in our analysis if they aren't knocking down our doors, but we have to remember our responsibility as people living in the belly of the beast. In this country, many of us receive material benefits from the domination of others that is done in our names. We also have opportunities that many people in the world don't have, to access and oppose the decision makers who run this game. It's our responsibility to embrace a broad view of social justice and to join in a fight against capitalism, racism, and imperialism, and fight to win.

GAY ART GUERRILLAS: INTERVIEW WITH JIM HUBBARD AND SARAH SCHULMAN

STEPHEN KENT JUSICK

SKJ: We're here to talk about resisting assimilation and the way in which you did that together in your cultural practice.

SS: Yes, the way we've tried.

JH: Yes. [Laughs]

SKJ: Okay, how did you guys meet, and when?

JH: I don't remember when we met, but I do remember when we bonded. It was that incredibly rainy night when we were putting up that poster.

SS: Gay Art Guerrillas! That's how we met. At David France's political party . . . where he invited all the gay people from the "left." There was this group called CRASH.

JH: Yes. The Committee Resisting . . . something, Sexism and Homophobia [The Coalition Against Racism, Anti-Semitism, Sexism, and Heterosexism].

SS: This is the late '70s. The gay left was so huge that there were multiple organizations. There was the Lavender Left, CRASH, some other stuff, the Committee of Gay and Lesbian Socialists. Right? And then there were all of those sectarian parties that had gay members. So your roommate, David France, who at the time was on the left and is now an editor at *Newsweek*, he threw a political party and invited all the gays and lesbians on the left who were all from these different factions. And that's where I probably first met you. And then we did our project called the Gay Art Guerrillas. It was you and me, Fred Carl, Ellen [Turner] (someone . . . she was a painter and worked at Oscar Wilde Bookstore), Ellen's lover Daphne, and a black woman whose name I think was Pauline. Anyway, we made up these posters and we called ourselves the Gay Art Guerrillas. I forget what the slogan was.

JH: I think it was something like "all dressed up and nowhere to go."

SS: That's it! It was because there was nobody who was showing gay and lesbian art. And we pasted it everywhere.

JH: Well, we tried but the rain was so incredible that night that we couldn't actually put anything on a wall. So we did it in the subways. That was our solution.

SKJ: I see. So that's how you bonded, doing that action?

JH: Yes, the two of us were working together. Somehow we got separated from everyone else.

SS: You see, one thing we have in common is that we are total workhorses. TOTAL! You know, if somebody needs to schlep the bucket, it's going to be me and Jim. And we would always do these crappy bullshit jobs, like pasting these posters.

JH: And we did that with the early festival. We would go out and just do the East and West Village.

SKJ: In '82 you were doing this CRASH postering campaign. And, that's pretty much all it was, right? It was this guerrilla postering, but it wasn't followed by an event.

SS: No. But it must have come from a discussion of the need for gay artists to have a place to show their work. I mean, there was no place. In these days, the lesbian theater was . . . you could not show lesbian work at P.S. 122, at the Kitchen, all the doors were closed, closed, closed. And Jim and I were having this discussion that you couldn't get gay film shown in experimental film venues, like that place across from the topless bar on White Street, the Collective for Living Cinema. And the gay festivals weren't showing any experimental film work either. So the real artists, you know, gay people who were formally inventive and engaged, had absolutely no place to show their work.

SKJ: So we're talking about 1982, and I know the festival didn't start until 1987. But, how aware were you of gay experimental film work at that . . .

SS: I was not.

SKJ: Okay, so how did you end up having that conversation?

SS: Well, we were talking about other kinds of work. I had a theater company that Jim used to come to, to see our plays. The theater is where the 7A restaurant is now, and our rent was $100 per month. And Jim, David, and Don Shewey were like the only men who ever came to see our work. Well, and Nelson [Gonzalez] and Nicky Paraiso, and that was it. So, very few men were interested in lesbian work, and I had a theater company at the time (from '80 to '85). But I wasn't interested in film yet—not until I got involved with Abigail Child. That's when all of that got started. The other thing that was happening in '82 was that Roger [Jacoby, Jim Hubbard's lover from 1971–1981] had AIDS and people were freaking out.

JH: No, Roger wasn't diagnosed until '84.

SS: '84, okay. Because at that time in '82, '83—that's when people were just starting to freak out. I remember you eating AL-721. I remember that day . . .

JH: Yes, David and I had manufactured AL-721. What was it? It was egg lipids. What you do is mix egg yolks, lecithin, and something else, and you put it in an ice tray, because it tasted vile. And so you iced it and then spread it on bread and ate it as quickly as possible. It was supposed to, you know, cure AIDS or whatever.

SS: Of course, it was bullshit. It was one of the many inventions at the time. This was around Rock Hudson, because for some reason I associate you eating this stuff with Rock Hudson.

JH: Yeah, that makes sense that it was a little later.

SS: And I also remember David picking up his shirt and showing me his chest and asking me if I thought it was KS. So everybody was panicked. So that was all going on. For me, in 1986, I fell in love with Abigail Child. Big mistake! [Laughs] And she was, um, straight and in the closet about our relationship. And she was a fairly well-known experimental filmmaker in the day. And she insisted . . . construed herself as a misunderstood genius and had no audience because her work was so superior and blah, blah, blah. And I was a populist, and I would even say a communist, which is something Jim and I shared, to an extent. And I believed . . . oh it's so hard for me to say this now. But, I organized the first forty-four years of my life (I'm forty-five now) around the belief that if you just explain something to someone clearly enough, that they could understand you. It has been very hard for me to come to terms with the fact that people do not want to know what's true. I still can't even face that. But I believed in people and their ability to do good and to understand. So I thought, as Abigail had explained to me, if experimental film could convey certain formal experiences of living that would organically resonate with human beings, then all you had to do was create an environment in which they could be welcomed into it and understand it. What Jim and I put together was that gay people were the perfect audience for experimental film because they had no representation at all, and their lives didn't follow conventional narrative.

SKJ: I understand how gay and lesbian people could be the perfect audience for experimental film, but why get involved in experimental film at all then?

SS: Because I was in love with Abby. Because I wanted her to come out and be honest about our relationship. But she was so under siege, she was so undermined by the prejudice about formal invention, that I guess somewhere in the back of my mind I was trying to create a community where she could feel recognized and so she could come out of the closet. I'm serious.

JH: Right. Well, my version of that was that I couldn't get any shows. I had just finished *Homosexual Desire in Minnesota*.

SKJ: You were an experimental filmmaker. And you had been making films for a long time by this point already.

JH: Sure, I started making films in 1974.

SKJ: Experimental work?

JH: Yes, it was always experimental. I don't think I recognized that at first. Okay, what happened was that in 1974, I had graduated college. I didn't have the slightest idea what to do. I had gone to San Francisco because my father was there and I knew he had to give me a job. So I had this silly job working at a health food store in downtown San Francisco. And I was walking down the back side of Nob Hill smoking a joint and said to myself, you've always wanted to make movies, why don't you just go ahead and do it. But I had no idea how to do it. So I started looking at schools, and went to UCLA for a weekend. I was horrified. These big macho straight guys were stalking around, bragging about "bringing in the film south of five," you know, meaning less than five million. And I ran the other way. Then I went to a Stan Brakhage show at the San Francisco Art Institute. I went two nights in a row, in fact. It was the world premiere of *Text of Light* and James Broughton introduced Brakhage. And I said, I want to study under that queen. But Broughton was still married at the time. This was just the time when Joel Singer was in his class and was causing the great *scandale* and stealing Broughton away from his wife.

SS: Of course, he had already made *The Bed* . . .

JH: Oh sure, he had been gay on and off throughout his life. His life was like a checkerboard of homosexuality and heterosexuality. But anyway, I started making these experimental films because I realized that's the only way you can have gay content in a film. You know, in Hollywood at that point, and even at this point, there's still not any real gay anything.

SS: That's why my theater company was in the East Village. I wasn't allowed to cross 14th Street as a playwright until 2002. So we were forced. Jim and I have always been out, in our work, and if you did that you were forced into the margins. I mean, for me, I was never that formally inventive. I mean, I am compared to the uptown world, but compared to downtown, I'm really not. But the convention was so unaccepted that you were automatically thrown into there whether you liked it or not.

So anyway, we got together and had this conversation, because I wanted to prove something to Abby, really. And because I was such a workhorse, and so are you, that when we have an idea, then we actually do it and make it happen. The first person we went to talk to . . . well, first we had a conversation about where to have it. I wanted it to be in the Chandalier Club [sic].

JH: Oh really? I don't remember that.

SS: Well, you said no and said it had to be at Millennium, because the point was to have it in an official film space. It was to insist that these films are part of the larger experimental film world. It's so funny now because gay film has eclipsed experimental film so hugely, because we have a popular audience that they don't have. But in those days they controlled everything.

JH: What's amazing is that here it is in 2003, and I'm still trying to prove it to these people. I just finished editing this number of the *Millennium Film Journal* on lesbian and gay experimental cinema. Okay? Now here they are finally doing it fifteen years after they should have. Right? But, the year after we started the festival, they should have asked me to do this.

SS: Let's talk about Su Friedrich. That's a really interesting person in all of this. And we needed a big opening-night show. And the most famous lesbian artist, probably in the world, at the time, was Su Friedrich, who was out of the closet.

SKJ: You know, I do believe that in the program notes from that first festival you even promoted [her] screening at the Whitney.

JH: Oh yes, probably yes.

A Queer Kind of Film

September 15 through 20.
The First Lesbian and Gay
Experimental Film Festival
opens September 15 at
Millennium, 66 East Fourth Street, N.Y.C.
with screenings at 7 and 9 P.M.

61 Films by 37 Filmmakers

SS: We were proud of her. Well, she offered us the world premiere of her new film, *Damned If You Don't*. It was just incredibly generous of her, I mean *incredibly* generous of her to give us that because it gave our first year credibility. And that was very much in the tradition that Jim and I were in. The prevailing idea of the time was, as Marx said, "Each according to their ability, each according to their need."

SKJ: Could you talk about your conception of the festival as something that gave back to the community? The rest of the community that you were involved with was not just filmmakers. You had to tap into writers and the press, like the *Voice*, for publicity and stuff like that.

SS: Jim and I have always been about community building and institution building. I think it's sort of a Jewish thing, something you do as part of your responsibility to your "tribe." But anyway, what happened was incredible. Our audience was a gay audience, not an elite audience. It was regular gay people who came to our thing because it was the gay thing that was happening. And they were able to relate to a very wide range of art. These were people without much of an art education, for the most part. I think that we proved you can take complex work and invite people in if it's relevant to their lives in some way, and it can expand their aesthetic sensibility. I think we proved that.

SS: Like the way we organized the publicity. Jim and I went out every fuckin' night with those buckets and we pasted the schedule all over the place. Just the two of us, every night! And then the way we handled the press screenings. I would call critics myself, and I would call them four times, ten times, whatever it took. I still do that now.

JH: It was grueling. There's this other set of *prima donnas*, the press, and you could never get them all in the same room at the same time. So we would end up doing individual press screenings. I remember we did thirty hours of press screenings for a festival that was twenty hours long.

SS: You know, the big coup the first year was that I got Todd Haynes his first review. It was for a film of his called *Assassins*, which was his Brown thesis film, I believe. And I called Elliot Stein, must have been four hundred times. So he finally came in, we talked about it, and he gave it a rave review. I remember Todd's face. I'll never forget it, because he was really still a boy then. And he asked, "What should I do now?" And I said to send him a thank you note. You know, because that's how much we cared.

Like when we showed Jennie Livingston, what was it, *Paris Is Burning* (this was later at Anthology). She had an apartment that she shared with Ray Navarro and Anthony Ledesma. This is when Ray and Anthony were still alive and had TB, and she kicked them out, which was a whole big thing. Well anyway, I was over there one night. And she had a video of this film she was working on, *Paris Is Burning*. There were a bunch of us there and we watched it. But the film couldn't be shown because it was on double system, and they didn't have enough money to make a print. So I said, "We'll show it because it's double system. It's experimental." So Jim and I booked this thing. No one had shown it. We rented this fucking double system and then we were like, "Oh my god, we have this film about black gay men." So we started going down every night to the piers where there was this whole voguing culture. It hadn't been discovered yet because Jennie was the first person to film it. And we went up to people to say, we really think you'll like this film and you should come see this film. It's a film about you. We just went down there and handed them the leaflets. And the night of the film, everybody came. Hundreds of black gay men came. I mean, there was a line around the block and we had to show the film . . . how many times?

JH: We did three screenings, which just pissed her off incredibly. It just happened and we didn't even think twice about it. I mean, we actually called her and left a message on her machine.

SS: And, I was like, "Jennie, it's so great! We went to our people, and we told them we have a film for you, and they came!" And we were so excited. But she was furious at us because she thought we were eating into her theatrical distribution. So she insisted that we pay her three times the fee. You see, we were communists, so we paid everyone the same fee. Because we knew you could work for ten years on a ten-minute experimental film, so why should they be paid by the minute? Well, she insisted she be paid three times as much. She came furiously and seized her print. And then we got a phone call from her lawyer saying that they were going to sue us, and sue me personally. At that time, I don't think I even owned a chair though. I mean, honestly, we were so poor, I think I just told them I don't even have any personal assets.

SKJ: Okay, but I actually want to go back to the first year, and the way in which you organized certain things. It wasn't a corporate structure, or a commercialized structure, even in the implementation of . . .

JH: It was just the two of us.

SKJ: Didn't you have something like a "drop off your print" party, for the filmmakers?

JH: Well yeah.

SS: Everything was always artist-oriented. The mandate was that the artists had to get paid before we could get paid.

JH: Right. But first of all, it was all film. There was no video because people weren't making video at that point. It was just starting. This was even before video-8. So, every film we showed we had to preview. People would come to my studio and show us their films, or we would go to them and look at their films. And we'd tell them right away whether we wanted to show it or not. Then we'd send acceptance letters. And a couple of weeks before the festival, I guess, Sarah and I would sit there for an afternoon and we would have all the filmmakers come and drop off their films.

SKJ: Was that just a practical thing, or was there a social element?

SS: It created community, and creating community is what it was all about.

SKJ: Because you were operating in this community-building mode, I'm curious about how you handled rejecting people, both in person, and over long distance. And also, can you talk about the first year, and how localized [the festival] was?

JH: The first year, half the films were old and we knew about them. And then the other half were new. And only one filmmaker came through the call for entry. That was Larry Brose. One day, I got this little package in the mail, at my studio, and it was the complete works of Larry Brose. All these Super-8 reels. It was wonderful.

SS: It was some amazing film. And it really expressed how we were feeling about AIDS at the time. But I was always in love with Chantal Akerman, so we probably had shown every film of hers by the end of my stay there. And she was against being in gay film festivals so we had to get them all "sideways." So we had to order her prints from other places.

JH: Yeah, we'd rent them from this place in L.A. But when we called, they'd never be there. So we had to just keep calling and calling.

SS: So, we outed her. But as for rejection, aesthetically we were extremely benevolent. I mean, we really tried to look with open eyes and open hearts at everything, and people's formal ideas. What I think we really stopped at were certain kinds of representation. Very vulgar, and very stupidly distorted representation was hard for us to swallow. I remember there was one film in which people were dressed in Nazi uniforms and burst in on a gay couple in bed. To me, that kind of representation always makes things more palatable than they really are. And it was, in a sense, a kind of propaganda for those horrific experiences.

JH: Yeah, I think as Jews we were insulted.

SS: So, often it would be for representational reasons. Certainly, we never censored anything for sexual, violent, or political content. All of this was before the "sex wars." The other thing we saw happen before our very eyes was the MFA-ing of experimental film. The first people that we showed became the teachers of the second generation that we showed. The first generation had experimented and figured it all out by themselves. But the second generation studied experimental film as a genre of film with certain properties and rules.

JH: Yeah, Abby was probably the only person with an MFA that we showed the first year.

SS: I've spent a lot of time catching up, because Jim still knows five thousand times more about film than I do. But I had to watch a lot of archival work. We used to go to the Museum of Modern Art and just watch. So I was trying to catch up and understand, like the Warhol films and the [Mike and George] Kuchar films. Did we ever show *Chelsea Girls*?

JH: No, we didn't because, remember, at first the Warhol films were unavailable, and then, they were monopolized by the Whitney and MoMA. Well, first we showed that unknown Warhol film, which we knew what it was. It was a section of *Loves of Ondine*, that Ondine thought was boring and had Jerry Tartaglia cut out, out of Ondine's print. Jerry had maintained this piece; he just kept it. So we showed that. And of course, the Warhol Foundation came running to see what this was.

SKJ: But why did you show that, for what reason?

JH: Well, we were being provocative. And we thought we were the legitimate venue for showing Warhol and we weren't allowed to. So we did what we could.

SKJ: I wanted to ask about finances and money at the beginning. I know you said you paid people, but I was wondering about the funding and how you pulled it off.

SS: At first it was all just box office.

SKJ: Didn't you have to put money down, to rent the venue, let's say?

JH: First of all, you have to realize that the economy was completely different. I had a part-time job, less than half time, at Citibank doing word processing, and could make enough money to support myself. So I decided that, if I have to lose a thousand dollars on this, I can afford to do that. In fact, it didn't work out that way. I fronted all the money for the festival except that first festival we got fifteen hundred dollars from Manhattan decentralization funds, which you can still do for a new organization. Other than that it was box office, and I got paid back. I can't remember, though. Did we pay ourselves for the first festival?

SS: Maybe a hundred. I wanted to say something about the philosophy behind this. From all the political movements I had been in, I had come to believe that if a political movement is actually meeting people's needs, they will join it. If a cultural event is doing its job, then it will earn back its costs. But, once you start pumping these things with lots of money, you replace the need to be accountable to the public. So we really tried to do this by box office, and we were quite successful for quite some time, I think. When the two of us ran it, we ran it quite cheaply and we paid artist's fees the whole time. For the seven years I was involved, we paid artist's fees.

JH: Then we got NYSCA [New York State Council on the Arts] grants starting in the second year. But they were a relatively small percentage of the money—the rest was all box office.

SS: Our tickets were very cheap and we let people in for free. You know, you knew everyone in the community and you knew who was poor. People who needed to see it would be able to come see it. We never turned anybody away.

SKJ: How did you communicate that?

SS: It was known.

JH: Back then, every gay event and lesbian event, the price was always five dollars, more if you can, less if you can't.

SS: We both had personal credibility with the community. We would tell people we were doing this really interesting thing, and people would come. Okay, we would have to call some people a hundred times, but eventually they would come review it. We would say, we're doing this festival, come show your work. They would. So people knew us. We had personal relationships with people so they knew that they could come and get in for free if they needed. The other thing was that the political movements were really exploding at the time, and ACT UP, we'd always let ACT UP be part of the festival. There was always someone there tabling. I would call and ask them to come table. So the festival was also a place where people got political information.

JH: Yeah, I remember someone came the first year. Now that you're saying this, I remember someone [Robert Garcia] at Millennium getting up and talking about ACT UP.

SS: I was in ACT UP at the same time that this festival started. So the ACT UP community really overlapped.

SKJ: That's really interesting. I didn't know there was that.

JH: Well you also have to remember, talking about credibility, that there were only five other gay and lesbian film festivals in the world at this time. And none of them were particularly friendly to experimental film. So these people really didn't have a place to show, because the avant-garde showcases weren't showing them.

SS: But our community went way beyond film. It was political gay people, artistic gay people, regular gay people who wanted a place to go on a Friday night. Where could lesbians go on a Friday night that was interesting? Nowhere. So the women's shows were always on Friday night. That was another political decision that we made. Because women had nowhere to go, we made the best nights be the lesbian nights. And they would be packed. Always.

JH: Millennium seats one hundred four people. We had two hundred fifty for Barbara Hammer's show.

SS: Right. Well, anyway, about the move into video. I think part of it was when I had an affair with [videomaker] Cecilia [Dougherty].

JH: I think the first video we ever showed was in '89. It was Phillip Roth's *A 25 Year Old Gay Man Loses His Virginity to a Woman*.

SS: Starring Annie Sprinkle.

JH: The reason . . . Phillip lied to us. He said he'd have a print by the time of the festival. So, we had to set up monitors in the aisles of Anthology. They had no video projection. So the next year we decided we have to integrate. I also have to give credit to Gregg Bordowitz, who was relentless in arguing for the inclusion of video.

SS: Video activism was also happening. So there was a cultural transformation going on. Video was an essential part of the political movement. Well anyway, I was having sex with Cecilia Dougherty, and we premiered her new feature, which was called *Coal Miner's Granddaughter*. That was the lead lesbian opening night feature.

[A]nother interesting thing . . . was when we showed Shirley Clark's *Portrait of Jason*.

JH: Not one of our best moments.

SS: No, it was complicated. We were showing this film that was historically the first overt representation of a black gay man. And yet, it was profoundly racist in and of itself.

JH: And homophobic.

SS: Right, but the thing is that there was not a cultural discussion yet that was sophisticated enough for that film to be watched as an object. We knew that it was going to be watched subjectively, not objectively. So we decided to only show the part before it became really, really exploitative. So we turned off the projector before the film was over. That was terrible. It was our only censorship experience. Our biggest mistake.

SKJ: Why?

SS: Because we should have shown the whole film and taken the hit.

JH: And had a discussion afterwards. We could have done that.

SS: That year, we had a focus on films by and about black gay men. It was the first time, I believe, that there were enough films by and about black gay men to do that in any festival. We showed a film about the guy who was the Mapplethorpe model.

SKJ: *Eye to Eye,* by Isabelle Hegner. You also showed *Looking for Langston*, by Isaac Julien, *Tongues Untied*, by Marlon Riggs, and *Black and White Study*, by Cramer. Later, how did you see either the community or the festival's role or engagement with the community change? How did it function as a community organization over the years? At least, as an organization that was supposed to have accountability?

SS: I didn't see a change during my tenure. I mean, I left for personal reasons. Basically, I had spent seven years of my life facilitating other people's work. You know, it's a little sick. And then I went on to spend five years of my life facilitating the Irish Lesbian and Gay Organization. I have problems. I have big problems, of which these are emblematic. But, I was also very proud of the way that we transferred power. We gave a financially healthy and intact organization to younger people. I think that was great. And Shari [Frilot] is now one of the lead programmers in the world. That was one of our best moments in the world, when that transition happened.

But, after that, I watched from afar. And I personally began to get alienated from the festival. After I left, I could never get a schedule about what nights, which shows, what people were going to be showing, and at what time, in enough time in advance in order for me to go. This has been for years and years and years. So to me, that was symbolic that people didn't really want me to go. It becomes so "insider" that the outreach just isn't there. And then artist's fees got waylaid, and then there was corporate sponsorship. I wasn't as interested aesthetically in a lot of the choices. There was too much of a focus on sloppy sexuality as the only subject. I just got less interested, personally.

SKJ: Let's talk about corporate sponsorship and what relationships you had to that? There was a relationship to the commercial culture in that you had to deal with the gay bars. You had a party at the Tunnel I think one year.

JH: Yeah, but it was a different kind of relationship. The gay community always had this base, in the bars. And political organizations always had a relationship with the bars.

SS: Especially in the East Village.

JH: Yeah. I think that's true in most cities, though. I've lived in Pittsburgh, Minneapolis, San Francisco, and that was true in all those places. So there's a difference between having a relationship with a local entity, even if it is corrupt, and with an international vodka company, or something. The corporate stuff I think you're alluding to . . .

SKJ: I'm asking about your eschewing it in the beginning.

JH: We didn't eschew it. It didn't exist!

SS: We never would have considered it. It never would have crossed our minds. We were so out of the mainstream, I mean, come on. We were SO marginal. We couldn't get reviewed in the *Times* for years. I was calling [gay New York Times film critic] Stephen Holden at home . . .

JH: We still can't get reviewed in the *Times*.

SS: But when I started to hear from Jim, "Should we get Camel cigarettes," I went, "Egh." I was in the Lesbian Avengers at the time (in '92) and we had started the Dyke March [with ACT UP Women's Network]. This was when the Gay Pride March was becoming this big corporate event, and the Dyke March refused any such sponsorship. There was a concerted effort at that point, then, to keep some part of the community community-based and not have a logo slapped on it.

SKJ: The Dyke March wasn't even permitted by the city?

SS: No permit. I'm from the old school and that's my way. I don't like gay community things having logos on them from companies. I don't think you need it.

JH: Well, there was a real change in the financial base of the festival. Then [in 1992?], there was a financial crisis in the state. NYSCA was cut and we were cut back to three thousand dollars. So, for the first time, we were in the red. In fact, the festival never really recovered from that finan-

MIX

13

Get Lucky

13th New York Lesbian & Gay
Experimental Film/Video Festival

November
10th -14th
1999
Anthology Film
Archives
PopcornQ
www.mixnyc.org

cial shock. But also, you talked about giving it over to younger people. And, younger people generally have a different relationship to mainstream culture and to capitalism than we did. And, they never saw the problems in corporate sponsorship, except in those surprisingly rare instances where corporations made demands on us.

SS: Well, I think the aesthetic of what is cool really shifted. For us, the thing that was cool was being of the people, of being cool, of being regular. That was the community-building side of it. But then glamour became cool. I think one of the key moments for me was when Christine [Vachon] and Todd [Haynes] and Barry Ellsworth started Apparatus. Suddenly there was this kind of Ivy League aesthetic, a whole different aesthetic than Jim and I were in. When Jim and I applied to them for money, and they came to our studio to interview us, they made us feel bad. I remember when they left. We felt really, really bad about ourselves. We weren't cool enough, or good-looking enough. We weren't fancy enough. We just felt bad. That was the deciding moment for me.

SKJ: You were talking about male representation of sexuality, and about orgasms. You know, there's a certain kind of lesbian who doesn't really want to see cocks. That was obviously not one of your issues.

SS: I would say that personally, I don't really care. But that was not the job. We weren't programming what we personally wanted to see. We were trying to facilitate a community expression. So that didn't really matter. [To Jim] You fought for lesbian films, not because you needed to see female bodies, but more for ideological reasons.

JH: There was an underlying, almost unspoken, commitment to keeping it all 50/50. In fact, I was the one who insisted on having lesbian night. You were against it at first.

SS: Yeah, I'm sure that's true.

JH: Basically, it has always been a principle for the festival that shows are inclusive, you know, everyone together—men, women, trans people. Well, we didn't have transgender films in our first year.

SS: That's not true. We had a transgender film our first year, Marguerite Paris's film [*All Woman Are Equal*]. Yes, we've had transgender film since the beginning.

JH: So there would be one gay male show, and one lesbian show. And then "date-night" shows.

SS: We wanted to give people a place to go where they could have fun. It wasn't just all film; it was supposed to be fun, too. The same principle was true for political movements. It had to be that you were making your life better by going to MIX. Not that you were doing a service or performing an obligation. That was really, really important.

SKJ: In terms of infusing political work into the programming, what did you do?

SS: They weren't really separate. The act of having a gay and lesbian experimental film festival was like saying "fuck you" to dominant culture or representation. It was such a crazy thing to do, to think that you could create a sort of underground popular culture out of such an esoteric category. It was hugely successful with all different kinds of people. So in and of itself, it was inherently clear that our politics were expressed in everything that the festival was. Every element reflected our politics. Everything we've been talking about—scheduling, pay schedule, the way people were treated—everything reflected our politics.

SKJ: I'm hoping to get you talking about what you told me once [about] the policy "to print whatever people gave us" for the program notes.

JH: Exactly. But, with the program notes, for the first six years they were just Xeroxed sheets.

SKJ: And how was the Xeroxing done?

JH: At Citibank.

SKJ: Illegally at your job . . .

JH: Well, it wasn't "illegal." I think we had other euphemisms for that.

SS: Yeah, but that's how everything used to be. Everything was done that way. Everyone knew some dyke—there was that girl [Kate Huh] whose name escapes me now, who worked at the copy store. And for years, she used to do everybody's stuff for free. ACT UP, all the artists, that's how we were all living. You have to understand, we were criminals. Literally, our lives were illegal. Nobody wanted us. Our families didn't want us. The art institutions didn't want us. We were totally rejected and reviled. Our stories were never allowed to be told. We were despised people. That's who we were. And a lot of us lived in a dangerous neighborhood, precariously poor and unprotected. And we were making this art event. I was a waitress when we started, and Jim was an office worker, temp or whatever. And so was everybody else.

JH: So if the subject is assimilationism, you have to remember that assimilation was only possible in the last few years. When we started to do this festival, although it was getting to the end of that era, the choices were being out or being in the closet. You couldn't be assimilated. You couldn't be an out Republican.

SS: You couldn't be a successful gay artist. It was not possible.

JH: No, it wasn't possible. Really, we did not have that choice. A lot of this, people can analyze this in retrospect, just grew out of the lives we were leading.

SKJ: There were still these positions you took, like making photocopies at the office.

SS: That was normal. Everybody did it.

SKJ: But also as a community situation, did you feel an obligation to provide a regular venue for people's work so that someone who had a new film every year . . .

SS: We showed people's new work regularly.

JH: As Sarah has said, we saw this as a community. So when people made new films, we expected that we would show them. And in fact, I still think that. I still try to promote that aspect of the festival.

SS: It's funny because we showed all this sexually explicit stuff. We showed all this porn, you know. We showed everything. But, Jim and I are not like these super-sexy people. We're kind of schlubby. But for some reason, it didn't really bother us. It never came up.

JH: Well, that was what people filmed. There's virtually no sex in my films, which is kind of interesting in its own way. But that's what experimental film allowed you to do. It allowed you to show gay male sexuality and, later, lesbian sexuality.

SKJ: You speak of the transition [to new directors and a new organizing structure in 1992–1993] as being one of your greatest moments. But, it also seems to me to be when the politics began to be evacuated from the festival.

SS: I can't comment on that. Not because I don't feel that way, but because I don't really know. I've totally just stepped away from it. I have to say, though, change happens and the world has changed. You can't stop that. I feel good about the way we handled it. I feel good that we were able to hand over a fiscally sound organization to younger people. What they made of it, and the world that they live in, and the way things are now, I can't really control that.

SKJ: But you live in this world. You as a political person, as an activist and a political person, continue to have a relationship to . . .

SS: To mass marketing culture. Sure, and I continue to do that. But, it's not just in MIX. It's the whole world that's going that way. That's one of the things we have in common. We both come from the Russian Revolution. We come from this kind of Jewish analysis. We're both still Jews, and we're very influenced by communism and all of those kinds of ethics. But people who are born fifteen years later are not going to have the same kinds of influences. Not at all.

SKJ: I think community-based ideas are much harder to realize today. I think the community is much more atomized and fragmented.

JH: There is no community.

SS: Yeah, I agree.

JH: It just doesn't exist anymore in the way that it did fifteen years ago.

SS: The marker for me is that in the old days, if there was a lesbian who worked somewhere, I could call her. And she would call me back and tell me how we could use her organization, or how we could use where she lived to help gay people. Like if I would say, "This is Sarah Schulman, da, da, da, I heard you're working there, listen I can send you this, I can send you that, we can use these resources, I can do Xeroxing, blah, blah, blah." We were the conspiracy. That was the relationship between us. It didn't matter if we knew each other. Now gay people identify with the power structure that they're working for. And that identification is a lot stronger than their relationship to each other. So, therefore, there's no community.

CHOICE CUTS

CHARLIE ANDERS

I've turned missing the clue bus into an art form.

I ignore insinuations, askance looks, vituperative snorts, and pantomime gasps. Partly I tune them out, partly I've genuinely attained sublime obliviousness. Often I don't know someone was giving me a dirty look until a friend tells me later.

If you disapprove of how I look and want to let me know, you'll have to pay for an ad in the paper like everyone else. (Note to self: This could be a way to jump-start advertising in *other* magazine. Offer a page of classified ads for people who wish to register their disapproval of someone else's life choices. It could be huge. We'll call it the Critics' Corner.)

I'm thick-skinned despite my painstaking skin care routine, because I couldn't possibly wander the streets en femme *and* give a damn what people thought. The way I see it, I've made two choices: one choice to live, love, and dress differently than penis-owners are supposed to, and another choice to be as open as possible about the first choice.

These were both informed selections. I read the literature. I consulted trained professionals. I used only as directed. I didn't operate heavy machinery while genderfucked. But I was brazen nonetheless.

I'm not the only queer who insists that I chose much of the way I live and love. There's a web-site at http://www.queerbychoice.com, and an e-mail list for people who believe they queered them-selves up. But this is definitely the minority view, and it's one that could get a person into trouble.

For one thing, asserting your own choices means crawling into the swamp of nature-versus-nurture debates. The Queer By Choice site doesn't seem to question the idea that behaviors have one simple cause (genes or experiences, take your pick). Instead, the site pushes its own theory: that people can "choose to feel" a particular attraction. It quotes a lesbian-by-choice who compares her past attraction to men to a taste for cheese: it turned out to be an acquired taste, and she chose to de-acquire it.

I can easily believe that I had a predisposition to color outside gender lines, both in whom I loved and in who I became. I have enough early memories of same-sex crushes and girly fantasies. But I was reasonably happy living as a straight guy for a while. It's possible I could have stayed a guy and expressed my femininity through Zen rock gardens or alt-folk-rock.

I chose to be a queer girl because it's way more fun than the alternatives. I was tired of feel-ing trapped in a straitjacket. I like being able to have lovers of more than one gender, and I get a kick out of cutting a feminine swath through the world.

Chances are, you already have your own opinion about how you got to be the way you are. You may be absolutely certain you were born as queer as you'll ever be. And maybe it's true for you. I don't claim to speak for everybody. I definitely think it's simplistic to say that attractions to genders are like cheese, and if you just expose yourself to enough Stilton you'll start to enjoy it.

Why does it matter whether my perversity was a choice or ordained for me? Partly because it feels like I'm bucking the trend in mainstream queer culture.

These days, queer people are supposed be hardwired for it. As one car manufacturer put it in a series of ads that appeared in San Francisco's queer Castro district a couple of years ago, "We're just built that way."

KNEE-JERK CONFORMISTS

The involuntary queerness story is the linchpin of many queer people's strategies to claim nor-mality. "We didn't choose this" becomes part of "We're just like you in every other way." Because, of course, if it wasn't for that one difference, queer people would all be just like Republican hate-monger Orrin Hatch. Even the women.

"Straight-acting" gays and "soccer-mom" lesbians always seem to be the ones who claim the lack-of-choice defense most vigorously. It's no more our fault than a blink in response to a finger jab at the eyes. It's always struck me as a weird version of pride. Aren't people usually proud of their decisions and the things they've built for themselves? The implication of the "we're just built this way" argument always seems to me that if queer people could choose, of course they would choose to be straight.

And it reminds me of David Brooks's argument that we're turning into a nation of Bohemian Bourgeois, or bobos. According to his book, *Bobos In Paradise*, bobos embrace "alternate lifestyles," but they're still basically yuppies with soul patches. The bobos' materialism and conformity, one layer beneath the surface, make them no threat to the right-wing agenda that Brooks favors.

Many denizens of San Francisco's Castro district remind me of Brooks's analysis. You could call them homo bobos, or hobos for short, if that word wasn't already taken.

Saying, "I chose this" automatically puts you beyond the pale. It implies a value judgment. It leaves open the possibility that other supposed straights could choose to go off the rails as well. Can you imagine anything scarier to the straight world? We could start an ex-straight movement, proclaim that straightness can be cured! All the worst nightmares about queers recruiting would come true.

So I don't have much time for people who try to fit me into their prefab narratives. It seems like if you're going to be a productive member of queer society, you have to treat your queerness as something like a nervous tic.

At least we've stopped viewing sexual orientation as a mental disorder. But if your gender identity isn't strictly Joanie or Chachi, then you're still expected to lay claim to a mental illness. Transgender people who want hormones or surgery must first get a psychiatrist to diagnose them with gender identity disorder, or "adjustment disorder."

I had one session with a gender therapist recently. When I said I felt that I'd created my own gender out of shiny ribbons that I'd found here and there, my therapist advised me not to say that to other people, for fear they wouldn't accept me.

Maybe you can measure how threatening a group is by the level of society's pressure on it to claim victimhood. Using that yardstick, making a jaunt outside your gender is as terrifying as crib death. You're only allowed off your leash if your assigned gender makes you crazy.

It makes you wonder how many people would change their gender, temporarily or permanently, if there were no stigma. Presumably, the ones who feel tormented beyond endurance by living up to the letter on their birth certificates are the extremes. Somewhere out there is a pretty big iceberg, even by iceberg standards.

I've been excited by the rise of the genderqueer movement, which seems to question the whole idea of two genders, as well as the traditional tranny script. People seem less and less committed to the idea that you have to transition completely from one state to another—like moving from Pittsburgh to Zimbabwe, only with more paperwork and medical bills.

This gets back to the fact that I want to own my choices as choices. It would be hard to transition without turning my transhood into the correction of a mistake, nature's clerical error. I may eventually try to become legally female, but only if I can find a way that doesn't take away my own agency as a gender-buster.

I want to keep on being openly frivolous, breaking the rules for fun rather than out of necessity. Most of all, I don't ever want to portray myself as a helpless victim. I've had more options than most people, including living in San Francisco and having a steady job where the closest person-to-person interaction I have is over the telephone. I've chosen to explore desires and aspects of my personality that I might have been better off ignoring. But it's been a fun ride, despite the bumps.

I might get beaten up for looking different. I could lose my job. Or I could become a victim of rape. But I'll never call myself a victim of my own queerness.

A LUMP OF COALITION

It's easy to make political arguments based on lack of free will. Nobody can really hold your identity against you if it was thrust upon you. That makes it easier, in some ways, to push for nondiscrimination legislation, because you can compare queerness to "inborn" traits like ethnicity.

It's a lot harder to face up to opponents of queer rights and say, "Yes, I'm deliberately flouting your rules, because I like it."

But while it may be easier to argue that we didn't ask to be this way, it makes our coalition a lot smaller. You leave out people like me, as well as other potential allies.

I'm sure gay-bashing Senator Rick Santorum (R-PA) can't see any difference between me and Log Cabin Republican-esque blogger Andrew Sullivan, because we're both Jesus-deprived colon-scratchers. I'm always amused to read Sullivan's reaction when a Republican bashes gays—he's always *shocked* to see it happen in this day and age.

Common enemies mean a common cause. And politics means you help to build a dam with whoever lives in the flood plain. We could build the biggest, sturdiest dam if we could abandon the "allergic reaction" theory of queerness in favor of a broader fight for sexual and gender freedom.

I'm standing up for everyone's right to choose to live and act and dress the way he or she wants. Gays, lesbians, and bisexuals should join forces with polyamorists, genderqueers, kinksters, and everyone else who breaks consensually out of boy/girl roles and missionary-position heterosexuality.

Built-in differences only call for tolerance (as long as you don't differ too much, or in too many ways). Tolerance is conditional and subject to revocation. Freedom of choice is absolute.

For me, it's important to say that I stepped outside the pale on purpose. I don't own any dysphorias, compulsions, or genetic anomalies. Just decisions.

LEGALIZED SODOMY IS POLITICAL FOREPLAY

PATRICK CALIFIA

In June 2003, when the Supreme Court decided, in *Lawrence v. Texas*, to decriminalize sex acts that people have been doing ever since they had genitals and other orifices, I was as happy as any other AmeriKKKan queer. San Francisco's gay pride parade followed soon after, and the city was full of delirious fags and dykes, bisexual (speak it under your breath) men and women, and even those do-they-have-to-be-so-obvious transgendered *people* ("Well, you can't call them men or women, can you?" say the gym-toned gay Democrats and the lesbian soccer moms), celebrating the good sense of our highest court. All of them far too stoned to follow such a long sentence. Like Nancy Reagan, I just get high on life, so maybe I'll get invited to help her change Ronnie's diaper. Anything's possible now that I'm no longer a sex offender.

Frankly, I didn't think I would live long enough to see this much sexual sanity in the United States of Gunpowder and the Indian reservations it made possible. Especially not under the reign of failed energy magnate George W. Bush. Maybe the Supremes felt that they owed us something for letting Bush steal the election in the first place? My personal dance of gratitude falters, because I very much fucking doubt it.

Bitter, table for one. Or two, since you're here now. Stick around, I've already ordered for both of us. Service is slow, which is odd when you think about how many self-proclaimed bottoms there are in this town, so let me throw out a few conversation stoppers while we're all chipper enough to deserve a chewing-out.

I'm a queer freak. I'm a promiscuous, bisexual, female-to-male transsexual and a sadomasochist. Do you mind if I grope your ass, lick your ear, and whisper, "Since my dick isn't long enough to go up somebody's ass, is it at all helpful to me to know ass-fucking is now as legal as taking fertility drugs to conceive a litter of southern Baptists?" You didn't say no, so I'm at least innocent of sexual harassment. Here's my next question. If you've been accused of witchcraft by your Puritan neighbors, and they hang you, does it really matter a lot if one of your neighbors doesn't watch so he can take a discreet leak on your pansies?

Go on your merry way, then. All the more high dudgeon for me to consume on my lonesome. Oh, dammit, I told you to bring the irony on the side, not ladled all over it like gravy. Yuck. Dear me, now the manager's headed this way, and he says, "Do we have a problem here?"

The problem is that I don't even know how to start telling you what the problem is. It's bigger than the one that got away. Even bigger than the one you had last night at Blow Buddies.

The problem is that even though they've decriminalized sodomy in Canada and authorized monogamous gay marriage in Ontario, Canadian customs agents still seize books that depict anal sex or images of bondage, fisting, or any sort of sexual fun between two men or two women. There's almost no pornography depicting the bodies and desires of people like me, so they don't even need to confiscate it to make my sex life invisible. At the same time as the Supremes give their blessing to oral and anal sex and other variations from breeder screwing in the dead-bug position, the Department of Justice has declared a new war on "obscenity" in this country. You can have queer sex, but you'd better not photograph or videotape it and sell those representations to other happy practitioners of buggery. Our elected representatives continue to angle for ways to get depictions of sex off the Internet, and that includes information about birth control, abortion, and how to have sex without getting infected with HIV, hepatitis, or other STDs. Agencies that do HIV prevention work are being accused of circulating material that advocates queer sex, and are being harassed with federal audits.

The problem is that even in the Great Gay Mecca of San Francisco, 85 percent of the gay men I know have to snort, smoke, or inject crystal before they can get their freak on. We're all very happy after we've taken our party favors, but if we were happy in the first place, would we really be making sure we didn't leave home without a bump and a straw? Is the music so loud because we don't really want to talk to each other, or because we can't stand the voices in our own heads? Trying to get rid of internalized homophobia when there's so much hostility all around us is like, shudder, washing your hair in dirty water. But, hey, it's our fault that syphilis rates are rising, because fags are self-indulgent and irresponsible.

We have more codified gay rights than we did when I went to my first gay bar in 1971. But there are still too many straight people who hate us. And there are still far too many deviants who can't see beyond the edges of their own oppression, to see how all the freaks are connected in a crazy quilt of sexual repression and misrepresentation.

The Human Rights Campaign still won't advocate writing transgendered people into ENDA, a proposed federal antidiscrimination law, and when gay civil rights laws are being debated at the local level, more often than not the lesbian and gay activists who are pushing for those laws actively resist extending that umbrella of protection to transpeople. These are the same people who would have pushed other Jews out of line to make sure they got one of Raoul Wallenberg's fake German passports out of the Third Reich. Let's keep on making sure there's never enough to go around, shall we? The surest sign of being a shit is the drive to make other people live in it. Ah, the sweet smell of capitalism, the rim seat of economic systems.

Sodomy is legal, but what if you want to wear a latex straitjacket and whimper, "Oh, sir, please flood my pig pussy with your dirty spunk?" while carrying on, hard dick up against a bruised but greasy and greedy butt? Leather people have been deplored and harassed in every single gay rights march we've had in Washington, D.C. And I'm not fingering Fred Phelps or the Sons of Saint Patty here. (Eeeuw. Gotta wipe that off my imaginary digit.) Mainstream lesbians and gay men apparently think that those of us who are drag queens or wielders of bullwhips enjoy being turned into the home-movie stars of homophobic Christian propaganda. In fact, it's a problem for us too. We don't want to do anything to set gay liberation back, but we also want a chance to celebrate who we are. We've already been shoved into the closet as far as we can go without getting turned into pathologized mashed potatoes. Unlike same-sexers, we're still in the damned DSM-IV, tagged along with trannies as a Mental Disorder.

The cross-waving addicts of flaming holy writ are not just after you, bubba, with your domestic partner and Jack Russell terrier. The religious right has targeted leather conferences, fetish parties, and S/M clubs all over the country in a well-organized campaign to prevent us from meeting or playing in public. Just as bars were once threatened with losing their liquor licenses if they allowed homosexuals to congregate on their premises, hotels and other establishments are turning us away because the vice squad has had a little talk with them. Kinky people come to these events and clubs in part because it's often not safe for us to have the kind of sex we want to have in our own homes or apartments. We don't usually meet compatible tricks at the laundromat, PTA, or down the hall in our offices.

People in the leather-S/M-D/S-fetish community lose our jobs, have our children taken away from us, get thrown out of housing, are made to leave job training or school, get beaten up or killed, and have to cope with the stress of being stereotyped and hated. We are depressed and angry. We are isolated and self-destructive. And that's just the BDSM activists I'm talking about. When will there be some kind of legal protection for us? Can we join gay men and lesbians in doing sensitivity training for the police so they'll stop trying to close our bars down and listen to us when we get assaulted or blackmailed?

In the wake of the 9-11 bombing of the World Trade Centers and passage of the U.S. Patriot Act, our elected representatives handed the Justice Department sweeping new powers of censorship, unlimited surveillance, and the ability to repeal *habeas corpus*. Your government wants to know what you check out at the library and where you go on the World Wide Web. The Feds want to know where your charitable contributions go and which foreign languages you speak, how you worship and where you go if you leave the country. You'll probably never know you've had your pockets and your credit report turned inside out by the Powers That Be, because it's illegal for anyone who rats you out to tell you Uncle Sam is looking over your shoulder at ads for piercing jewelry, VCR head cleaner, and used jock straps. Have you seen any coverage of the Patriot Act in your local homo bar rag, perhaps between the ads for gay dentists and lesbian realtors and the outcall masseurs?

Transgendered people have been singled out for special scrutiny under the guise of rooting out terrorism. Our ability to change our legal documents, work, or travel freely has been curtailed by an attorney general who seems to think he is the reincarnation of both Senator Joe McCarthy and J. Edgar Hoover. Talk about unsafe sex. Throw a blanket over that image, will ya? Doesn't anybody have a condom I can throw them?

This is my life. I have a full beard and a driver's license that says I'm a girl. I can't change it because the Department of Motor Vehicles wants an affidavit that says I have had genital surgery. Even if I had health insurance, it wouldn't cover that procedure. So if I want to travel, I have to do it with a passport that doesn't match my gender. If you hate taking off your shoes at the airport, think about what they're going to want *me* to take off. I can't pay my rent, much less buy a penis. I don't even think I could afford an hour with somebody else's penis. I fuck anyway, of course—I enjoyed witnessing and executing penetration long before I became a testosterone-based life form. But the dildo in my strap-on harness is illegal in several states. New Right think tanks have written model obscenity legislation that includes banning sex toys along with titty mags and boy-boy X-rated videos. If I try to sneak my dick into my native state of Texas, perhaps when I am over there petitioning a court to revise my birth certificate, I'll have to tell the nice rent-a-cop at the airport that it's a dog retrieval dummy. But I won't be making that trip any time soon because, guess what, no frankendick, no piece of paper that says you are a guy. All of a sudden, nobody wants me to use their bathroom. Better start walkin' like a camel, because I'm going to have to hold it forever.

And the sad thing is that oblivious straight people usually treat me better than gay men or lesbians. The fags are afraid I've got cunt cooties, and lesbians have never been nice to "dykes who just gave up when it got too hard to be a butch woman so they traded it all in for male privilege." Yeah, I've got so much male privilege that I am constantly sick to my stomach for fear I'll say the wrong thing, be seen reading the wrong book or talking to the wrong person, and be read as a tranny and stomped. My male privilege only lasts as long as nobody knows. Kind of like the way everybody is nice to you at work until you invite your queer lover to the company picnic? No more heterosexual privilege.

Now that sodomy is legal, the part of my sex life that I refer to as "foreplay" is no longer a criminal act. Until the handcuffs come out. Then it might be assault, even if the person in the handcuffs is dribbling quarter-cups of precum and consent. Sodomy is legal in England, too, but they still sent three gay men to prison for participating in S/M activities with one another. The Operation Spanner case included about a dozen defendants, and the bottoms were convicted of assaulting themselves. And you thought it was hard for Scott O'Hara to suck his own dick! In the last few years, people in New England and San Diego have been arrested at play parties and charged with public indecency, assault, possession of weapons, and other rot. So why do it? Especially, why do it someplace other than my bedroom?

I won't deny that I'm an exhibitionist who enjoys casual sex and mayhem with strangers. But I also want to participate in the public life of a community. If I stay home and watch television or go to the supermarket, I am not going to see any people who are like me. S/M play parties are not just opportunities to do elaborate scenes on equipment that won't fit in a studio apartment. They also offer a chance to see old friends, make new ones, teach someone how to play safely, learn a new bondage trick, eat potato chips, show off a new outfit, show off a new relationship, ease loneliness, and bolster self-esteem. Where else am I going to find people who will think I am just dandy because I can cane someone for an hour without making them bleed? Assimilate that.

When the term "queer" first came along, it was such a relief to be able to embrace a label that encompassed so much of my experience and identity, but normalization is as relentless as a marching troop of army ants. "Queer" is on the verge of becoming nothing but a synonym for "gay." Just the way "bisexual" has come to mean "gay," under the rubric of being inclusive. Please come to our inclusive safer-sex workshop for gay/bisexual men, where we will only talk about your MALE sex partners. You can't expect Kinsey 6 men to stay in the same room with the word "vagina." There's not enough Viagra in the world to erase that trauma. And what about those diversity-loving political leaders who blithely refer to transgenderism as a sexual orientation? Hello, not all transgendered people are gay, and the norms for gender identity are not enforced the same way that norms for sexual conduct are regulated.

"Gay Liberation" never included sadomasochism. Never saw any potential for pride or dignity in the eroticism of physical restraint and the judicious application of intense physical sensations. Didn't believe in the spiritual surcease of being forced to slow down, go within, escape the confines of the flesh, and fly up to a blissful realm of communion with the divine. Never saw any value in the establishment of a fantasy realm in which people actually get to decide what they will experience, and can let go and trust that their limits will be respected and everything that happens is done for their benefit. It's too big a reminder of what we don't have in real life—justice, consent, loving kindness, acceptance, pleasure, attention.

Living in a human body subjects us to unregulated and unfair pain and suffering. And we all cooperate in a system that multiplies that agony. Even when we gratify our basic needs by eating or sleeping in a warm bed, we enjoy those privileges on the backs of people who are hungry and sleeping on dirty streets, in the cold. At least my slaves can take off their collars.

I don't want to give up the term "queer," because it still bugs people like the middle-class gay homeowners in the Castro who have halted plans to open a shelter for homeless queer youth in their beautiful neighborhood. I use it because every time I say it, I get an unpleasant jolt of memories of being called vile names or bashed, and I guess I hope that if I say it with enough aplomb and non-chalance, those memories will lose their power to subdue and terrorize me. The jaws of assimilation have closed around the word queer, but they haven't managed to crush it into dust just yet.

But I think the term "freak" has to be reclaimed as well. A freak is somebody who is unusu-al, stared at, upsetting, revealing by their difference what is wrong with the status quo. When a freak appears, the world is instantly divided into gawkers and the unique and solitary individual who has given them pause. There are those who cannot hide their shameful or alarming attrib-utes, and those otherwise apparently normal people who love them. The cloak of the exile falls upon them as well, because their eyes and hearts have persuaded them to be loyal to people who are shunned. Freaks are entertainers, jesters, satirists, artists, beautiful in a way that few can endure or savor, intelligent in a way that makes others angry.

If you don't want to be a gawker, you've gotta join the circus. Goddess knows I wish I could run away to one.

QUEER PARENTS: AN OXYMORON? OR JUST MORONIC?

STEPHANIE SCHROEDER

What does it mean when a lesbian/gay/bisexual/transgender couple—or single person—or other configuration—"chooses" to have a child or children? Does it dilute the queerness of that person, couple, family? Of the queer community? Does it play right into the hands of the right, whereby the lesbian moms or gay dads next door are tolerated because we people the PTA, coach our kids' soccer teams, and chair school fundraising committees, while the nellie queen upstairs or the leatherdyke next door is shut up and shut out? The nellie queen and the leatherdyke are out as queers about town. They front for those of us who pass, but where are the queer families when the community needs them?

It seems that queer parents, even activists and former activists with the most radical credentials, are diving headlong into a new kind of "activism": "inclusiveness," family values, and queer parenting. Is this REALLY activism? Does being a parent, even a gay or lesbian one, translate into any radical concept? It certainly *does* change the definition of family, especially when there exists an unconventional convention of parents, but is it de facto radical to be a queer parent? Doesn't it actually dilute the community, the energy, and talent pool of committed activists? Does writing a check for a cause or organization we used to people, demonstrate for in the streets, or get arrested over really replace frontline bodies and grassroots activism? Is it okay just to send a check because we can't get a babysitter?

Is raising a feminist son or daughter of the queer community an end in itself? I've been wrestling with these questions since my former partner and I "decided" to have a child five years ago, after five years together. I never actually envisioned myself as a parent: I had a decidedly miserable childhood, and when I was growing up lesbian, lesbians didn't have children, at least not that I knew of. I also didn't think I would ever want to give up my own private time, life adventures, activism, and writing assignments for the mundane, dreary, crazy dailiness of raising a child. Yet now I have a bright, sunny, cheerful, and handsome son, who brings joy to me at odd moments, like when a broad grin spreads across his face after he's shown a brochure about the Big Apple Circus and asked if he would like to attend—it really does send chills down my spine to see such simple and innocent joy on his face and in his heart. It makes me experience, for a glance in time, the pure and simple joy of a happy childhood.

But the dark side of parenting that I struggle with daily, the other half—or more than half—lurks in my brain at all times and sets me thinking about other things that I rehash over and over. Shouldn't we be spending our time ensuring that the coming generations of GLBT persons have all the data they need, the his/herstory to draw on to know that they are not alone; that there need be no teenager (or younger child) who has to commit suicide, be abused by his/her parents/guardians, or thrown out of the house to make a living on the street because of homosexuality or gender identity; that no genderqueer need hide in a heterosexual marriage and live a miserable straight existence for fear of repercussions from family, friends, and society. I want homos and trannies to be publicly exposed and to expose publicly ourselves and our sexuality, exalt in it, and show the whole world the full glory of our lives, not just the sanitized family part, not just the professional working-person part, not just the "we-are-just-like-everybody-else, except . . ." because if there IS an "except," then we truly ARE NOT like everybody else. In fact, if we are an exception, then we as a queer people are exceptional. Sexually and otherwise. My friend Joan Nestle, a lesbian feminist sex radical activist, has written that we should walk through the world as queer sexual beings at all times: "If we do not battle [Amerikan colonization of other countries] as open sex radicals fighting the forces of death, all the small freedoms we have won will disappear."[1] We MUST be exceptional to have the energy not only to fight for our own lives, but for the lives of others as well.

However . . .

We all know that as minority groups exist, persist, and fight against the status quo, making themselves forces to be reckoned with and defying convention, they eventually become convention, or at least parts of the group become assimilated and normalized. More than occasionally, these "success" stories—like Log Cabin Republicans, closeted celebrities, and lesbian daughters of Republican Vice Presidents—betray their own people.

A few recent examples of what I will refer to as the "family-inclusive/assimilation agenda" are detailed below:

Chastity Bono, in an interview with *The Advocate*, labels herself an "assimilationist," basically saying, hey, we're just like everybody else and we just wish you would let us "in," dammit—who the "you" is has ranged, in Bono's case, from her parents, celebrity actress/singer Cher and her late father, arch-conservative Congressman Sonny Bono, to the mainstream television audience of *Ellen*, to the targets/members of GLAAD, HRC, and readers of *The Advocate*. Hey Chastity, what are you working for if you just want to be accepted—you are the offspring of two very famous and wealthy individuals. You needn't dirty your hands by dabbling in the queer community UNLESS there really is something amiss in you, and going mainstream actually doesn't make you "just the same as" a straight person.

Kelly Taylor, founder and former publisher of *Alternative Family* magazine (now *Proud Parenting*)—"the premier magazine for gay, lesbian, bisexual, and transgender parents—and their children"—wrote in her "A Word from the Editor" column in the May/June 2000 issue entitled "Kids, Hide Your Eyes: A Family-Friendly Guide to Pride 2000" that "I have come to realize that many of the things I enjoyed as a young lesbian watching in awe have now become my worst fears." Taylor is referring to the dykes on bikes who lead the Gay Pride parade—too loud for the tender ears of her young daughter—as well as leatherdykes with piercings, and other examples of our community that offend her new-parent sensibility. Taylor laments the (imaginary) refusal of pride parade organizers to take the special interests of families and children into consideration: "I am deeply saddened by many of the organizers who are unwilling to accommodate a celebration for the Pride in all of us." It makes me wonder which "us" becomes important to celebrate when a child enters a queer family. Is it now the children who take precedence, and anyhow, why are leatherdykes, drag queens, radical faeries, and motorcycle dykes offensive on any level? If, indeed, as Taylor goes on to say, "Our children are the voices of our future and deserve 'a place at the table,'" why are children of queer parents sitting at a different table than their parents?

Whose table? What place?

Bruce Bawer caught hell with his theory of assimilation, expressed in his book titled with the same phrase Taylor chose to use in her editorial, "A Place at the Table." Radical activists were outraged—what had this movement come to? Begging for crumbs beneath the table of the mainstream breadbasket; a seat next to a Republican at an election fundraiser; Andrew Sullivan writing for *The New York Times*? This meant erasure of difference, erasure of a different—indeed radical-by-nature—culture.

I remember that in one interview, Dorothy Allison spoke about how she doesn't want to hide the community, *her* community—lesbians, faggots, FTMs and MTFs, butch dykes and fem women, the S/M community—from her son. In the most straightforward way, Allison was responding to the typical question by a horrified liberal to gendertrash who likes rough trade: Honey, I got nothin' to hide.

The miasma of the interloper queer family and the questions surrounding it haunt my mind, mixing with thoughts of my own child (who was sitting on the couch next to his grandmother enjoying a *Winnie-the-Pooh* video in the mid-sized Manhattan apartment I lived in when I wrote the first draft of this piece in late fall 2000). This makes it all the harder to say what I really think: that queer people having children conservatize not only themselves and their children, but tar the entire queer community as well. They shift the movement in a different, and highly problematic, direction—into the mainstream. The Main Stream, get it? Swimming with the straight fishes—"breeders," as we used to call that particular brand of people who gloried in children but did nothing much to help society.

I am just throwing out ideas here, raising questions, talking about issues. I don't have any answers except to say that I am getting extremely restless, wanting to reconnect to the individuals and institutions—both grassroots, ad-hoc situations and formal organizations—that represent me, my interests, and those of my queer brothers and sisters.

Of course, I understand that there are also institutions that represent children of queer families, that there are formal organizations for GLBT parents, families, and our allies. I also realize I span a tensile bridge: taking my son to school and arriving late to work, leaving community organizing meetings early to take him to dinner, or missing a weekend vigil for a transexual sister to spend "my day" with him.

I do know that the normalizing factor, as one of my childless lesbian/feminist friends calls the gayby boom, is noticeable in MY life. For example, when my son was an infant and I pushed him along Upper West Side sidewalks, I got more than my share of approval and attention. Hey, I was a lady with a baby. My relationships with people changed, especially with straight women, but with men, too. Even being a lesbian didn't throw most people off since I was now a legitimate woman, a MOTHER. At work, in the store, in the street, the moment anyone found out I had a child, I was accepted, taken for granted as a "normal" individual. That I am lesbian, queer, was secondary. I also have the luxury, if you want to call it that—I don't, frankly, it's a real hassle—of looking very conventional. Just a tall slim woman with long hair and clean Midwestern good looks. My former partner, as well, looks conventionally feminine, of the hippy childbearing Jewish variety. We were two unthreatening women, living amongst others who are just like . . .

But no. I am not and will not be just like . . . everyone else. I will proclaim my allegiances to the queer community, to myself, to my new lover and son as a lesbian and I will not accept being accepted—for something I am not. And I want—no, I insist—that more members of the queer community think about the challenges, delights, and heights that make us queer, that take us places—both literally and figuratively—that straight people will never go to, have never been to, will never know. Queers must take these things into consideration before exchanging their activist/community membership cards for shitty diapers and college tuition bills.

NEVER A BRIDESMAID, NEVER A BRIDE

CAROL QUEEN

I'd solidified my convictions about marriage and kids way before I came out as queer. My early philosophy was influenced by the countercultural mores of the 1960s as well as the abysmal example of Mom and Dad. I pretty much had these sentiments down by the age of twelve, and mind you, I hadn't even heard of Emma Goldman yet. I was going to fuck anyone I pleased when I grew up; I wasn't going to marry anybody; and bringing children into a post-nuclear world was a karmic error that would follow the perpetrators past the grave. Nothing that's happened during the ensuing thirty-five years has done much to change my mind.

None of this means that I decry the solace and pleasure of family (I even recognize that a scant few of us came from nurturing and delightful families of origin). I appreciate the drive that draws so many of us together as partners. I even understand why you people want to pull pictures of your kids out of your wallets. See, look at these photos of my cats! Aren't they precious? Look, this is Teacup, walking through a carpet tube! She's so smart! And Bracelet holding a stuffed bear with her paws—did you ever see anything so cute?

Hey, I'd even send 'em to college, if they wanted to go. Fortunately, I've chosen a species to love that doesn't need a degree to succeed in life. But I digress.

From the time I began to go to slumber parties, where I invariably was the only girl present who didn't want to wait to have sex until she was married, I've looked askance at engagement rings and bridal showers, crudely decorated honeymoon cars, and the sticky-sweet taste of wedding cake. (I used to feel the same way about bachelor parties, too, until I worked a couple of them. I never jumped out of a cake, though. That's so retro.)

Even when I came out as queer (I knew about Emma Goldman by then), I was in no hurry to plan my wedding. Ironically, the reason I came out to my dad had to do with a lesbian wedding, a lovely little outdoor ceremony planned by my college Gay Studies teacher during summer break. I had to get my dad's permission to go (in those days he paid for everything, including bus tickets to weddings), which involved me telling him what prompted the trip in the first place: When I had finally let loose that Jill was my *Gay Studies* teacher, and she was marrying a *woman*, my dad violently crumpled the newspaper he'd been reading and yelled, "Jesus Christ! I suppose that means you're a homosexual!"

"Bisexual, actually, Dad—but if you can only imagine things one way or the other, thinking of me as homosexual will be fine."

Jill and her lover had a nice little ceremony with tasty cake, which I figured presaged a higher quality of marital commitment than the typical heterosexual. I'm sure it was good while it lasted, but within a few years they had broken up. (Let's spend another minute considering the question of cake, since I am so obviously fixated on it. They make that vile icing perfectly white and sculptable, and damn the flavor. Doesn't that in itself telegraph a *huge* warning about marriage?)

I wondered what it must feel like to call someone "my wife" (or, for that matter, "my husband"—I couldn't really picture either situation). My mother's career as a wife effectively ended her autonomous dreams, and she wound up an unhappy alcoholic stuck in a tiny, uninteresting world. "Husbanding" didn't seem so great either, when it meant you had an unhappy alcoholic and two unhappy kids to shepherd around.

In the queer world, we called each other "lovers," an appellation I couldn't imagine my parents ever using. Straight people de-emphasized the connection between partnering and the erotic (well, the older ones did, anyway—the ones who got married; in those days there were scads of heterosexual lovers too, also under the philosophical influence of Emma Goldman). Queers re-emphasized the sexual—especially the boys, who had their own special bathhouses wherein they could do precisely that. The word "lover" had another kind of larger political significance, too, as in, "An army of lovers cannot fail." I firmly believed (Jill and her wife to the contrary) that we were redefining what it meant to be together, rejecting hetero ways in favor of erotic personal affiliations based on the value systems of people who saw and treated each other as equals. Such coupling (or triplings, for that matter) would not fall prey to the sex-role stereotyped problems to which straight marriages were heir.

Later, we had to alter the slogan a little, to "An army of *ex*-lovers cannot fail." But I quickly adjusted, because I had figured out that queer lovers could in fact fail, and spectacularly; but if you stayed on good terms with your exes, after the obligatory and hopefully brief period of hating them for ruining your life, you could get back on footing, perhaps even firmer than when you'd been together.

Granted, as we congratulated ourselves on avoiding the pitfalls of hetero gender-role stereotypes, three things were happening: many hetero people worked very hard to discard those stereotypes and to remake marriage as an institution; queer people rediscovered how hot gender roles could be; and some queer people put their noses to the grindstone so they could step up to the altar and call each other "husband" and "wife."

Having come of age, and come out, in the heady years just after Stonewall, when more queer men I knew joined Faggots Against Fascism than wanted to join the Army, I always viewed the assimilationist queer folk around me with bemusement. I respect pretty much any queer organizing, even the Log Cabin Republicans (if only because of the childish fun it is to point and laugh when their favored candidates mistreat them time and time again). It is clear to me, with thirty years of hindsight, that every kind of queer organizing has moved us out of the shadows, although I have not always personally appreciated the type of limelight some have chosen. But I could never have predicted that joining the Army, getting ordained, and getting hitched would be the big issues they are as the new century dawns.

Certainly, oppression in any context is wrong. Naturally, queer folk are irritated when straight people get benefits denied to same-sex partners. There's nothing to *like* about being discriminated against—except, perhaps, the way that, through anger and creativity, it shows the way to the road less traveled. As we have seen time and time again, pissed-off (or even simply irritable) queers making a point can cause the culture to shift—sometimes not a lot, often not enough, but these shifts are no less significant for that. Queers who flounce off to live our own lives often find straight people eventually come tugging at our coattails, wondering what we're doing, how we're doing it, if they should do it too. Who doesn't have a wistful "straight but not narrow" friend who's confided, "I wish *we* had a parade."

And don't even snap back, "Butcha *do*, Blanche, you have the Macy's Thanksgiving Day Parade, the Rose Bowl, and every other fucking parade all fucking year," because what Poor Wistful Straight Friend really means is: "I wish I could celebrate my sexuality like you do."

Yes, the correct Gay Studies answer is: We do this because we have to. We do it because the larger culture doesn't celebrate us at all (well, at least before *Queer Eye for the Straight Guy* it didn't, and now every-damn-body wants us to throw out their old clothes and redecorate for them. Wow, now *that's* progress). We do it to flaunt—for each other, mainly, but sure, you can watch from the sidewalk. We do it to create ourselves, celebrate ourselves, make ourselves visible as big and loud and proud and *here*. In the old days, pups, we did it for those reasons even when some of us wore paper bags over our heads. (Yes, I attended more than one demo in the '70s where paper-bagged queers shouted "2-4-6-8, gay is just as good as straight"—proud enough, but also worried about keeping their jobs if they were to be caught on film by a TV crew. I always said we ought to all wear Groucho Marx noses, but no one ever took me up on it.)

(Let me just pause a sec here and make it plain that *I* was not wearing the paper bag, people. No, *my* shining face was pictured in *The Eugene Register-Guard*, front page, because my gay youth group was busy suing the school district for access to ad space in student papers. I would have done the Groucho Marx thing, though, because I've always felt the queer movement needed just a touch more Dada.)

But then the next question is, if heteronormativity is still so ubiquitous that it needs no Straight Pride parades, whom will we become if enough of us squeeze our asses onto the park bench of Normalcy? Because you know that's what the military/marriage nexus is all about.

I took my friend Arugula DeVoon, a female drag queen, to the 1993 March on Washington for Lesbian, Gay, and Bi Equal Rights and Liberation. She had come out in San Francisco and was, like me, an alumna of the Lusty Lady Theatre, a peep show that allowed women of all sexual identities a place to grow larger-than-life femme personae, even if they strode in wearing Doc Martens. Arugula had never been to a predominantly political queer march before, and she was excited to be there. She wore a 1950s foundation garment with the cups cut out, so that her own very splendid breasts could serve as the garment's focal point, and she had personally sewn a couple of zillion strings of pearl Mardi Gras beads onto it. She didn't ride the Metro in this get-up; she changed in the restroom beneath the Lincoln Memorial. There we encountered a lesbian from the Midwest, or perhaps the D.C. suburbs. She was wearing a sweatshirt with fuzzy protruding pussywillows on it (I do not think any irony was intended) and a mullet. She did *not* appreciate the excellent beauty of Arugula DeVoon; in fact, by the time Ms. Mullet was finished ranting, Arugula was in tears. The gist (I bet you can already guess): "I'm here to march for my civil rights! When they see *you*, it'll ruin everything!"

Sobbing as we trekked up to tell Abraham Lincoln what had just happened, Arugula managed to say, "I thought this was about letting people be *themselves*!"

If some of our elder philosophers—Harry Hay, Judy Grahn—are correct, queers are here to culturally diversify every society into which we emerge. We are here to expand the very notion of what "being ourselves" can mean. Many of us are also here to devote more of our life's energy to cultural production (art, teaching, and so forth) than to producing the next generation. Instead of raising it, we help birth the alternative ways of seeing that the next generation (or the one after that) will embrace.

Fortunately for Arugula, the Sisters of Perpetual Indulgence were up on top of the Lincoln Memorial, and they welcomed her as a lost sister. As speaker after speaker trashed Bill Clinton for his absence from D.C. (the putatively pro-gay president had flown the coop when the people who helped elect him started to arrive), queer after queer from all over the U.S. rushed up to Arugula and asked to have a photo taken with her. "I've got to send this to my mom!" gushed one guy. And, of course, when she, with her Mardi Gras bead accents, met up with the fags from New Orleans, it was homecoming all over again.

Note to Missy Mullet: Not only is Arugula better dressed than you, she has more pride. Pride is supposedly what brings us to things like marches, and when this culture gets comfortable with Arugula (and all the men who are dressed like her), they won't even *notice* you—except perhaps to say, "Eccch! Pussywillows!" But I'll tell you what—when that happens, you'll have some civil rights you don't have now.

Civil rights, snivel rights. Again, I am not suggesting these goals are completely inappropriate. I don't want a world where fiercely independent people never fall in love, never create family (whatever that means to the people involved in creating it). I want every one of us to be able to care for our lovers, make the lives we want, in the way that works best for the kinds of people we are. I don't want us or our partnerships to be second-class.

However, any queer who has set her or his sights on traditional marriage hasn't been paying attention. Look, I know how much fun it is to go all Martha Stewart and impress your grandma—and I even know that some of your grandmas would dance at your weddings. But marriage is in crisis in this culture, just like Pat Robertson said—it's just that *we're* not the ones who put it there. A vote for gay marriage is a vote for gay divorce—don't ever forget that, nor how quickly legal supports can turn into legal bonds. Really, go talk to a bunch of divorced people before you decide hetero-style marriage is where it's at. Is there any chance you've been watching too many screwball comedies?

Even the touted "queer marriage" alternatives—domestic partnerships and civil unions—require us to assent to a less tightly corseted version of marriage. Now we may be getting somewhere. But, interestingly, in some places these alternatives are open *only* to same-sex couples. My partner Robert and I can register as domestic partners in San Francisco, for example—but we can't with the State of California, until we're senior citizens. (Huh?) To the extent that a domestic-partner agenda is created as an alternative for those who *cannot* legally marry, it does nothing but shore up the notion of marriage. It isn't a real alternative at all.

"Why don't you get married, then?" Bi-identified queers with other-sex partners hear this all the time. Well, let me ask you this. If you had one lover who was white and one who was not and the law only allowed you to wed the Caucasian one, would you? (There *were* such laws in the U.S., and not so long ago.) Why would I want to sanctify one of my relationships (or potential relationships) when I can't get the same respect for the other one? For that matter, why would Robert and I want to take advantage of a cultural perk so many of our friends are disallowed? We don't. Not to mention the fact that we're more likely to want a third (maybe even a third and fourth) person to join our life than to live monogamously. Not many people (including pro-marriage queers) are quick to say the state should allow us the same marital privilege if "us" equals more than two. I recently read a long article from the conservative *Weekly Standard* arguing that the reason to oppose gay marriage had nothing really to do with gays, but rather because once gays could marry, how would we stop the polyamorists from wanting the same thing?

Emphasizing marriage rights in a queer community where many people have chosen alternative relationship configurations, including living single, cuts off or de-emphasizes all the other ways we can choose to relate to one another. Unless we mindfully make marriage one choice among many, many equal choices, we've elected to minimize diversity. We should have dozens of choices, so when the mainstream queer rights movement clamors loudly for marriage, it masks all of us for whom that isn't a great goal; it does not honor our difference.

Oh, but you say you don't want to be different? Butcha *are*, Blanche, ya *are*. Not only that, lots of heterosexuals are as well. The queer movement was truly the key in the closet door, but what those of us worrying about being normal don't realize is that it wasn't just homos and genderqueers in the closet. Everybody was in there! Even *heterosexuals* did not want to live *Leave It to Beaver* lives. I find it deeply ironic that while the LGBT movement focuses its resources on the enormous battle that is gay marriage, straight people are busy signing up for polyamory workshops, renting *Bend Over Boyfriend*, and identifying as queer because *they think we hold the key to living free lives!*

We all need more choices rather than fewer. I won't be the least bit disturbed, really, when one of those choices is gay marriage—unless our other choices have shrunken and not grown. There are as many ways to be wedded as couples (and triples and more-ples) who want to commit to each other, even more reasons than insurance, inheritance, and love. The bottom line is, we live in a culture that puts barriers in the way of even heterosexuals who want to create authentic, lasting, and equal partnerships.

One of those barriers is marriage—it does not truly facilitate our day-to-day relationships, though sometimes it cages us in them. It does not create what was not already there. If you have chosen someone, and you don't wake up every morning knowing your commitment is strong and your love real, your love as permanent as it will be, how will marriage help you? If you *do* have such a relationship with someone (or more than one), how could marriage make you cherish it more?

Our cultural rituals create possibility and identity, but they also exclude. And I find no joy in the Ms. Mullets of the community, who cling to the values of a rejecting culture and proceed to reject others in turn. That culture is in crisis anyway, and desiring to join it more or less on its own terms seems to me like swimming toward the *Titanic*. Write yourself a ritual, throw yourself a party, put on a tux, stand barefoot in the Pacific, invite all your friends. Hell, insist that your

NEVER A BRIDESMAID, NEVER A BRIDE

mother buy you a toaster. But don't get all romantic about Church and State. They don't feel the same way about you.

IS GAY MARRIAGE RACIST?

A CONVERSATION WITH MARLON M. BAILEY, PRIYA KANDASWAMY, AND MATTIE UDORA RICHARDSON

This conversation was inspired by the question-and-answer section of a panel presentation of the same name, which took place at New College of California in the spring of 2004.

Q: I understand that historically marriage has been an oppressive institution, but can't queer people change marriage and make it just? Can't queer people—by virtue of our experience building our own family structures, support systems, and definitions of love and commitment—transform marriage?

Mattie Udora Richardson: The United States has never been a just society as far as African Americans are concerned. The very first promise to freed slaves was that they would be allotted forty acres and a mule—a promise which has yet to be fulfilled. African Americans have repeatedly attempted to transform the institutions of the U.S. to meet our needs and to create a space for us as full citizens. We have tried to reform the state from the inside, becoming police officers and elected officials; we have relied on legislation to "correct" racism—to no avail.

Black families have been maligned by state and local officials as "pathological," as they were described in the infamous Department of Labor report issued by Daniel Patrick Moynihan in 1965. Even though our families have always been defined as deviant, African Americans have often looked to heterosexual marriage to afford us respectability. Historically, neither the granting of marriage rights to Blacks during Reconstruction in the nineteenth century nor the relatively recent dismantling of interracial marriage laws in 1974 has legitimized or protected Black families from destructive state interventions like incarceration and the seizure of children by the state. In fact, marriage has been used against African American people, held as an impossible standard of two-parent nuclear household that pathologizes the extended families that are integral to both our African ancestral and African American cultural lives.

I think that, as a people, our continued search for American inclusion is a tragic one. The U.S. will never embrace Black people as we are, no matter what legislation is passed. Just because there are laws on the books does not stop the state from invalidating and destroying Black families by incarcerating our loved-ones by the millions, terrorizing our neighborhoods with local paramilitary police forces, and placing our sexuality under constant scrutiny by state welfare agencies. Until we as Black queer people speak our own truths, what passes for gay rights will do very little for us. Let's not jump on the white lesbian and gay bandwagon without assessing our own political needs and goals.

Marlon M. Bailey: I do not want or need the U.S. state to ratify or legitimate my intimate relationships to merely prove that I am human. I am not heterosexual, nor do I want to be heterosexual; therefore, personally, I have no use for a heterosexual institution like marriage. Yet, I see this forum as a very important opportunity to begin to grapple with some of the complexities of same-sex marriage, especially when we begin to see it in the context of race, class, gender, and sexuality. Not everybody's relationship to the state is the same; therefore, people's different investments in same-sex marriage or lack thereof should be discussed.

Q: My lover is in the hospital and I can't visit her because I don't have spousal rights. Wouldn't gay marriage help me to help my lover?

MR: First of all, I think that everyone should have the right to choose whomever they want to visit them in the hospital and to make decisions for them. Sadly, it's often women's spouses who put them in the hospital in the first place. I want to choose who visits me in the hospital, who makes my medical decisions, and who receives my Social Security benefits. Maybe I want my nephews to receive my benefits, not my partner. It should really be up to me.

This question about hospital visitation is always linked to the issue of gaining access to spousal health insurance. I think it's ridiculous to have health care contingent on employment status. In fact, I want all of my lovers to have health insurance! I'd like for society to truly honor families in their diversity and to actually have a commitment to the health and well-being of everyone—regardless of citizenship, marital and employment status.

Q: My lover and I had a brutal custody battle when we split up, and since she was the biological mother, the courts gave her full custodial rights and prevented me from seeing my child. Wouldn't legalizing gay marriage allow me to see my daughter?

Priya Kandaswamy: Not necessarily. While many of its advocates argue that gay marriage would secure parental rights for gay and lesbian couples, I think this actually depends on a lot more than marital status. In the U.S., race is the strongest determinant of whether or not the state chooses to recognize your parental ties. Black families are the most likely of any racial group to be disrupted by Child Protection authorities, and 42 percent of all children in foster care in the U.S. are black. If being married doesn't protect straight black families from having their children taken away, it's unlikely that it will protect queer black families. It is incredibly important that we organize to have non-biological ties to children recognized and respected. While marriage might offer limited protections to some people, it will not change the racist and homophobic practices through which Child Protective Services determines who is fit or unfit to be a parent. Unless we change these practices, I don't think that any of our parental relationships are really secure.

MB: We should not assume, in a racist, sexist, heterosexist, and homophobic society, that all people will have access to the so-called rights and privileges that marriage purports to offer. Black people, especially Black queers, have never been able to rely on the state to see us as equal citizens entitled to the rights and privileges granted to our white counterparts. For many Black people, marriage has never been the answer to these problems simply because Black people's social institutions are not seen as institutions worth honoring. We are locked out of these so-called protections even when we adhere to the social strictures that are supposed to enable such protections.

Q: My lover was recently deported because he couldn't get a green card. We are domestic partners, but the courts didn't recognize that status. Wouldn't marriage have kept us together?

PK: It is true that theoretically if you and your partner were able to have a legally recognized marriage, it may have allowed your partner to remain in the country. However, I think that there are a couple of important things to consider before taking this as a reason to endorse gay marriage. The first question that I would ask you is: Was your partner really deported because the two of you couldn't get married? Or was s/he deported because of racist immigration policies that readily exploit immigrant labor while at the same time forcing millions of immigrants to live in constant fear of deportation because the state refuses to grant them legal status in this country?

It is true that for some immigrants, marriage can be a path to obtaining legal status. However, not only is the process of gaining legal status through marriage contingent on the INS's recognition of your marriage as one made in "good faith," but this process also places a great deal of power over an immigrant in the hands of their citizen spouse. The requirement that immigrants prove to the INS that their marriages are legitimate and not just a means to legal status has meant that immigrants of color, who by virtue of the racist discourses surrounding immigration are more likely to be seen as "cheating the system," often have a much harder time gaining legal status than white immigrants. In addition, many feminist activists within immigrant communities have drawn attention to the ways that an immigrant's dependency on her citizen spouse for legal status in this country can produce or at least exacerbate exploitation and abuse within a relationship. As a result, in many cases, immigrant women are faced with the dilemma of having to choose between remaining in an abusive relationship or deportation. Given that domestic violence is not only a problem of the straight community, I think it is important that we take seriously the inequalities that gay marriage might produce in relationships between citizens and immigrants. It seems better to me to focus our political energies on fighting for broader changes in immigration policies that might enable immigrants in this country to live better lives regardless of their marital status.

It is really important that you bring up the particular concerns of queer immigrants as these concerns are often very marginalized within queer political organizing. I think that a radical queer politics must address the multifaceted forms of oppression that queer immigrants face in this country. This means not simply thinking about queer immigrants in relation to their citizen partners, but developing a complex analysis of the ways that capitalist exploitation of immigrant labor, xenophobia, nationalism, racism, patriarchy, and homophobia affect the lives of queer immigrants. Most immigrants in this country come from places in the world that have been dev-astated by U.S. military operations or U.S.-sponsored economic policies. When they get to the U.S., many of these immigrants are forced to take poorly paid jobs with long hours, few benefits, little upward mobility, and few, if any, labor protections. To top it all off, they are denied most public services, and often their very presence in this country is criminalized. So, it seems to me that a radical queer politics needs to, at the very least, take a firm stance against U.S. military and economic colonialism abroad, support struggles of workers everywhere, and oppose racist state policies that criminalize immigrants. This seems much more in line with the long term interests of queer immigrants as a group than struggles for gay marriage.

Q: Obviously gay marriage shouldn't be the main priority for queer struggle—I know that this is just a first step, but don't we have to support gay marriage if we want to further struggles for full equality and civil rights for all queers?

MB: The crux of this movement is led by white, middle-class gays and lesbians who would large-ly benefit from same-sex marriage (the Log Cabin Republicans, for instance). These people already have a considerable amount of upward mobility, so marriage is the icing on the cake. However, what these white queers are not concerned about, or at least it has not been expressed, is the vast majority of people of color who do not enjoy such social mobility and who are largely disenfranchised, and who need health care and don't have it, etc. There has been no sustained cri-tique of marriage from the white queer community, no mention of how it has been situated as a marker that Black people are compared to. While Blacks are seen as being outside of marriage and therefore deemed a dysfunctional people, meanwhile the state is consistently engaged in var-ious schemes that undermine Black social institutions that support our kinship structures. And let's be honest, the white queer community, in large part, is extremely racist. Therefore, Black queers should be highly skeptical of any movement where we are being asked to jump on the bandwagon because at the end of the day, we are not the ones who stand to gain anything.

MR: The mainstream white lesbian and gay leadership is extremely arrogant to assume gay mar-riage as a "last barrier" to full citizenship when many of us will never see full equality or civil rights. Lesbian and gay mainstream marriage advocates have proclaimed that their inclusion will complete the U.S. march towards full equality for all of its citizens. This argument is a slap in the face to everyone who continues to experience institutionalized oppression in this country. The fact that they reflexively refer to African American civil rights struggles as their point of comparison for equality that has been "won" does two things. One, it falsely establishes that Black people and gay people are mutually exclusive population sets. Two, it is a boldface disregard for Black history and an act of disrespect to Black people who continue to face the violence of racism every day.

Furthermore, not every queer desires to base their families on the model of the two-parent household with 2.5 kids. Every time white lesbian and gay leaders trot out some well-heeled homosexual couple who own their own homes, have six figure salaries, and live the American dream, they do violence to the numerous forms of intimate arrangements and loving parenting that do not conform to mainstream ideas. For example, not so long ago my partner and I accepted the challenge of caring for my teenaged nephew. During that time I had to interact with several state and local agencies that did not recognize us as a legitimate family even though I am a close blood relative. The first institution that challenged our legitimacy was the school my nephew attended, which did not see my partner as an equal guardian with me. The second was the state welfare office. Being a graduate student earning poverty wages, I applied for general assistance for such necessities as food. I was humiliated and denied aid because my sister did not relinquish her parental rights.

In reality, this is a lesbian and gay agenda, not a queer one. Our families are more "queer" than simply having two parents and children; we have kids enter our lives from our extended family, from our neighbors and friends. We have multiple intimate partnerships; we live in bodies that are not exclusively "male" or "female." Many of our genders and the genders of our lovers are not recognized by the state at all. Upon closer inspection, marriage is not even a first step for addressing the needs of queer people.

Q: I agree with your points, but isn't it true that at the very [base], marriage is about love and any way that two people can express that love for one another is progress?

PK: I would disagree with your assumption that love is actually at the foundation of the institution of marriage. Rather, I would argue that marriage is a legal institution that is fundamentally about preserving property relations. Not only does the marriage contract have its historical roots in the ownership and exchange of women, but it has been a key mechanism through which material wealth has been kept within particular families. In addition, the centrality of anti-miscegenation laws in U.S. history also demonstrates the ways that marriage has functioned to police racial borders and preserve white privilege.

Ultimately, whether people love each other and whether people get married are two very different questions. The state recognizes a very particular kind of relationship in its recognition of marriage, a relationship that is structured by the idiom of property. However, this is not the only kind of love relationship that exists, nor is it the kind of love relationship to which we as queer people ought to aspire. For me, radical queer politics has always been about challenging the boundaries of what counts as "love." One doesn't have to be in a monogamous, long term, same-sex relationship to love other people. One of the things that I think is most unfortunate about the gay marriage movement is that its implicit message seems to be that framing our relationships in ways that the state might recognize is more important than defining our practices of love on our own terms.

CHILDREN, THE TRUCKS, CHAINMAIL, TIME, THE BORDER, SKIN PROBLEMS, THE FEDS, AND THE URBAN ECO-VILLAGE OF YOUR DREAMS

SYLVIA AND SYLVIA'S CHILDREN: A BATTLE FOR A QUEER PUBLIC SPACE

BENJAMIN SHEPARD

The other day I saw a strange item in the *Village Voice* Choice weekend listings:

> Spring for some brioche, some chocolate, and a bottle of Beaujolais, and picnic at one of these divine destinations: Downtowners should bus it to the West Side's Hudson River Park, where the benches face at a series of seriously seaworthy piers afford views of that old French gay, the statue of liberty . . . [1]

It was odd to read about Manhattan's Christopher Street piers promoted as a tourist destination in the city's "alternative weekly," yet that is what they have become. Queer street kids have used the space as long as anyone can remember. Yet, in recent years the image of a street youth enjoying a drink on the piers has come to embody an ongoing class war over the city's "quality of life."

Only a couple of years ago, the piers were considered very specific queer space, a mecca of sorts. Pier users often called them "the Trucks" because of all the trucks lined up in which men could meet and have sex. Few straight people or tourists crossed west of Hudson Street to go to this Oz-like autonomous zone, where generations of gay men had created a free zone for sexual contact and community. Yet in recent years, much of the radical potential of the space has been white-washed away—as the piers fall victim to gentrifiers, politicians, and urban planners on the one hand, and a blandification of gay culture on the other.[2]

Yet the "malling" of Manhattan—and of queerdom itself—is not without its opposition and resistance. What emerges in this essay is the story of a flashpoint in a class war pitting corporate control of public space against a burgeoning "do-it-yourself" public space activism in which queer difference is honored over assimilating sameness. Part one considers the legacy of one grand activist who fought for queer spaces, while part two offers stories of how her radical approach to queer activism continues with a new generation.

SYLVIA

The "Grand Dame" of the gay liberation movement, transgender activist Sylvia Rivera, helped build a series of enduring queer family networks on the piers. "As a Stonewall veteran, I feel it's my responsibility to make sure these kids have a place to come," Rivera explained when she was living on the piers in the early 1990s (Mateik and Gaberman, 2002).

As one of the most famous of the street youth who fought back during the police raid at the Stonewall Inn in June 1969, Rivera came to personify the aspirations and flaws of the modern gay liberation movement. Born on July 2, 1951, Rivera spent her life fighting for solidarity among transgender people, queer people of all colors, homeless people, sex workers, and other liberation groups, such as the Young Lords, Gay Liberation Front, and the Street Trans Action Revolutionaries. As the years distanced activists from the causes of the riots, Rivera often clashed with mainstream gay groups that advocated for assimilation, and West Village gay residents who supported redevelopment of the piers. Rivera spoke for the queer youth who experienced the piers as perhaps the only place they could consider home.

While Rivera is credited with throwing the "first brick" during the Stonewall Riots, she claimed she actually threw a Molotov cocktail, declaring, "This is the revolution." For Rivera, that revolution meant fighting back against the police, who had harassed her since her days as an eleven-year-old prostitute working the streets of Times Square. Rivera was on hand for the first gay pride parade, the Christopher Street Liberation Day march in 1970. With no roadmap to guide her, Rivera worked with the founding members of the Gay Liberation Front (GLF), and later the Gay Activists Alliance (GAA). GLF's vision was a politics of global solidarity with liberation movements around the world, while GAA focused more on specifically "gay" issues. As a member of GAA, Rivera involved herself in campaigns such as the fight to pass New York City's first gay rights bill. For several years Rivera straddled these competing streams of the gay liberation movement. A willingness to engage in direct action was her claim to fame.

"One of my first organizing campaigns with the political aspects of the gay liberation movement was petitioning for the gay rights bill," Rivera recalled during a 2001 interview assessing her career. Arthur Evans (2002), who worked with her on the bill, recalled:

> My favorite memory of Sylvia Rivera was in early 1970 in New York City. The Gay Activists Alliance was collecting petitions for a bill in the city council that would outlaw job discrimination against gays and lesbians. We took our petitions to a meeting of the Village Independent Democrats in Greenwich Village. Carol Greitzer, the liberal councilwoman from Greenwich Village, was present at the meeting. Greitzer refused to take—or even look at—the petitions. Sylvia Rivera grabbed the petition-laden clipboard, marched up to the front of the meeting, and hit Greitzer over the head with it. The liberals started to listen up. GAA leader Marty Robinson called the process "climbing up the liberals."

Rivera was ever-present, doing whatever it took to pass the bill, including getting arrested with Evans and Marty Mumford. She later explained, "I was the only drag queen that got arrested for petitioning for gay rights. We were included in their bill. All of a sudden, I started becoming more and more an organizer and a front-liner. Drag queens could be out there. What did we have to lose?"

Debate was often noisy during the early gay liberation years, as cultural leaders such as Rivera, who sought to transform restrictive notions of sex and gender, clashed with more politically minded leaders, who sought incremental changes without radically altering the status quo. Lesbians and gay men debated the meanings of male chauvinism, homophobia, and transvestism, and structurelessness tore at GLF's foundations. By 1970 Rivera and the late Marsha P.

Johnston—another Stonewall veteran—co-founded Street Transvestite Action Revolutionaries (STAR) as a caucus of GLF. STAR, one of the nation's first transgender rights organizations, served as a nudge for the nascent gay liberation movement to pay more attention to transgender issues. It also provided housing for those involved at STAR House, a shelter-like crash pad for trans street youth. "In the beginning, we were the vanguard of the gay movement. We were very well-respected for the first four years," recalled Rivera.

Yet Rivera's conflicts with the movement continued on several fronts. Women in GLF were uncomfortable referring to Rivera—who insisted on using women's bathrooms, even in City Hall—as "she." The pressure mounted. The year 1973 witnessed a clash that would take Rivera out of the movement for the next two decades. As her lifelong friend and fellow Stonewall veteran Bob Kohler recalled, "Sylvia left the movement because after the first three or four years, she was denied a right to speak."

The breaking point came during the Pride rally in Washington Square Park after the 1973 Christopher Street Liberation Day march. To the dismay of Lesbian Feminist Liberation (LFL),[3] drag queens were scheduled to perform. As LFL passed out flyers outlining their opposition to the "female impersonators," Rivera wrestled for the microphone held by emcee Vito Russo, before getting hit with it herself. Rivera later explained, "I had to battle my way up on stage, and literally get beaten up and punched around by people I thought were my comrades, to get to that microphone. I got to the microphone and I said my piece." Rivera complained that the middle-class crowd cared little to nothing about the continued harassment and arrests of street drag queens. Bleeding, Rivera screamed, "Revolution Now!" and led the crowd in a chant of "Give me a G, Give me an A, Give me a Y . . . What does it spell?" Barely audible, her voice breaking, she groaned, "GAY POWER." Russo later recalled that only the sudden appearance of Bette Midler averted outright violence, as trans opponents and supporters battled over the mike. Midler, having listened to what was happening on the radio in her Greenwich Village apartment, rushed to the scene, wrested control of the mike, and started singing "Friends" (Marotta, 1981: 296–7). Rivera would not return to formal queer organizing for some two decades.

In the years after STAR's demise in the early 1970s, the movement became more and more assimilated. And for many, the transgender legacy of Stonewall was left behind. While the American Psychiatric Association did away with diagnosing homosexuality as a psychiatric disorder in the early 1970s, the term "gender identity disorder," used to label transgender people as mentally ill, remained a psychiatric classification in the *Diagnostic and Statistical Manual of Mental Disorders*. By 1987, the New York City Council had passed the gay rights bill Rivera and GAA had fought for, but without language protecting transgender people from employment discrimination.

From the late 1970s to the early 1990s, Rivera lived in Tarrytown, NY, before moving back to New York City. For a number of years in the 1980s Rivera, who suffered from chemical dependence, was homeless herself. Yet she continued organizing—this time a community of transgender squatters who lived on the piers on the West Side of Manhattan. As she had done with STAR House, Rivera played the role of surrogate mother to a community of homeless transgender and queer street kids on the piers.

In June 1994 Rivera was tapped by the leaders of the Stonewall 25th anniversary celebration to lead the march. She later recalled feeling like she was being recycled from off the shelf. And her relationship with mainstream gay groups remained tenuous. For example, Rivera was formally banned from the New York City Lesbian and Gay Community Center. (Different people have different stories as to why Rivera was kicked out, yet most agree it had to do with her drinking.) Yet her activism continued. "I did not leave the movement because I've always felt that this is what they want. They want us to go so that they can hide in their little closets as if we don't exist," Rivera explained.

In 1998 Rivera was arrested with over a hundred others during a political funeral for Matthew Shepard. Her presence inspired many to compare the police attacks on that demonstration and the response to the Stonewall Riots themselves. Yet Rivera was quick to point out that transgender people die as a result of similar attacks without fanfare on all too regular a basis. Her lover Marsha P. Johnson died mysteriously herself on the piers.

By the summer of 2000 Rivera organized rallies to draw attention to another such case, the murder of Amanda Milan, a transgender woman, in Times Square days before the Manhattan Pride march. Over the course of the following year, Rivera successfully organized Milan's political funeral and countless other demonstrations. Unlike Marsha P. Johnson, whose death was never investigated, Rivera made sure there was a coordinated effort to find out what really happened to Milan.

Through Rivera's linkage with the issue, Milan came to symbolize the unfinished business of a GLBT movement that had all too often, in Rivera's words, "left transgender people at the back of the bus." As transgender issues emerged in the press, Rivera noted, "If things don't pan out, then it is going to be totally the old way. If it takes arrests to bring the media to the plight of this community, I'm willing to take all the arrests that I have to . . ." In her final weeks, Rivera fought for New York City and State transgender rights legislation, which was finally gaining steam. She even met with Empire State Pride Agenda over the bills from her hospital death bed the week she died in the winter of 2002. Within three months of her death, the New York City Council passed, and the mayor signed, the transgender rights bill for which she had spent three decades fighting.

In the weeks following her death, Rivera was remembered as an activist who had fought to break down the walls between movements to make the world a better place for everyone. Many confessed that they had not seen Rivera's wisdom until she was gone. "You gotta listen to the crazies," Kohler reflected. While those in the movement had not always paid attention to her, Rivera had become an icon to young activists. Many recognized a heroine not interested in assimilating to a status quo that consigned transgender youth—or anyone else—to the margins. "These kids finally had somebody of their own, their own Evita," Kohler explained. "They would see someone from the streets who was theirs. Sylvia changed lives."

SYLVIA'S CHILDREN

In the months after Rivera's death, attacks on the pier kids and the spaces where they converged intensified, with many arrested or told to move along for doing little more than occupying public space. "We face constant threats of violence from police and residents," explained Mervyn Marcano, an organizer for FIERCE!, an advocacy group by and for queer youth of color (Henry, 2002). In the fall of 2002, FIERCE! organized a rally and speak-out on the issue, entitled "Reclaim Our Space." During the October 5 rally, activists recalled the late Rivera's struggle, implicitly linking their cause with hers. In many respects, her legacy continues with a new generation of activists who recognize the liberatory potential of a radical queer public that aims not to gain acceptance, but rather to create a politics in which difference is honored and no one is left behind.

A NEW "PROBLEM" IN THE NEIGHBORHOOD

Queers hanging out in public were once considered a staple of West Village street culture. Yet within the climate of the Giuliani/Bloomberg "quality of life" crusade, the presence of gender insubordinate young Black and Latino queer youth, as opposed to white men with moustaches, is often viewed as a problem. Complaints of prostitution, public sex, and drug and sexual commerce continue to inspire the local Community Board to encourage aggressive policing and street sweeps throughout the West Village, including the piers. Others question whether it is the same people who run these "Community Boards" who are making the complaints, thus producing the panic to which they then are "compelled" to respond.

Tools utilized in this class-cleansing process include anti-vagrancy, zoning, nuisance-abatement, and quality-of-life statutes, all enacted by cities to restrict movement in public space. As Mervyn Marcano explained at the rally, "They disproportionately target queer youth of color. It's resulting in increased prison populations of queer youth just for loitering or urination on the street."

Dakota, a long-time pier user who first started hustling there in the 1970s, described the current scene for sex workers who work in the city's public spaces. "They are all going to jail. I got fifty-three misdemeanors for prostitution convictions."

Adonis Baough, a former pier user who has spent his life in and out of jail, suggested that the police presence shifts the way he understands public space: "Public space means I could stand there wherever I want, whenever I want. So, it's no such thing as a public space. Because if the police come after me, then it's not a public space, it's a police space."

PROFILING THE NEW "PROBLEM"

After witnessing random sweeps of youth on piers and being told, "The residents don't want you here," FIERCE! began organizing against police harassment in the summer of 2000. "Fighting back" became a constant refrain of the October 5 rally.

Jay Dee Melendez described residents "putting water and piss and garbage out of their windows onto the youth" during the rally. She was followed by Gail from the Audre Lorde Project, who does outreach in the area. She explained that the pattern of abuse was becoming a city-wide problem:

I've been working for about five or six years with the victims of police violence. And we see it all with Giuliani and with Bloomberg now with the "quality of life" campaign. The police say you gotta give up your right to walk. Whose quality of life is this improving? It sure isn't improving mine. And I can't come down to the piers on a weekend with my friends without the police stopping me and asking me what I'm doing, where I'm going, when they start putting curfews on the piers. And if you're white and you're rollerblading that's all right. It might start here in the Village. It might involve queer youth and transgendered people here, but it's also happening up in Harlem, it's happening in Brooklyn.

James Place, a twenty-eight-year-old person of color and former hustler who is constantly stopped by police, elaborated: "When you see those white kids down there, the police don't ever stop them. Loud, making noise, and drinking and smoking like they got licenses for it, but they don't get stopped." Yet when people like Place even walk along the piers, the police assume "that I am up to no good or out to rob somebody." "Often, I go there to just to hang out. And yet they want to stop me. There's a lot of police there. Every other corner you see a cop."

Boo-boo, a forty-three-year-old transgender woman of color who first started going to the piers when she was in her teens in the late 1970s, actually lived along the piers in a tent with two girlfriends in the 1980s. "I had tent, a portable pail for washing, a hot plate, and a TV set plugged into one of the electric poles that gave you juice. It really was a home." She sees a more benevolent motive to the increased police presence.

I used to think the police were there just to hassle us. Now I think they are there cause they know what the thirteen- and fourteen-year-olds who go there face down the road if they stay. They used to find so many bodies there I thought there was a serial murderer. One of my friends had her implants cut off. Another had her penis cut off and put in her mouth before they threw her in the water. The violence was too much to imagine. To cope with it, you would have to turn to drugs. Now, I think I'm the last one left. Most everyone else either died from HIV or the bashings.

Other people interviewed suggested the harassment had as much to do with homophobia—or fear of difference in and of itself—as race. When asked if people of color were being unfairly targeted, L.P., a Latino man and long-term pier user, explained:

> I wouldn't really say that, because I've seen a lot of my white friends who got it even worse. When they did talk back, the police brutalized them harder and more than they did to the minorities. With minorities, a lot of us would fight back. The white kids didn't know how to fight really and they would really get it. But I have to give it to 'em, some of the softest ones were the ones who would chain themselves to something. And they wouldn't let go and they wouldn't give up no matter how much you beat them, no matter how many times you arrested them, no matter how much food you denied them, no matter how much legal process you denied them. When you went into court, they still screamed about gay rights and transgender rights. And they were truly defiant through all of the black eyes and those stuns with the cattle prod-like stun gun things they were carrying in the olden days.

ATTACKS ON QUEER SPACE

The struggles over the piers continues to happen within a specific political context of crackdowns on public sexual culture in Manhattan. Over the last ten years, the city has tightened the screws on displays of public sexual culture, first shutting sex clubs and then harassing people who use cruising spaces such as the piers or the Central Park Ramble.

Adonis, who still frequents the Ramble, talked about the increased pressure:

> I've actually been told "get out the park." No, I'm not getting out the park. I'm on a public path, not in the Ramble in the dirt. I was in public space. You cannot tell me to leave. But they just said, "do you want to

spent the night in jail?" Then I walked away, but that kind of threat might have scared a lot of people. Not wanting to have their business brought out in court. Not having their job find out why they had to go to court. Most times the cases are dropped. I was walking out of Central Park at 1:01 am and the police saw me and gave me a ticket. The judge laughed and tore up the ticket. But you still have to use your energy to go down there or a warrant will be put out for your arrest. You do that and what do you tell your job? What do you tell anyone?

The crackdown is part of a campaign designed to privatize, sanitize, and control public spaces such as the piers throughout New York City. It began in 1994 as a cornerstone of Mayor Rudy Giuliani's pledge to clean up New York City. Existing "quality of life" legislation falls under Article 240, Title N, Offenses Against Public Order, Public Sensibilities, and the Right to Privacy. Such "offenses" include "rioting, unlawful assembly, criminal anarchy, disorderly conduct, harassment, loitering, public intoxication, and criminal nuisance in a public space" (McClean, 2002). Yet there are countless additional antivagrancy ordinances that regulate public space, including the short-lived "Under 20 Rule," designed to restrict public gatherings to fewer than twenty people. This 1999 rule was later struck down. The same could not be said after 1995 when the New York City Council passed a zoning law intended to restrict and shut down adult-use spaces such as strip clubs, bookstores, video stores, and movie houses. Mayor Giuliani hoped to shut down almost every adult business that dealt with sexual materials or entertainment.

When quasi-private interior spaces targeted by the zoning law were shut down, people with nowhere else to go moved outside. But visible signs of public sexual culture were further targeted, with the police carrying out undercover sting operations resulting in stepped-up arrests of men charged with indecent exposure, soliciting sex, and other "lewd" acts. Some were based on entrapment, while others were wrongful arrests. During one three-day sting by the Port Authority police in 1997, ninety men were arrested in the men's bathroom in the PATH station concourse of the World Trade Center (Schindler, 1997).

Adonis elaborated: "If two heterosexuals were in the park making out and the police walked by, they wouldn't say anything. If two homosexuals were doing things, they would say something." Many of the "quality of life" initiatives appeared to specifically target queers. Selective enforcement of a Prohibition-era cabaret law, zoning ordinances, a ban on dancing, and fire codes were used to produce a constant flow of legal assaults narrowing the types of clubs and bars functioning in Manhattan. Before summer of 1997 some seventeen gay businesses, nine theaters, and eight clubs—including five in close proximity on Fourteenth Street—were closed for violations of the state health code banning oral, anal, or vaginal sex on business premises. That summer, fifty queer businesses faced some fourteen hundred inspections (Schindler, 1997). Many clubs could not endure the legal barrage and were forced to close their doors.

TWO POTATO AND AIDS FEAR

One such space was the Two Potato, a bar at the corner of Christopher and Greenwich Streets, close to the piers. Many suggest that the current controversy surrounding the piers began with the debate over the Two Potato, now called Chances Are. L.P. and several others I interviewed recalled the Two Potato as a "legendary" gathering place for queer and transgender people of color. Like the West Village in general, the Two Potato provided a refuge when the AIDS epidemic hit. "At night people could spread out to Fourteenth Street and over to Two Potato on the water and just drink and wild out and have sex, and feel like we were still normal," L.P. recalled. Yet the feeling of safety engendered within the queer spaces of the West Village was placed in jeopardy by phobias accompanying the epidemic. As L.P. explained, "We'd have to do a lot of fighting because there was a lot of prejudice."

The pattern is simple enough. Moral guardians use fears about the AIDS crisis to justify restricting access to spaces such as the piers and Two Potato, supposedly in the name of community health and "the children." What unfolds is a general "not in my backyard" thinking stirred up by the "quality of life" campaign.[4] The result is simple. "He [Giuliani] used the excuse of AIDS. He was saying that [public sex] was a way to spread the virus, but responsible adults who knew about it used condoms. They were consenting adults," Adonis explained.[5]

Yet as sites for camaraderie, public sexual spaces are unique. "Everybody had sex and nobody gave a fuck. You could go into any club and stick your dick through a hole in the wall and there'd be somebody on the other side to suck it," L.P. recalled. "Sometimes you could go to any club and literally almost have sex on the dance floor." Dakota, who no longer goes to the piers, recalls similar scenes. "It was outrageous. It was crazy. They [the residents] walk out their doorway and find somebody getting a blowjob. It was real."

One of the important elements of the piers and other public sex spaces is that they break down class and social roles. Charley Shively (1974–2001) specifically notes that "the trucks" were a place where "a faggot will make it with someone he will not have to live with the next day." Within such spaces, "occasionally the vision of luxury, even ecstasy, of a mutual faggot sexuality can be found."

Yet as the AIDS era wore on, anxieties about the epidemic coincided with countless other cultural phobias and inequalities. L.P. explained that just getting off the train at Fourteenth Street could be an ordeal. "If you got off the train and you looked gay, you might get beat up by a group of kids. 'Faggot, we don't want you in New York.' And the police were no help. The cops would stand there and watch because they were in agreement that this was the gay man's disease and that they didn't want to get any bodily fluids on them or get involved. Let the faggot get what he deserves." For L.P., navigating from the Bronx to the Village "was like going through a gauntlet." Between the antivagrancy laws, a social purity crusade described as a "quality of life" campaign, and AIDS hysteria, L.P.—like many other queer youth—engaged in a struggle against what amounted to a panic over queer space.

Back to the Two Potato, L.P. explained, "We used to hang out outside." But in recent years, "They would come two or three times a night. If we were at the door at Two Potato, the residents would tell the police they have to shut it down." Contact with the police only increased. "If the bathrooms were filled and you were going to go take a leak around the corner, they followed you around the back so they could pick you up. It was called a lewd act in public," he explained. Residents viewed the bar as a site of drug use, prostitution, and violence, including slashings. They also complained about patrons such as L.P. who "hung out" in front of the club. "I went to jail a couple of times because I refused to move from in front of the club," he said. On one occasion, L.P. recalled:

> I told them I had paid money to be in that club and I had just come out
> to get a breath of fresh air and it was hot. And I was not going to move
> just because they was yelling through their loudspeakers and they were

saying to move. No congregating on the sidewalk and they were blocking the sidewalk.

Other neighborhood residents objected to the frequent drag shows—some featuring full
nudity—that took place there. Patrons maintain that the space was targeted because of the Black
and Latino transgender crowds that flocked there (McLean, 2002).

As the police contact intensified at the piers, the Two Potato, and other spots, Adonis and L.P.
became increasingly aware of their rights to use public space. As L.P. explained:

> I started to learn the law that if there was more than five people, that was
> considered a public gathering. So we tried to break up the groups to
> threes and stand around defiantly to let them know. And quote the law
> that if there was no more than five, then it was not a public gathering
> and we had as much right to stand there as anyone else.

As Adonis explained:

> Well, most people got arrested because they were doing explicit sexual
> acts on the piers. And they got caught. Or drinking a beer, or playing the
> music too loud, or dancing and not paying the officers no mind, and they
> get mad and they arrest them. Now, if whatever they charged them with
> didn't stick, they still had to go through the system. They had to suffer
> for those three days. The police don't really care after they do their
> paperwork.

In August 2001, after years of "quality of life" complaints, the Two Potato's liquor license came
up for review prior to renewal and the bar was closed (McLean, 2002). For L.P. and countless others, the impact of the club's closure and the subsequent erection of fences at the piers was immediate. "It made it very hard for us to function," L.P. recalled. "You couldn't hang out by the water
anymore. They were doing construction on the highway, so you couldn't really go down there."

GENTRIFICATION

Along the road, the less affluent felt squeezed out and unwelcome. Tim Doody worked on the October 5, 2002, "Reclaim Our Space" rally. He explained that an emphasis on property and real estate had distorted the values of the space:

> It's Giuliani justice—the same thing that is happening with community gardens is happening with the West Village—profits over people. It is time and again. A lot of the original people that were in these areas all over New York City have been shuttled out for the new breeds that have disposable income, not much culture, not much of a lot of the things that once made New York City so vibrant.

Imani Henry elaborated on the stages of the gentrification process taking hold:

> If you are a rich developer and you want to make sure that this is prime real estate, then you are going to do everything in your power to get community boards and the kinds of clientele that can afford to pay $3,000 for a studio. And you are going to get the police to do watches on the streets and harass people and close clubs down, and file phony violations on spaces, and literally physically arrest, brutalize, and beat people to get them out of that area.

The point was to make the people who rent those $3,000 studio apartments feel at home. "You are not supposed to see drag queens," Henry explained. "God forbid there are no trans women. There are no sex workers. There are no youth. There are no people of color."

SYLVIA AND HER CHILDREN

Sylvia Rivera struggled for over thirty years to force the city to accept and protect the right of transgender people to walk or work in public space. In many ways, the youth who continue to struggle for queer spaces are working from the same vantage point. Queer space is about creating room for the spectacle of difference as opposed to assimilating sameness. As long as autonomous zones pop up, the possibility remains.

Boo-boo recalled a visit to the space in the summer of 2003 after fences went down in the summer, opening a panorama across the waterfront:

> There are other spots, others piers, yet there will never be anything like the Manhattan West Side piers. Don't take this wrong, but there were a lot of lost souls out there. Some days I go down there, look at the water, just remember and meditate. That was our fantasy world. But I don't care how many curfews or arrests or laws the police push, they will never stop the children from going down to the West Side piers.

REFERENCES

*Baugh, Adonis. 2002. Interview with the author. 25 October.

Crimp, Douglas. 2002. *Melancholia and Moralism: Essays on AIDS and Queer Politics.* MIT Press: Cambridge, MA.

*Dakota. 2002. Interview with the author. 13 November.

Evans, Arthur. 2002. Rivera recalled. *Bay Area Reporter.* February 28.

Henry, Imani. 2002. Homeless, hungry and harassed. *Workers World.* October 17.

Henry, Imani. 2002. Interview with the author. 5 December.

Kohler, Bob. 2002. Interview with the author. 10 June.

*L.P. 2003. Interview with the author. 3 January.

*Boo-boo. 2003. Interview with the author. 15 July.

McLean, Rebecca. 2002. Junior Colloquium Paper, Columbia University. May 2. Unpublished paper.

Mateik, Tara, and Denise Gaberman. 2002. Sylvia Rivera Tribute Tape. Paper Tiger TV. New York.

Marotta, Tony, 1981. *The Politics of Homosexuality.* Houghton Mifflin Company: New York.

*Place, James. 2002. Interview with the author. 13 November.

Read, Kirk. 2003. SF Street Theater: The Hot Pink Police Riot *Gay Today* Vol. VII Issue 72, May 15. http://www.gaytoday.com/viewpoint/031003vp.asp

Rivera, Sylvia. 2001. Interview with the author. 27 June.

Rodgers, Steve. 2002. Interview with the author. 20 December.

Schindler, Paul. 1997. Is It a Gay Thing or a Giuliani Thing? *LGNY.* August 3.

Shively, Charley. 1974/2001. Indiscriminate Promiscuity as an Act of Revolution. In *Come Out Fighting: A Century of Essential Writing on Gay & Lesbian Liberation.* Edited by Chris Bull. Nation Books: New York.

* These names are aliases.

UNSUITABLE FOR CHILDREN

GINA DE VRIES

Y ou know, I think I'm just unsuitable for children," I said to my girlfriend Sarah.

We were on the bus home from a recital at the summer school where she worked, teaching civil rights history and health education to a program of one hundred twenty rising seventh, eighth, and ninth graders. I'd been a student in the same summer program when I was twelve—now I was twenty and back in San Francisco on summer vacation. I wanted to see what the program was like eight years later, and I was excited to meet Sarah's students and see what they'd come up with for the end-of-summer celebration. I'd biked across town to the recital in a go-go dress and fishnets, and still managed to arrive ten minutes early. While Sarah was teaching, I'd spent my summer days doing porn modeling and writing for income, and volunteering at the Center for Sex & Culture in Hayes Valley. I'd spent that particular day sorting and categorizing a recent donation of fag porn, an irony not lost on me as I walked through the doors of the Pacific Heights prep school where the program was held.

"I just feel like I should have one of those 'Parental Advisory: Explicit Lyrics' stickers tattooed on my forehead."

"But Gina, you're great with kids! My students really liked you . . ."

"You know that, and I know that, but dude, all I talk about is sex and porno! What parent is going to want me to talk to their twelve-year-old about anything, let alone the stuff I *want* to talk to kids about? I'm queer and a slut and a pervert and—"

Sarah attempted to stop the lather I was working myself into with gentle humor. "Honey, so am I. Remember why you're sleeping with me?"

"Well, how do you do it, then?!" I cried. "How do you keep yourself from being 'inappropriate'? How the hell do you walk the line between educating as much as you possibly can without getting your ass booted out of there? I want to teach kids about consent and pleasure and how cool their bodies are and how to keep themselves safe. I was wracked with guilt for being sexual at that age, let alone for being queer, let *alone* for thinking about the crazy kinky stuff I thought about! I think it'd be fabulous to teach middle-schoolers that all that stuff's okay! But see, most parents wouldn't! If I had your job I'd get fired in five minutes!"

It's not like I didn't think about sex or feminism when I was in middle school. In fact, sex and feminism were all I thought I about at that age, especially since most of my sexual fantasies (like the one where I was a young nelly faggot getting his dick sucked by an equally pretty queen, surely influenced by my obsession with David Bowie) weren't exactly in line with the mainly older, second-wave lesbian-feminist community that reluctantly took me in. But maybe that's a whole other essay.

Our conversation left me thinking about the kind of sex education that I got as a middle- and high-schooler—what worked for me and what didn't, what made my queer, kinky sexuality feel validated and sexy, and what made me feel gross and invisible. More than one person has said that I was a particularly sexually precocious kid. I came out at an extremely young age, and whenever I talk about coming into my sexuality, most people—even most queer people—discount my case as "special." I usually get a response along the lines of "Oh, you were just a particularly self-aware eleven-year-old, Gina. Most kids aren't like you were, and they wouldn't need the kind of information you did."

My reaction to that line of rhetoric has always been complicated. When I came out in 1995, even in the supposed queer mecca of San Francisco, I was certainly the only out sixth-grader I knew. I remember how scared I was when I first acknowledged my crushes on other girls, and a lot of that fear had to do with knowing that people—even other queer people—wouldn't believe me. I began attending queer youth events and support groups at the Lavender Youth Recreation and Information Center (LYRIC), the organization I credit with saving my life and my sanity as a scared adolescent. LYRIC gave me a sense of community and family, a refuge from the taunts and violence I faced every day at school. But still, my first few months going there, the most common reactions to my age were, "You're *how old*?" and, "You're too young to even *have* a sexual orientation!" For a long time I thought that I *was* the only young one, or at least one of very few who was thinking about these things.

I now know that there's a lot wrong with telling someone that their individual experience is so completely unique that they won't find representations of themselves anywhere else. I visit LYRIC when I'm home on break from college, and now there are tons of people in middle and early high school in attendance. In fact, the last time I visited there were probably more people of middle school age than there were college kids. I left feeling a mix of amazement and relief. I might have been the only twelve-year-old at LYRIC eight years ago, but that certainly isn't the case now.

Also, while being vocal about my sexuality at eleven was unusual, thinking about sex—and sex tinged with "taboo" elements—was not at all unusual. As I got older, I heard stories from friends of all ages about what they'd fantasized about at twelve, and younger, and what they still fantasized about. There was the friend of my first boyfriend who, starting at age seven, had rigged up a suspension bondage contraption from which she would hang herself for hours at a time. There was the bisexual-identified faggot who made his own dildoes and buttplugs when he was six, and the friend from high school who started out as a foot-fetishist and soon discovered she also had strait-jacket and WAM (wet and messy) fetishes. Clearly, I was not the only young person thinking about queer and kinky sex—and some of my friends' stuff blew my thirteen-year-old "femme dyke as nelly fag" fantasies clear out of the water.

But the question remains: how can we support children and teenagers in the discovery of their sexuality, especially if it's of a queer or kinky flavor? The best sex education I got as a young person involved my friends telling me about their sexual lives in a frank, open manner—allowing me the option of backing out or saying, "This is too much for me to handle," or "This scares me," and also giving me room to ask questions and talk about my own experience. This is, in part, the place where my opinions come from about people sharing their experiences around sexuality with youth. While it might not be appropriate for a teacher to share this information with hir class, it's critical that queer role-models and mentors share this information with queer youth.

For example: At fourteen, I wrestled with some of the kinkier elements of my sexuality and tried to reconcile my submissive and masochistic sides (which I didn't recognize as such at the time—I just thought I was sick) with an early childhood sexual abuse experience (which I didn't yet classify as abuse, it was just "something bad that happened when I was younger.") A twenty-four-year-old dyke friend of mine, without telling me how to name my experience or my sexuality, simply listened to my worries. She suggested that I get my hands on a wide variety of porn, and spend some solo time playing, exploring, and figuring out what turned me on. She reminded me to be satisfied and guiltless about my explorations, as long as they weren't hurting me or anyone else. Finally, she reassured me that it was okay to have limits, and that in my explorations, I might not like everything I saw or tried, or might fantasize about stuff I'd never even attempt in real life. To this day, that's some of the best sex advice I've ever received—and I wasn't even having sex with other people yet, nor did she imply that I should be. Rather, she encouraged me to discover myself as a sexual being, on my own terms and at my own pace.

Conversations with older friends also allowed me, on some level, to learn from their experiences. The same friend spoke very frankly to me about her own sex and love life—the trials and tribulations of pursuing nonmonogamy with a less-than-respectful lover; the casual sex she began having after their bad break-up, what she liked and didn't like about the encounters; the S/M erotica book she'd read that hadn't done anything for her but that she recommended I take a look at if that's what I might be into. I got to hear about relationships and encounters and experiences I wasn't having, and the knowledge that other people pursued polyamory, S/M, and casual sex made my own desires feel less bizarre. It also educated me about how to get what I wanted in a way that wouldn't hurt or frighten other people.

The other routes through which I found support for and education around my sexuality were the safer-sex workshops held at LYRIC and queer youth conferences. These workshops took for granted that youth were interested in, and perhaps having, sex—this sounds obvious, but the contrast between "These are the kinds of barriers you use when you're giving head" and "This is how you might protect yourself if you were ever to engage in intercourse, which you should only do if you are married and plan to have a baby"—was huge. My main memory of attending safer-sex events is that, while I didn't start having sex until I was sixteen, I always felt welcome and encouraged to speak—even as a twelve-year-old virgin. So much of the rhetoric of the anti-sex-education movement is "If you teach kids about sex, they'll do it." First, kids having sex isn't necessarily a bad thing, and second, if anything, going to safer sex workshops kept me from jumping into bed with the first person who expressed interest in me. I learned how to figure out what interested me, and how to set boundaries and say no when I wanted or needed to. In these workshops, I learned that I didn't need to have sex right away to prove to people that I was queer. My experiences not only gave me the confidence to say, "This is what I want and how I want it" when I eventually began having sex—I also gained the confidence to say, "Yeah, I'm a virgin, but I'm still queer; so don't use that 'you haven't had sex' argument to tell me I don't know who I am."

I despise the way the mainstream gay movement has ignored the issues surrounding sex education in the United States. In-school activism, when spearheaded by gay adults, does not reflect the needs of queer youth, and often sidesteps the issue of sex education altogether (not to mention issues of age and ageism, dis/ability, race, class, and sexualities and genders that aren't strictly "male" or "female" and "straight" or "gay"). Older, usually more conservative gay activists talk about the state of youth today and quote statistics about queer teens without actually consulting the youth movement they claim to represent. If people want to see what is happening among queer youth activists, they can go directly to the source: queer youth social, support, and activist groups; school gay-straight alliances; and the important activist alliances formed between younger and older activists.

However, this kind of youth-driven activism is not what gets the most attention in the mainstream media, or in the mainstream gay movement. As a young person, I want to make it clear that I do not advocate writing off older queer activists. I have learned a huge amount from the queer activists who have come before me, and I owe an enormous personal dept to the older people in my life who were there for me when I was first becoming an activist (and to the older people who are still teaching me). However, part of why my relationships with older activist friends and colleagues have been so good is that I have been fortunate to work with adults who are committed to youth liberation, and who have the same radical politics I do. I referenced activist alliances between younger and older activists at an earlier point in this essay, and this is what the mainstream queer movement is missing. We need alliances between youth and adults, and safe spaces and activism exclusively for youth, instead of adults speaking for queer youth without their input.

School-based queer activism in the hands of adults tends to focus on rights for gay teachers and protection against discrimination for queer middle- and high-school students, or students perceived to be queer. As a queer student who was frequently and violently harassed in middle school, I appreciate the work that's been done to make schools safe for queer and gender-transgressive youth. However, creating a safe school environment also means creating curricula that are inclusive of queer issues, including but certainly not limited to sex-ed curricula. According to a fair number of adult gay activists, the heralded solution to "gay issues" is for schools to tack a "gay day" onto their sex ed programs, explain that being gay "is all about love" and that gay people "are just like straight people," and leave the scary and personal questions about actual sex at the "none of your business" level.

As someone who spoke in schools as a teenager—often to kids who were older than me—about queer issues, I did get tired of being barraged with the obnoxious "Uh, how do you do it?" questions from the homophobic set. But forbidding students to ask questions about sex, pretending that their curiosity about the subject doesn't exist, and expecting them to be satisfied with "Being gay is all about LOVE!" isn't any better. It's not that love or romance aren't important— I could be described as an almost-slutty romantic when it comes to how much I love my girlfriend, friends, and family—but sex and love are subjective and based upon people's personal definitions and experiences, and need to be treated as related-but-separate entities, especially when approaching sex education. By universally equating queer sex with love, and love with long-term relationships, the gay movement is selling itself short.

When students—queer or not—ask questions about queer sex, they're searching for answers about their sexuality and sexual behavior. For kids who are insecure about their own budding sexuality, it's very easy to mask fear and curiosity with rude comments about cocksuckers and lesbos. I don't think that only talking about romance and commitment can tackle those comments or answer peoples' questions about sex. In fact, straight, vanilla, monoamorous kids could just as easily benefit from the kind of explicit, nonjudgmental sex education that I got as a decidedly queer, pervy, slutty kid. What the queer movement needs is to reform the whole system of teaching kids about sex and sexuality, not just insinuate ourselves into already sorely lacking sex-ed programs.

It's my hope that someday every student, regardless of their eventual sexual path in life, will get the kind of sex education I got from my friends and mentors. In the meantime, I'm doing my part as an older youth to continue that education and activism with my friends.

PRAISE FOR THE PRANCY BOYS

CLINT CATALYST

Anyone who's scanned the Homo personals has seen it: "straight-acting." Men who are "straight-acting" seek "straight-acting dudes" to do "normal guy things." The words are polite euphemisms—"discreet" and "no obvious types"—but the message smacks all the same: Be a fag, but don't emulate one.

The operative term here is *acting*. Hetero thespians ham it up through homo roles in sitcoms. Shouldn't fags behave like fags in real life? Republican gays clad in Gap khaki whine that little Lord Fauntleroy types are an offensive representation. They want acceptance and respect. Who doesn't? But why shouldn't it be on our own terms? Personally, I find whining offensive. Uber-femme as she may be, when was the last time you heard a sharp-tongued trannie *whine* about anything?

However, what's more offensive is the thought that I should play the part of someone other than myself to benefit the comfort level of society—particularly homosexual society. In my case, pulling off masculine realness is not, well, *real*. Since I-can't-even-remember-when, I've been disinterested in sports, if not downright lousy at them—excluding Double Dutch. Redneck classmates found me a laugh riot, mocking my swishy prance (gently described by one friend as "walking from the hips") and clocking my sibilant speech ("sounds like ya got a tampon shoved up in there, faggot"). At home, my father urged that I speak into a tape recorder so I could play it back and "hear how [I] sound." Clearly, I threatened his terms of masculinity. And he's not alone.

Even in San Francisco, alleged gay mecca of the globe, I experienced sissyphobia. With my soft facial features, I'd wear suits and ties to my shitty temp office assignments and get called "dyke" by Castro boys while riding the bus. Bored beyond tears with shagging supposed straight guys who'd refer to me as their "Big Exception," I'd try hitting on fags and get told, "Sorry, you're not my type. I like men."

Moreover, I took up smoking under the auspices that I'd get one of those deep, raspy cigarette voices and finally get called "sir" on the telephone. Instead, strangers still call me ma'am, and I'm stuck with stained teeth, a smelly apartment, and yet another habit to kick.

For the folks who have that casual-dude energy coursing through their bloodstream, that's great. But gays should not grow up alienated just for us to alienate each other. It's too predictable, like any other cycle of abuse. Plus, the conformist, competitive notion that by "toning down" we are "growing up" ultimately blunts the radical edge of what it is to be queer; it truncates our colorful journey of identity.

Said another way, it's like living in West Hollywood and working a gay job by day and working *it* in the gay nightlife, wearing delicate shiny shirts picked up from the gay dry cleaners, yet coquettishly left unbuttoned to reveal the pec implants purchased from a gay surgeon and shown off by prancing around the gay-owned-and-operated theater hopped up on gay health clinic steroids and wheat grass purchased from the friendly gay boy who's new to the city, and impressed by the monstrous SUV purchased from a gay car dealership with its rainbow-striped bumper sticker that says "Celebrate Diversity." Then logging on to the local Gay.com listings and describing yourself as "straight-acting."

Let me make myself clear. This is not a campaign for everyone to be like me. That'd be a total yawn. Instead, this narrative is about praise for the prancy boys. Granted, there's undecided gender-fucks, dagger dykes, faux-mos, po-mos, FTMs, fisting-top daddies, and lezzie Looners who also need props for broadening the sexual spectrum, but they're telling their own stories.

The Cliff's Notes of me and mine are this: the only moments I feel alive are when I'm just being myself—not some stiff-necked temp masquerading as normal in the workplace, not some insecure gay boy aspiring to be an overpumped circuit queen, not some comic book version of swank WeHo living. If that's considered a political act in the homogenized world of twenty-first century homosexuals, then so be it.

adèle m pederson 2·23·04

REVOLTING

JOSINA MANU MALTZMAN

We never even considered going to Pride and *not* protesting. We gossiped for days about what we were going to wear, carefully planning our mutual displays of dissent. Vile, my charming co-conspirator, was handcuffed to a briefcase and shackled to a plastic medieval-inspired ball-and-chain . . . and dressed in nothing more than the quaint little chain mail codpiece she stuffed herself in. With the words "CHAINED MALE" scribbled across her chest, Vile was an exemplary flaming faggot.

It was my cock's public debut, pinned against my hips by the inner-tube harness over my tinytight shorts. On my back was written with a large marker, billboard-style: "THE DOLLAR MAKES ME DRY BUT ANARCHY GETS ME WET"—a line I lifted off a friend from Seattle who used it similarly two years before (*none* of this is original, darling). Electrical tape across my bare chest spelled out the words "PRIDE SELLS; QUEERS BUY." Simple and to the point, no?

Good queers? Bad Queers? Who decides? In that moment it felt good to claim the "bad queer" title for myself. A few years later I was forced to reckon with the sour taste of this question in another intimate context.

It was spring 2002 and I was at a counter demonstration to the "Salute to Israel Day" parade in New York. I will never forget a brief moment I witnessed in which a fellow from the Naturei Karta handed a non-Jewish protester a flier expressing the Naturei Karta's criticism of israel. She looked at him, his peyes and overcoat—a man who obviously takes his covenant with g-d *very* seriously—and then at the flier. The leaflet explicitly describes israel as out of compliance with g-d's orders, and how it should not be supported in its atrocities against our brethren, the Palestinians. She looked back at him then, and said with the utmost sincerity and condescension, "Good for you!"

GOOD FOR YOU?!!!

There it is, the pat on the head from the kind-hearted liberal. Thanks, that's really why we're here.

I assumed from the guy's lack of outrage that he was used to this, but I was fuming. That liberal was amazed at finding a "Good Jew," was stunned that not only a Jew but someone so visibly *Jewish* could possibly grasp the importance of the Palestinian struggle or the role of israel as an imperialist power.

Gathered there were a variety of protesters, many Arab and Palestinian—demonstrators from numerous ethnicities. How ironic that this liberal was also *surrounded* by Jews, "bad" Jews and "good" ones, queer and trans, and observant and secular—all of us. Now I look at this picture, at the Naturei Karta member who is just as likely to protest a queer march as an israeli one, at the israel supporter who was telling my friend she was only on the pro-Palestine side of the fence because she is too ugly to find a husband, and I'm sure there is a wonderful yiddish joke to sum it all up—I just don't know the punch line.

Not an hour later an israel supporter looked me up and down in a split-second eternity, taking in all my tattoos and the meaning behind the sign on my chest that read "ANOTHER JEW AGAINST ZIONISM." Her response to my existence, indignant for my sake and full of self-conviction for hers: "You're not really Jewish."

To hell I'm not. *Feh*.

I am a Jew, a queer, a freaky pervert, a brawler. In no specific order. My white skin and class privileges allow me to operate in numerous subcultures and "pass," but nevertheless it is blaringly obvious to me that I am an outsider.

In our private struggles between privilege and oppression, sometimes privilege wins. That is to say, capitalism in the u.s. rewards assimilation. Out gays can now operate in the professional world with the Human Rights Campaign at their side. Some Jews have resources that enable them to change their last name and even anglicize their features, in order to escape anti-semitism. Transpeople who pass in the gender-binary system can choose not to be out in order to maintain relative security. Caucasian queers can easily slip into the comforts of the lgbt "community," ignorant of the white supremacy that dictates who belongs.

In this treacherous world, everyone "deserves" to be safe, and the idea of it is seductive. For those who have been swishing since they first stood, there's no way to run and hide. For many, the question is how to win the fight? Unlike many of my peers, I get to choose who knows I'm Jewish; no one has ever thrown pennies at me while I walked down the street, no stranger has called me a "dirty Jew"—only the people I thought were my allies have done that. Through talking with friends about the violence they have faced in their lives, I am just now realizing how often I exploit my ability to blend in, and how I must intentionally blow my own cover. Once a nazi attempted to befriend me, not realizing until I told him: *I AM THE ENEMY.*

Living in fear of the very real threat of anti-Jewish violence turns some of us into cheerleaders for the bully on the playground, or the bully's sidekick. The heckler who not just picks on but terrorizes those who have little power or means to defend themselves. Aligning ourselves with the aggressor doesn't abate the grotesque stereotypes they give us: money pinchers in control of the world's resources who are in cahoots with the devil. Neither *conversos* nor those from the pale escaped these accusations, because it doesn't matter your monetary or social capital—which is why no amount of assimilation today will erase the foreboding pendulum we hear creaking above us.

I used to speak to various audiences about my brief experience in Palestine, and why I am a Jew in candid support of the Palestinian independence struggle. In my *spiel* I would identify zionism as a racist political ideology, having little to do with Judaism—religiously, culturally, or ethnically. Once, while speaking at a university, I engaged in an argument with a professor. He declared that my view, of Jews needing to take a stand against anti-semitism by challenging the imperialist motives of the u.s. and israel, was "like blaming the victim of a rape."

Unlike him, I refuse to be a victim.

Israel is expelling and attempting to eradicate an entire people with a violent occupation, in the name of Jews everywhere. To embrace an identity of victimhood that accepts an uncomplicated history of Jews is yet another form of assimilation. It is buying into an ideal of security that is militarily enforced, and selling out a rich legacy of anti-capitalist and anti-fascist resistance.

I don't look to the tyrant to dismantle tyranny. We'll do it our fucking selves, thank you. When we make connections between marginalized groups and struggle together across identity lines, when we live in accordance with our own truths, we are living in defiance.

When I think on assimilation, I think of the *kapo*. Have you ever heard this word? It might ring familiar to many of you Jews out there. A *kapo* is the person who polices their own, the snitch, the sell-out. There were many *kapos* in the camps and ghettos of the *shoah*, some were Jews, some were Poles or Czechs, they were all prisoners. They were the ones who would crack the whip for the gestapo, monitor the movements of their peers, kill another on ss orders for an extra piece of bread or another day of pathetic existence. Today I use the word more loosely, but I derive the same meaning: those who believe their oppressors are right and righteous; those who would kill their own family to sit at the master's table (or eat the scraps), even if it's their last meal. I keep my eye out for the *kapos* of queers, Jews, and genders—those aspects of my life that I feel social power pushing against my very existence. And I make damned sure that *kapo* is not my role.

The assimilated homo doesn't understand why I don't protest the Boy Scouts of america for being homophobic, or why I don't give a shit about gays in the military or—gasp!—legal marriage rights. I presume that the assimilated gay world finds it very divisive of me, protesting my lesbian and gay sisters and brothers instead of the straight world at large. What they don't get is this: I don't give a shit about the straight world. Sure, dominant society is just that: DOMINANT. No consent here. But, you see, I'm not trying to make room for myself in it. We fagulously freaky queerbos are not looking for a seat at the table of normality. Funny, the lgbt movement is eerily reminiscent of junior high. The kids that try so hard to fit in, inching up the ladder so they can spit on the heads below them . . . those kids don't get how the deviants just don't care—we're not vying for a rung and we refuse to prop up the ladder. We're not primping and pruning ourselves into the fashions of convention, waiting by the phone for that invitation that finally tells us YES! YES we've been accepted! We've been invited to the party that counts! *THE* party where all the cool straight people hang out and they've finally realized that we're JUST LIKE THEM!!!!

Back to Minneapolis, 1998. Vile and I entered the parade, waving and smiling alongside a marching band of christian homos twirling glittery crosses as batons. It was hard to glean a reaction from the crowd except for a few confused looks and even fewer gestures of solidarity. When we arrived at the park we continued our prance, spiraling through the event with the hope of leaving behind a trail of whispers and possibly discovering new friends. People were definitely looking, but were they paying attention? At one point a person approached us with a camera and asked if they could take our picture for next year's Pridefest promotional material.

"Oh *honey*!" we exclaimed, "Don't you understand? We're not proud! WE'RE REVOLTING!"

THE PRICE OF "COMMUNITY": BISEXUAL/BIRACIAL PERSPECTIVES

BEVERLY YUEN THOMPSON

Because of my Chinese-White mixed-race and bisexual identities, I have always felt outside of identity-based groups that focus only on one aspect of who I am—that's why I began this project. I wanted to explore the ways in which other bisexual/biracial women were negotiating their places within established identity-based organizations, and the ways in which they were breaking out of those established models to create something new. I brought this group together to explore concepts of multiple and mixed identities, and the ways in which bi-bi girls construct our own communities.

Single-identity organizations have not manifested the promise of community or support that we have needed, and many of us have created more personal, hand-picked communities. The desire for sameness in identity politics becomes problematic, and sometimes oppressive, for those with multiple identities. Similar identities do not necessarily guarantee similar mental outlooks, and therefore disappointments are inevitable—and not only for those with multiple identities. Bi-bi girls have revolutionized our personal concepts of community as we integrate the ideals of identity politics into our lives, yet move to include individuals who share similar progressive politics, responsibilities, and models of acceptance.

This article is based on interviews between eight bisexual and hapa women and myself—Lucki, Lani, Janet, Karin, Steph, Sharon, Eve, and Sabrina—for a book on multiple identities. Perhaps it will point to the future direction of identity-based communities, as alliances are built upon common commitment and struggles for solidarity against multiple forms of oppression and exclusion.

Beverly: The problem with identity-based organizations for those of us with multiple or mixed identities is that they're based on additive models where "other" identities need to be managed or ignored. But difference is not something to be "managed," it can act as a force that revolutionizes identity politics. I wanted to therefore ask about your experiences with mono-identity groups.

Lucki: I live on the East Coast and the queer community there is really white, it's really lesbian, and it's really separatist. None of which really work for me.

Lani: I fell in love with a man in 1980 after I came out and couldn't leave the community—that's what lesbians usually do when they fall in love with men—they leave. And, I didn't want to leave 'cause it was my community so I didn't. I stayed out and became the professional bisexual in San Francisco, the professional bisexual in the lesbian community in San Francisco in the early '80s. It's hard, I think that the history of lesbian and bisexual women is so much push-pull mistrust hurtful stuff—a lot of it's internalized misogyny.

Janet: When I first started coming out I didn't know where to go. So I went to mostly mainstream bisexual meetings. It's mostly all very white American and some of them had more polygamous ways of living their lives and so I couldn't really identify with a lot of them. But I started moving towards other directions, like I started joining more Asian women's stuff. Then I saw it's different.

Karin: As I was trying to figure it all out, I would go to gay and lesbian meetings and I would be the only person of color in the room sometimes. And that made me feel like I don't really identify with these people, you know. And not being able to identify with this "community" made it harder for me. So that's a way that racism kinda helped keep me in the closet, there weren't people around me both of color and queer. At least early on, until I started meeting some more folks.

Beverly: Another thing I've noticed in mono-identity groups, is the way in which physical appearance and passing alter the reception you receive. A lot of times, the white queer groups I've been a part of want me to speak at some event, making me into a token because I look Asian. That kind of behavior makes me feel really alienated and question the depth of racism within the queer movement. But in Asian-American organizations, queer issues are often ignored and are difficult to bring up. Additionally, mixed-race folks might not receive the proper understanding from mono-racial organizations. What are your experiences with passing or imposed racial revision?

Steph: I think it depends on whom I'm with. If I'm with someone who doesn't know that I'm bisexual and is of color then I have to remain silent. Obviously my friends who are bisexual or gay know I'm a person of color, but it's not something we talk about.

Karin: When you're Sri Lankan, and there's so few of you, you're always stoked to meet another Sri Lankan. There's really not much of a community, so they always pull you in and totally embrace you. But the community I'm around and the most comfortable with, just because I'm familiar with it, is the Latino community. A lot of my friends are Latino, I speak the language and they usually think I am Latina until I tell them otherwise. So I'm very embraced by that community too.

Lucki: I'm Chilean and Chinese but I look Asian—I totally pass. People do not think I'm mixed when they meet me. So when I go somewhere new, people assume that I'm Asian and I get sucked into that group really fast. More of my friends out here on the East Coast are Latino. Most of the people in California are Chicano, which is really different from being South American. I mean I'm pretty tight with some people in the Latino community but I think I'm much more a part of the API community in San Francisco than I am in the Latino community there.

Sharon: Some people have made me feel as if I kind of had to prove that I was half Asian for the way that I look. And so we got into these strange discussions about which would make you more Filipino. And what is "more Filipino"? Whether you can speak Tagolog or whether you look Filipino while you're in the United States? You know, it's kind of been a constant discussion and it's one that I don't dismiss, but it makes it hard when you're trying to build a sense of community.

Karin: I attended the Asian Pacific Lesbian Bisexual Network conference and that was the first time I really started feeling a part of a community. There were so many biracial women there and there were actually a lot of South Asian women and even a couple that were biracial. And it was like the first time that I was around a lot of Asian queer women. So that was the first time I really felt part of a community. But for me also to feel a part of a community is not just based on the fact that we are of the same sexual or racial identity—it also had to do with the politics. The conference was very political and the women that were there were very politically active, conscious and doing different kinds of stuff. So it was the first time where I had some sense of community, where I felt like I could really identify with all these folks around me. That's how I see "community." It's where you kinda deal with each other on different levels. All these Asian women still had conflicting identities between their ethnic and sexual identities. And so I felt like people there were just a lot more open. They weren't as rigid about one identity or the other. It was the only time I really felt like I could groove with this group of Asian American folks.

Beverly: It sounds like our communities are based upon an integration of politics, identity, and open-mindedness. But this contrasts with many established communities which are based upon a single identity. Mono-identity groups might work for some, but for those of us with multiple or mixed identities—we need to establish community in a different way. What are some of the ways that you have made your own community, instead of forcing yourself into existing structures?

Lucki: My community is something that I define personally. It's more handpicked people that I have commonalities with of some kind or another, whether they be racial or sexual identity based, or political or intellectual or artistic. To be perfectly honest I've never felt comfortable in a label-identified community.

Sharon: Well my tightest groups of friends, outside of any of these political external definitions, are artists. Groups that I feel included in, like when people ask me to come and be part of their group, are political activists, people of color communities, women's communities, techie communities, or queer communities. I'm definitely somewhat a part of all those groups even though I'm not always actively doing something with them.

Sabrina: I wanted to write something, so I started to write and kind of gripe, really. It was really just to vent things out on those issues. And it turned out that I started getting mail from all these hapa women also who were either straight or gay or in the middle, and they were like, "Well I'm glad you brought that up because I feel the same way." And I was like, oh my god—you know? And I didn't really realize that until I came out with my 'zine—that other women felt that way. But I knew that they were out there somehow, you know. And so, like, to me it was that my 'zine [*Bamboo Girl*] was a very validating tool for me to get in touch with other women who had similar interests.

Beverly: That's the reason I started my website also, snakegirl.net. I felt like I couldn't find a place for me out there, and so I started writing about issues that were related to mixed and multiple identity and found other people who related. It was a very validating experience.

Sabrina: I've made up my own little world with my 'zine. And that's also made me feel like I can validate myself, as well. And that's been very, very important to me because up until only recently I felt like I had no voice. And so I didn't really speak very much, I just wrote a lot, and it's only recently that I've really found my voice and that I've been able to start developing it. And so I guess those who really include me in helping me to express my voice are kind of like a community for me.

INSIDE THE BOX

NEIL EDGAR

Time has made me more of a salivating slut than any enhancement pill or miracle fantasy starring hot dead punk icons. Time, not in the sense of you looking down at your watch now to make sure you'll be at your important meeting on time. No. Not even like, "I wonder how much time it will take me to get that hot ass in my Sleeptrain mattress?" No, baby. My time is that of a special, set-aside sect of boys, men, and boyish men who despise the mockery of the clock's tick and the sludgy slowness of the seasons' drift. Ours is the "So, how much time you doin'?" or even "What kinda time did they give ya?" Time, deciphered in simple layman's terms to, "TIME SPENT IN A BOX."

A box built to break the hope of the human insects thrown within, virtual butterflies mounted on display. A box of disguises like the tricks of a prop comic—hats, faces, identities. The prison cell, a mold existing to squeeze you into their desired shape. What do they, the faceless forces of darkness, they who run the clanking, lurching system revving its perpetual death roar around me—what do they want to make me?

First, and most coveted by the greed industry sucking away humanity while I age another day—one that feels exactly the same as the last one—is my individuality, un-wired to their collective brain; I'm a boy who still knows revolution of will. Without that spark, I'm swallowed up into "them" like a dead carcass complete with maggots.

Never that.

When I walk the prison yard, not much sets me apart from the hundreds of other guys out there—besides my hair, which really isn't too extreme, just one line of spiky disarray in an ocean of Bic-bald, tanned, tattooed heads or slicked-back mobster do's. I've got a lot of tattoos on my body, but so does everyone else. I've got a distinctive swagger; so does everyone else. I've got a tough look in my eyes, not because I'm a hard-ass, but because doing years in prison gets in your head and establishes this headquarters for personal defense, like a mental body guard, and it shows. Everyone else has that too. Besides the noticeable differences of skin color, height, and physical frame, all convicts really look alike—prison does that; it's like involuntary solidarity on our part. We represent the blue prison-issue duds, we represent the rebel, we represent the enemy. We relate to one another, but we're always paranoid—of the Man, of the rats, of enemies. It comes with the environment.

They even have protocols to undermine individuality, to keep us in inferior mindframes, to take away our ability to express ourselves. There's this set of rules that constitute "grooming standards." No long hair, all cuts must be under three inches. No facial hair other than trimmed moustaches. They tell us this is enforced so they can identify us better, like in case of an escape, I guess, but this just doesn't make sense. Making us look more like one another makes us lose recognizable difference; without these rules, we would have long and short hair, shaved heads, goatees, full beards, Fu Manchus, handle-bar moustaches, chops, and dread locks, and I wouldn't be getting fucked with everyday and punished for having a harmless mohawk. This is just their power trip, more propaganda to prove that we are a dominated people without free right. Our clothes are all the same colors—dreary blue-gray and white, same for shoes. The population smears into one another, the convict mirrors the prison itself: uniform, dull, hard, automated.

Ah, but the beauty of the exotic image revolutionary, the idealist romantic, the iconoclast drag queen! The gurly prison punk—an extreme and crucial necessity. The anti-convict, who I adore, support, and see as a vital organism in prison society, who breaks molds and shocks mediocrity.

I see them all around me, and I wonder if the uniform they wear ever grows constrictive. These boy-girls with their curls, shaved legs, homemade colored-pencil-based makeup, smuggled-in g-strings.

My old friend Nicole, who has long since paroled, showed me photos of her on the streets. She slung those hips and filled the heels perfectly. She's a girl, through and through. This queen Reese shaved off his nappy braids a few days before his parole date. I noticed stubble on his chin. Going back to the "real world" where he was a "normal" black man with a wife and kids . . . who sneaked out to dark alleys or porno theaters to give head and feel liberated again. For only a moment, before . . . SUCK! Swallowed into the rotting carcass of that societal "moral" persona.

I wonder why the dress gets donned by so many boys here behind these walls who don't desire the world to see them as girls. No, they just want us to.

Sometimes I get so frustrated, being this tattooed, outspoken, punk rock, butch bi boy—hungry, horny—I feel alienated and set apart, even in a prison yard of hundreds. Why? Being a loner isn't always glamorous, I guess.

My sexuality is fluid; I'm open, eager, curious, explosive. No boxed-in libido like these skinned-in bones. Too many cages. So sick of floors and ceilings, walls on all sides. Sex is like drinking down an ocean of cloudless Montana sky, soaring, expansive, ever onward.

I always felt like that part of me was healthy, like it was compatible with any guy who gets a woody seeing Johnny Depp in tight pants and eyeliner. But, alas, fucking definitions, boundaries, molds, expectations!

All my drag companions are strictly bitchly, they will only receive. Like they never pitched a game in their life. Please. Here in the joint, it's all about becoming a "wife," shaving the pits and receiving butt-hole orgasms. I know half of these self-proclaimed bottoms jack-off alone in the cell to fantasies of butt-fucking the cutest hottie on their tier. But they have succumbed to the same bullshit that repressed homos or Christ-forgiven "healed" fags have—the exchange of one's own autonomy, whatever it is, however alien or un-trendy or out of vogue one's own self is, for some easy-to-assume, prepackaged iconology. If you're into homo sex and you're in prison, there's really only two kinda dudes. The bottoms, all purdy, and the tops, alpha male, protector, brute, hard and macho. Oh . . . and not gay. They just fuck. They'd never get fucked.

But me? Guess I'm just a dying breed. I scare away the ones who seem to dig me. Not that I'm some frigid celibate, but most of my sex inside has felt like compromise. You know, getting fucked (but jacking myself off) 'cause I need to be touched. Or getting my cock swallowed, but when I try to feel the swallower below the waist, I get slapped off.

I'm sick of all the insincerity. Is it me? Am I the problem? No. It's our minds, taught to compartmentalize, to assign, to define. But I'm thankful. I have my individuality. I have a heart that beats within this cage. I have a sexuality that rebels, that seduces, that dances in circles.

RIDING RADIO TO CHOKE THE IMF

OLIVELUCY AND SALMONELLA

OliveLucy: In April of 2000, I was a queer personal attendant writer who lived with seven other folks in an artist/activist house in Oakland. That was my legal face. Underground, I was crawling around in attic spaces, rooftops, and radio tech books, learning and applying the basics of amateur radio for the RadioActive Queer radio station. I was also working as a pro-domme.

I had traveled to Seattle for the November 30 anti-World Trade Organization (WTO) conference in 1999, where I'd been involved in creating a food, housing, media, and social infrastructure throughout the protests. That squatting action, at the formerly abandoned 918 Virginia Street warehouse, showed me that strangers with a common vision could come together and create alternatives to tired and violent capitalist systems that fail to meet the basic needs of humanity. The tools learned from that project inspired me to go to the anti-International Monetary Fund (IMF) conference in Washington, D.C., to work on independent media, specifically pirate radio, for the antiglobalization movement. I took a small paycheck from an emergency attendant service in Berkeley, and money from a domination session, to buy a plane ticket.

SalMonella: The Washington, D.C., protests against the capitalist rampage of the IMF were my jumping-off point into a whole new world. A few years earlier, I had started working on a pirate radio station, come out as a queer, and begun to develop a radical analysis of the world. The D.C.

protests proved to me the power of Do-It-Yourself (DIY) activism. In April 2000, I found myself in the deliciously ironic position of grabbing the world with my teeth—as I prepared to launch an illegal protest radio station in the face of the IMF and came out as a female-to-male transexual beginning to inject testosterone—while at the same time struggling shyly and bitterly to fit in and be cool in this new, sexy, crazy balls-out culture.

ARRIVING IN D.C.

OL: The primary physical infrastructure activists created for the anti-IMF protests included two convergence centers where activists could network about housing, action logistics, and affinity groups, as well as create props, costumes, and songs. Food Not Bombs also served free meals at these sites. A third common space created for the protests was the Independent Media Center (IMC), where protestors were able to use computers, watch multiple TV news stations, and create media that covered the actions. All spaces were offered to activists by the building owners. D.C. appeared to be running like any other U.S. metropolitan area when we arrived, except when we went to the convergence centers. There, people were animated by plans to organize direct confrontation with members of the IMF, as well as to create an incredible presence in the streets, forcing the mainstream media to cover our opposition.

OL: One plan up to that point was that the RadioActive Queer folks would join other amateur radio folks from around the country—Wireless Virus (Milwaukee), Prometheus Radio (Philly and NYC), a local D.C. pirate station, and a pirate station out of Minneapolis—to create Mobilization Radio, a station for the voices of anti-IMF protestors.

SM: Another plan was that RadioActive Queers would be a completely separate entity, acting as a mobile unit, using a 30-watt transmitter on a separate frequency from the Mobilization Radio group. We would specifically serve the protestors downtown, letting folks know where the hot spots were—a live in-the-streets communications team.

OL: An additional option was that a repeater would be used, so there would only be one station, and it would be less than 100 watts, but the repeater would allow a greater transmission that would extend throughout the central area of D.C.

OL: I remember one of the first nights we went to the tentative FM Mobilization Radio space that had a long stairwell leading up to a vacant apartment.

SM: Yeah. We met D, the guy I knew from my first pirate station. His friend had a microwave receiver that was pretty ingeniously made out of a coffee can. D wasn't as friendly as when we had worked together before. Things had this weird, serious overtone, like I'd just jumped in with the big kids when I belonged back in vocational school.

OL: There was a lot of technical talk about specific pieces of equipment like the yagi and other antenna designs that I was not familiar with, and there was a rooftop demonstration of the microwave receiver. D seemed to have good clout with everybody, and the other guys were very attentive to each other and the project, but didn't really talk to us. Everyone was straight except for us. And we were all white. I was excited to be there anyway, listening to all of the options for FM radio and web radio, like having a microwave link from the FM transmitter radio to the web radio. This form of transmission operates at a higher frequency than traditional FM broadcasting, and therefore the FCC cannot trace it.

SM: I felt slightly depressed and out of place. It was difficult to know how we would do it all. D was not being supportive of our still-forming plans. I felt like we were slightly looked down upon because our technical knowledge was a little less developed. We knew the basics, and we were hoping our more-learned friends would share their knowledge. But I think they perceived us as a bunch of rag-tag know-nothings. Perhaps the folks in our group who looked like bio-guys, and also coincidentally had a bit more technical talk rolling off their tongues, felt a bit more respect. But you and I, the weird genderqueers, I think we were pretty much dismissed. I remember leaving feeling extremely unclear about what we were about to embark upon.

SM: So we went back to J's house, uncertain of what folks would do, and then we got a call that the tentative location was not available. We asked J if we could use her apartment and she said YES!

OL: That was fucking exciting! We were like, here we go! We rushed down to a chain copy store and scammed tons of Mobilization Radio fliers that announced 87.5 FM would be broadcasting live, uncensored coverage twenty-four hours a day. With copper wire, rubber, PVC pipe, solder, and electrical tape we created a Slim-Jim antenna to bolt to the roof. At that point, we were using the equipment from Minneapolis and Milwaukee, but were not yet using equipment from the more technically advanced people. Our own equipment was holding its own, yet the transmission did not extend outside of the immediate neighborhood. Later, the other radio crew donated a Comet omnidirectional antenna to our project. Our broadcasting range increased, and we were excited to reach a wider audience.

BROADCASTING

OliveLucy: The Mobilization Radio crew broadcasted for three full days during the anti-IMF conference. I got a great interview with Pirate Jenny, this New York City DJ who had a weekly radical feminist show on Steal This Radio (NYC's former Lower East Side pirate radio station) called "Out of The Shadows." The interview was challenging for me, as a genderqueer person politicized by feminism in the early nineties. Pirate Jenny is a generation-and-a-half older than me and has been politically active for years. I wanted to represent the exciting ways politicized genderqueer people can creatively debilitate misogynist forces by gender-jamming, or portraying many genders. Pirate Jenny replied, "I do consciousness raising with a group of young women, and just did one with a young activists group from Columbia University. They felt alienated when they experienced misogyny or sexist behavior. They feared being attacked if they spoke up." I thought about my friend Greta Garbage, who is a transsexual woman, and who attended the anti-IMF protests in D.C. Was she included in Pirate Jenny's definition of "woman"? I did bring up my confusion when Pirate Jenny said, "There is a tremendous amount of violence against women today."

Are "women" a specific group of people today?

Are we talking about the power dynamics between white women and white men, Black men and a Latino intersexed woman, or a Filipino transsexual woman and a Vietnamese man? Discussing the histories of specific groups of women, or of individual women, helps me understand power dynamics such women are experiencing. Former U.K. prime minister Margaret Thatcher is not Sylvia Rivera, right? Then why is the language articulating the oppression of women omitting class and race realities?

I am fortunate to have dialogues with older generations of politically radical women. I believe it is necessary for generations to listen to each other, realize which direct action tactics have worked and which have failed, as well as to understand how movements can move forward together, without diluting specific issues that affect unique groups of people.

SalMonella: I got a good interview with some folks from Mexico who had done Spanish shows on the RadioActive Queers station back in Oakland. How amazing to see the Mexican punks all the way across the U.S.! The apartment/studio also began to be a revolving door for people from the IMC, the guerrilla gardeners representing from the SF bay area, and the Austin LoneStar Pirates, as well as random politicized people who wanted to do a radio show during the protests. We also aired TV, mainstream radio, and police scanner footage to offer listeners a juxtaposition of tactical info and responses to the protests.

OliveLucy: As queer and trans-based, it felt less uptight than straight independent radio stations I have been involved with in the past. Some of us made life changes in that radio station. There was faggot sex happening in the living room when I had a date over for a satirical "grumpy old folks" radio show. The name my date chose as a DJ name on that show became his new trans name.

SalMonella: Yes, unashamed, kinky sex was possible in that space. One night, something broke on the transmitter and I soldered it back together while Spiv, my new flame and member of our radio collaboration, held the box between his legs. It felt like we were having sex while the solder sizzled and melded the parts together. We didn't say anything. The sexual energy was off the wall.

DUPONT CIRCLE

SalMonella: I remember we took a break from the demonstrations, and were walking through the gay district and there were all these stupid yuppy gays with their cell phones. We wanted to jump them and take their cell phones so that protestors could use them to call the radio station from the streets. I feel like we went to the gay area because our friend Spiv thought it was going to be interesting. Another tactic we used was drag. Three of us brought suits to D.C., attempting to look like businessmen and infiltrate certain buildings. After I put mine on and went to the protest one day, a group of black block protesters loudly said something about an infiltrator and moved away. I wondered how anybody, freak or otherwise, could have mistaken my obviously young, genderqueer body, clothed in a strange big suit and carrying a dumpy briefcase, for either a police infiltrator or legitimate member of the mainstream. I think the intense attention to security culture clogged people's ability to use common sense.

WHAT CAN HAPPEN WHEN THE FEDS COME

OliveLucy: On the third day of the protests, I had been downtown at the IMC space, assisting with dubbing live interviews from the streets. I returned to the station and was prepared to do a show. The space was filled with overlapping voices, music, and bodies in motion. The renter of the apartment got a phone call from the apartment complex manager, who was actually hosting protestors and was down with the IMF resistance. She said the feds had just visited her apartment and were on their way to ours. We made an announcement to the folks inside the apartment about what was happening, and pulled the plugs as it is not illegal to have equipment that broadcasts radio waves under 100 watts, but it is illegal to actually broadcast. We were off the air, and POUND POUND POUND on the door. Me and another main force for the radio were standing in the hallway next to the door, so we looked through the peephole to see four suited people in front of the door with their arms crossed over their chests. We didn't answer, but dashed into the bedroom and phoned DAN, the Direct Action Network, as well as the IMC, and came up with the wingnut cover for all eleven of us to be "having an orgy" in the bedroom. During the next two hours, the knocking continued, and once they announced themselves as the Metropolitan Police, but the door never came down. We remained silent and didn't answer the door, as we hid underneath covers and continued our phone calls. One of us left the bedroom during the first hour to look out the peephole, only to find it covered. Phone calls informed us the block was overtaken with police and black sedans.

Troy (an activist we know from the SF/Oakland Bay Area): About two hundred of us decided to leave the jail solidarity campout and support the radio station, so we began marching. Of course we had this huge police escort, all of these unmarked cars and marshals started to follow us up the street. We took over the street, even though they kept telling us to get on the sidewalk. About two-thirds of the people were totally freaked out and got on the sidewalk, but the rest of us stayed in the street. It took us about forty-five minutes of marching, in the rain, to finally get to the radio station. As we turned onto that street, all we could see were police—tons of police cars. They had police barrier tape up and down the block, stopping anyone from going anywhere. I didn't know which building it was because there were police everywhere, but finally I saw a huge wall of riot police, and I thought, "Okay, this looks like it." We had a bunch of media following us up the street, FBI agents, and undercover agents (a guy with a giant fire extinguisher or pepper spray unit strapped on his chest). So we marched up to the building and there were already some protestors facing the row of riot cops.

Pablo (an urban gardener and housing agitator who has collaborated with people from the West Coast to the East): As I moved from the demonstration's legal office to the IMC, the radio raid news was spreading like wildfire. A whole crew of us got in a car and went to the station. Once we arrived, we're walking around the back, there's mad cops already, so we called our "comm" [communications] people. On the way to a payphone, a handful of random people, some who we knew, walked by us. We told them about the raid, so they went up to the radio station block. I guess those were the first folks there. Maybe around twenty to forty people. We called microradio stations around the country and lawyers that deal with pirate radio, and just honed in on letting people know our friends could go down; it was big drama.

OliveLucy: After a while we accepted that we were all eventually going to jail and might as well make something to eat because jail food sucks. It was suffocatingly silent in the apartment and outside. I made a delicious pho-like soup and we ate, then began to hear a large crowd noise coming our way. It continued to get louder, until it was immediately outside of the windows, and we realized it was for *us*. "Free our radio" was the chant—it was a proud rush to realize we had a huge posse outside the building.

SalMonella: I was walking around downtown, trailing a rather mundane march and doing the odd-person-on-the-street interviews, when I heard rumors of the station being busted. Everybody had converged on a park to rest, but the police were circling slowly. Folks made some sort of a big drum/yoga circle, and I burned with urgency as some people led some silly relaxation ritual. Finally, I got to announce the siege and encourage folks to join me on a march up the hill. The other option was a jail solidarity campout, so it was not difficult to mobilize the more energized folks to walk up the hill to the plain but urgent chant, "SAVE OUR STATION!" Suddenly, I found myself mobilizing about four hundred marchers to make the trek up to the besieged station.

It felt truly glorious and humbling, mobilizing all these folks to save our dear project. As we filled the street in front of the apartment building, the cops were only too eager to negotiate a retreat.

Troy: We stood around and yelled and chanted, and the cops continued to yell at us to get out of the streets. Then they said, "If you move out of the street, we'll get in our cars and move away." And that was the weirdest thing I had ever heard, and most people were like, "Don't believe the police." But then about two-thirds of the people got on the sidewalk and the rest of us were thinking if they were lying we would just get back out onto the street. So the rest of us got on the sidewalk, and the police got in their cars and DROVE AWAY.

Pablo: When the cops left, we were like, "They never let us win, I can't fucking believe it."

OliveLucy: We heard the cheering/chanting for a while, maybe a couple of hours, then someone poked their head out the window and saw a shitload of cop cars drive away. We were totally confused, but then some protestors outside screamed, "The cops are GONE."

SalMonella: Perhaps the converging masses of protestors prevented the FCC (Federal Communications Commission) from pulling any equipment-grabbing shenanigans. We felt this was our greatest victory.

Olive: (to SalMonella) Yeah, so then you called and said the cops were gone, and we told you to try to come into the building as a test to see if there were any Feds still in the apartment complex. A couple of minutes later there was our kind of knock at the door, ya know, you can tell the difference.

SalMonella: We were concerned about the legal ramifications of leaving the equipment in our friend's place, and we didn't want any FCC losers to remove it themselves! In retrospect, we should have gotten other folks, not connected to the station, to carry the equipment out. But it seemed nobody was available for the rather involved task of removing the antenna from the roof, so I grabbed two bystanders and we snuck up to the roof and removed the antenna. The operation went smoothly, despite our racing blood, and we left the area—pissed, tired, and relieved.

OliveLucy: So we got the equipment, called someone to pick us up, and jetted out of the building. Of course, the get-away car was nowhere in sight, so there we were with garbage bags full of the threatening equipment that brought out Feds and riot cops to that block, and we just stood in the alley, like an action movie with two kids trying to be bad-asses. Some guy from the National Lawyer's Guild came up to us for our story, no cops were in sight so we put the equipment in a dumpster, gave a media report in the alley, and by that time the get-away car drove up and took us away from the scene.

HOW TO CONTINUE MOBILITY

OliveLucy: After boxing up all of our radio equipment at an aftermath household filled with anti-IMF protestors, we pulled out a scammed shipping company account number and prepared the boxes for travel to their homes for free. I probably had twenty bucks or something to my name at that time and wanted to visit friends in Philadelphia, so SalMonella, Spiv, and I got on an Amtrak, put our backpacks in an aisle, and stashed our bodies in the train's bathroom for the ride to Philadelphia. People pounded on the doors on and off so we'd periodically get out and change bathrooms. One change, we got vicious looks from the people waiting or sitting by the bathrooms, but another time we got applauded, like it was a pervy marathon or something.

In Philly we ate well, told stories, and discussed the effectiveness of the protests. I had a really cute sex night with this queeny fag who got off on me being genderqueer. I was reeling that a bio fag acknowledged my gender and polysexuality. Most people took me for a dyke only. But, it was exciting to occasionally be in a room full of queers of different genders, like at The Need and Boys Of Now show we went to at the 4040 club in Philadelphia.

From Philly we went go to Chicago, then eventually back to Oakland. Five of us figured out how to get on "Pig" trains, the trains that have semi-trucks on their cars, and people ride between the axles.

SalMonella: After we left our friends in Chicago, OliveLucy and I continued on alone. There had been a lot of romance and hot sex wrapped up in the radio intensity, and the parting was sad and unclear for me. Things looked up as we crossed the green Midwest. We both read Joanna Kadi's *Thinking Class*, and began a long discussion about queers and class that continues today. That trip was one of the first times my life had veered significantly away from my middle-class comfort zone, and one of the first times I'd thought deeply about class. At that time, a life of scams, product liberation, and free travel was more a romantic and political lifestyle statement than an economic necessity, as it was for several of the folks I was working with. I still had money saved up from my post-college job, although I was saving that money for chest reconstruction surgery. I jumped on the DIY antiglobalization bandwagon of a free, travel-based, protest-motivated life—an amorphous movement that grew out of other movements in the early '90s, peaked around the 1999 Seattle WTO meeting, and continues. I am sincerely grateful to the folks who helped me into this life, and I surely don't regret a minute of it.

OliveLucy: Class is a carnival of information and games. In relation to the D.C. protests, it was possible for us to build a radio station with nearly no money because people collaborated with equipment and knowledge. When a media group is poor, folks must bring information and radio gear to share. One person can stream radio waves on the World Wide Web twenty-four hours a day if they have the computer, stereo equipment, MP3 hardware, DSL capacity, and music library. But, this coverage would most likely be more homogenous than the expressions by a group of people.

The queer foundation of the FM Mobilization Radio group was a new experience within mass demonstrations for me. Programming, sleeping space, and eating were less controlled and contrived with queer folks.

SalMonella: This was a period of relative discomfort within both of our lives. Some of this discomfort was voluntary, and some wasn't. Comfort is not a bad thing: comfort with our bodies, our friends, and some part of society is necessary for health. Comfort is also not constant; it moves in and out of phase with our lives. A lot of gay activism focuses on forcing the capitalist system to create comfort for a particular oppressed group. What about queer activism that attacks capitalism and focuses on using people power, community power, to create comfort for everybody? This is the kind of activism we were striving for with the Mobilization Radio project. Anti-capitalist activism sometimes involves more discomfort than comfort—fine.

OliveLucy: Right, while I don't glorify poverty, and have found it exhausting, I understand financial and living dis-ease is a reality for politically charged writers, musicians, and artists in this country.

But hey, we will always throw the best parties.

SEXING UP THE CONFLICT

QUERY

YOU ARE WELCOME

After lying profusely and brandishing my marked *Lonely Planet Guide* to corroborate my tall tales, the security agents allow me out of baggage claim and into Israel. My sleep deprivation, along with the lingering effects of hash I scored in Barcelona the previous night, helps me to maintain a steely gaze during all three interrogations. I'm in. I stare at the confusing barrage of signs written in Hebrew, roam and double back, looking for a currency exchange. "*Shalom!*" I turn around and see the shiny shaved head and yoga body of Gaddy. And I am confused but grateful 'cause he never said he would meet me at the airport. Before I can respond with more than a dropped jaw, he says, "Are you ready? We missed the march, but the after-party just began." Right, Gay Pride, Jerusalem.

Two of Gaddy's friends, Ronen and Danielle, sit in the back seat of the car. We head east out of Ben Gurion airport. My jaw drops again when I see "Jerusalem" written in Hebrew and English—this city of labyrinthine streets and millennia-old conflicts, this backdrop of the New Testament, reduced to a green sign on the side of the highway that says we have five more kilometers to go.

We get out of the car. The Dome of the Rock gleams golden down the hill, riffing off the setting sun. This pretty boy stands at the entrance to the club, his pale, lithe chest peeking enticing-

ly through the holes of a black mesh shirt. To his left, a dominatrix in shiny thigh-highs swishes her cat-o-nine tails. Inside, Johanna's punk band plays songs in Hebrew, Yiddish, and Arabic. She wears the dangly strings and black hat of Orthodox male drag, until she tears off her shirt, her tallis, and exposes her naked chest, "End the IDF" [Israeli Defense Forces] scrawled above her breasts in black marker. Then this DJ boy with dreads steps up to the turntables and spins the track by Peaches where she moans, in amplified surround sound, "Fuck the pain away."

Three hours later, we're back on the street. Ronen asks, "Do you want to eat Arabic at Damascus Gate or go to the New City for Western food?" He is soft around the middle. Wavy brown hair frames his cherubic face.

I tell him I want to go to Damascus Gate and kind of can't imagine what's next. Or when I'll get to crash.

"Okay, we will be Americans then," Ronen says, aiming a small grin at the other Israelis, "and only speak English."

Damascus Gate is a drawbridge-like entrance in a castle wall built by Romans around the Old City of Jerusalem. It leads into the Muslim Quarter. Palestinians throng the entranceway, coming and going and talking with their hands and vending batteries, falafel, and vegetables. They are a fluttering quilt of red and blue and black khaffiyehs and hajibs. A child runs with a kite in his hand. Five others chase after him. It is Friday. Orthodox Jews, a narrow stream of wide-brimmed black hats and straight-ahead stares, file in and out of the opening too—Damascus Gate offers them the shortest path to the Western Wall.

We climb down the stairs to the gate and—*Fucking gunshots! Where? It's not fireworks. People are jumping. I think I should duck. Where? Not that flimsy stall where the old woman is selling, what the fuck is she selling? Olive oil?* I feel naked, like in one of those dreams when you're the only one without clothes and everyone else knows what to do.

Armored vehicles screech to a halt on the street above, the soldiers blaring static commands through loudspeakers. The flashing blue sirens pierce darkness like strobe lights in a club at four a.m. But it is only eight-ish when I look back at Damascus Gate, the entrance like the snarling jaws of an immense monster who has just belched a warning. In a square cut into the wall above the gate—an eye socket—an Israeli soldier stands with his gun leveled down on the crowd. A

Palestinian man in jeans approaches me. He looks up from my orange socks to my spiked belt and patched pants, and then into my eyes. "You are welcome," he says, smiling.

OUTREACH I

Way west, past the Bauhaus-inspired stucco buildings, the legions of armed private security, and the sleepy sun-drenched cafes, along the sand where the Mediterranean laps the edge of Tel Aviv, I shield the setting sun with my hand and gaze up and down the boardwalk.

"Excuse me," I say to a passing cop, "can you tell me where Independence Park is?" He looks at me for four long seconds before pointing north and telling me to walk up the beach to the Hilton. I guess everyone knows about Independence Park.

I walk past the Hilton and see nothing but more sand. *This can't be it.* I re-trace my steps and try again. *Fuck.* Then I see this steep pathway for the first time. I walk up, higher and higher, until I am above the cliff face. Dense brush and windswept pines cover this plateau, providing infinite alcoves. Night has fallen.

I can still hear the Mediterranean surf far below. It is the summer of 2003 and I am three hundred miles from the U.S. invasion of Iraq, on the peripherals of another, longer war. I duck under a tree and strip down to a pair of shiny blue soccer shorts. Israeli men emerge from and disappear into shadowed recesses and walls of leaves. I choose a path, any path. After several minutes of walking, I hear the footfalls of an approaching guy. I pivot towards him slowly, my eyes the last part of me to make contact. *Hey, he's really cut.* I can tell, even though he slouches in his white T-shirt like James Dean. I zig and zag around the space that is between us and he does the same and we close that space, footsteps roaming two concentric circles that overlap, more and more, until—

He says, "You're nice with no shirt on."

"Yeah, well you should take yours off."

"Maybe you will come with me?"

"Sure," I say.

"One thing." He looks down for a second. "I am here with my boyfriend. Can he come too?"

"Yeah, yeah, no problem."

The three of us are off in the bushes, thrashing around on some discarded mattress. James is fingering my ass and jerking off. His boyfriend is slurping on my half-hard cock. I caress their heads. James clutches a fistful of my hair and his body twitches and turns rigid. I plunge two fingers into his ass and he cries out, gasping, heaving, as he comes.

We sit on the mattress and smoke cigarettes. James says there are more Orthodox Jews in New York City than in Tel Aviv. Then he says, "Aren't you afraid to be here? The Arabic are not like us. Our mothers would never strap bombs to their children." The white three-quarters moon shines onto our faces, the mattress, and his come on the mattress. When I look down, his beads of come are streams of stars, each sperm a pinprick of light trying to escape.

OUTREACH II

Palestinian license plates are white; Israeli plates are yellow. It's the same color scheme for the lights of so many Palestinian villages and Israeli settlements in the West Bank. The cynical say, this way the F-16s know who to bomb at night. All the vehicles that pass me have yellow plates. I get a lot of stares from their occupants. I'm standing beside this roadblock of boulders, rucksack on my back. I'm nervous and not sure what to do next; I'm not even supposed to be here—something got lost in translation from me to Abdul Latif to the van driver.

Earlier today, the sun had been up for only a few hours when Abdul Latif, the stocky scruffy mayor of Yanoun, gave me a ride in his ancient Volkswagen to the nearby village of Acraba. Abdul wears an easy grin and a two-inch scar over his left eye. I asked him what happened. "*Mustawtineen*," he said. "Settlers." The settlers from Itamar had bashed his face with the butt of a rifle during one of their invasions of Yanoun.

In 1991, settlers founded Itamar on the ridgeline above the centuries-old Palestinian village of Yanoun. They claimed Yanoun and the surrounding area as theirs, and in the name of God they say they're going to take it. The sheepherders, farmers, and other residents of Yanoun have never retaliated. The gouged eyes, beatings, and gunshot wounds got to be too much though, so all but one family fled last year. After a six-month vacancy, most of the families have returned to try again, accompanied by a rotating cast of Israeli and international activists. I was there for the duration of last week.

It was easy. I just hung out around the basin of the valley of Yanoun with sheepherders or children, or curled under a wind-whipped tree reading a book. In the morning, the three elderly women next door would leave plates of fried goat cheese, olives, hummus, and large disks of homemade unleavened bread on the doorstep with only the faintest knock. By the time I opened the door, they would be peeking and waving from the frame of their entranceway. In the evening, the other Westerner and I turned on the UN-donated generator that replaced the one the settlers destroyed, and the villagers enjoyed their four hours of electricity for the day. If they turned it on themselves, they would be attacked. Then, the Nezzers or the Abuhanis or the Latifs invited us to a modest feast in their home, and their daughters would translate the conversations that we couldn't have without them. It was a good week to be in Yanoun. The settlers only attacked in our dreams. They did scan the village with spotlights during the evening, and when the bright, wide beams hit you, you shined up like a desert apparition in a special-effects film. Settlers with binoculars mounted the towers on the ridgelines or rode around the surrounding peaks on an all-terrain Vehicle (ATV). Only one settler, named Vic, rode all the way into camp. He rode with a rifle over his shoulder and sharpshooters looking down behind him. All the children ran and hid. They were young, but not so young that they didn't wear the scars of last year's attacks.

In Acraba, Latif and I hugged goodbye after he found me a ride to the edge of town with two men in a van. But like I said, something got lost in the translation. So instead of taking me to a Palestinian taxi stand where I could hopscotch my way, cab by cab and roadblock by roadblock, to the peace camp in Mas'ha, the van driver took me out to a desolate pile of enormous boulders, one of the hundreds of roadblocks built in the West Bank by the Israeli army to quarantine Palestinians. Behind the boulders, an Israeli road dissects the countryside. You can tell it's Israeli 'cause it's paved. That, and all those yellow license plates zipping up and down the smooth surface.

Itamar is still way too close, and those settlers don't only hate Palestinians. Last fall, they broke the arm of a sixty-year-old American woman while she was harvesting olives with the villagers of Yanoun. She is just one of the Israeli and international activists who left the area with debilitating injuries.

After a nervous half hour, a truck with white plates rolls by and I wave. The driver steers the truck to the roadside and I walk up to his door, smile, and say "Huwara," the name of one of the villages between me and the peace camp. He nods. I climb the ladder into the rig. "*Shukran*," I tell him. "Thank you."

The driver, a Palestinian, puffs cigarettes through a plastic filter. He speaks only a few phrases of English, which is just about all the Arabic I know. He tells me his name is Mohammad and he is from Nablus and I say, "*La lilihtilal*, no occupation." He grins and high-fives me so I say "*Sharon sharmut!*" Now he is laughing. Me too. He hands me a cigarette.

Fifteen minutes later, we approach a clump of vehicles and he slows the truck to a stop. Ahead, Israeli soldiers with drawn weapons scurry around concrete barriers, their dark green jeeps positioned on both sides of the road. Zatara Checkpoint.

Palestinians talk about getting past a roadblock or a checkpoint, but they never really do get past anything, because as long as they're in the West Bank, these obstacles ensnare them in an immense web. Women have given birth to babies and sick men have died right at the checkpoints because soldiers won't let them pass.

We pull forward, one car length at a time, until we are the first vehicle in line. A soldier in wraparound shades points his automatic rifle into the windshield, finger hooking the trigger, and I stare into a tiny bottomless black hole. *Christ, what if he sneezes?*

Another soldier asks Mohammad for our identification. After looking at our documents, that soldier says something in Hebrew and the soldier pointing the rifle lowers it. He approaches my door and motions for me to open it with the gun barrel. He is grinning when he says, "You are America? You are New York City? What are you doing here? It is not safe, there is shooting." I lie and say I am here to teach English and spin fire chains for children. I mean, I do both, but I'm still, you know, withholding information.

Past the checkpoint and down the road a mile or two, Mohammad backs the truck into a dust bowl. He unloads an enormous dumpster from the flat-bed by pulling a few levers. Then he picks up a full one. Then we aren't going anywhere. We're just smoking.

He gazes at me. He gazes at his hands. He rubs his forefingers together as if the tips were pistons in an automobile and says, "You, yes?"

"What?"

He moves his hands down the sides of his head, tracing the outline of an imaginary hajib, the head scarf worn by many Islamic women, and then he arcs his hands as if running them along the contours of full, round breasts on his flat, male chest. He points at me and again says, "You, yes?"

"Uh, yes," I say, nodding with a polite smile. "I think so." *Those Old Testament stories of rocks being hurled into heretics' bodies, they make so much sense now. There are so many fucking rocks here, what else would you have used?*

I take a chance, form a hole with the thumb and forefinger of my right hand and thrust a finger from my left inside. Mohammad looks down for a second and then pantomimes, in rapid succession: hajib, breasts, hole, pistons. He points at me. I grin, say yes, and flash a thumb's up.

I realize a few things about living and dying and how desperation has built the thousands of word choices available to us. I also realize it's universal: truck drivers everywhere are perverts.

He points at me and then into the back of the cab. I jump over the seat and onto the mattress. I take my clothes off and pull a condom from my bag, along with some packets of EZ Glide. Then he jumps over the seat, prayer beads flopping from the dashboard to the floor mat. He cups my balls in one hand and strokes himself with the other. *Dear Muslims, Christians, and Jews: If you believe that Adam and Eve predated Cain and Abel, then you've got to admit that we've been fucking at least one generation longer than we've been fighting.*

I am laying on my back and Mohammad hovers over me, his lips wrapped around my cock. Suddenly he jolts, lunges for the window, and parts the curtains. *What the*—I am crouching, behind him, ready, but no one is there. *Ready? How can you ever be ready?* I try to slow my breath. *If there would have been someone there—*

I see their faces 'cause I can't stop seeing them. Bearded, smooth, frowning, or kind of smiling. Their jaws clench, unclench. Their eyes look through us to the sky beyond.

Just after that demonstration for political prisoners, some of those men who were shooting guns into the air took off with black bandannas and green flags—Islamic Jihad—and pointed those guns into the legs of a man. They claimed he behaved inappropriately with a woman and fired six shots. I do not know what happened to the woman. Nobody ever told me that.

I do not want divine justice and there is nothing outside but rocks and hills. Mohammad wants to leave, but I tell him please wait 'cause it's been way too long and I yank my cock until I come. He jumps back into the front seat. I join him and we say nothing. He drops me off in Huwara and we say bye: *Ma' asalama*.

CHECKING IN

We circle up on the dusty road headed to the Palestinian city of Qalqilya, the surrounding slopes first terraced by farmers thousands of years ago. We want to enter the city, but this is going to be difficult because Israeli contractors have almost finished Stage I of what Prime Minister Ariel Sharon calls a "security fence." He claims that Israelis must build this security fence to prevent Palestinians from sneaking into Israel to attack. But this so-called fence makes the Berlin Wall look like a rough draft, and Sharon tries not to mention the words "land grab" or discuss how the barrier snatches some of the deepest wells and most arable farmland in the West Bank, preferring to say, instead, that the security fence was built around difficult terrain and certain concessions had to be made.

Whatever your interpretation of Israel's motive, you can't argue this: the barrier runs along the inside of the Green Line and, as it passes Qalqilya, separates to form a loop around the city, a loop of twenty-five-foot-high seamless concrete blocks and even taller sniper towers. Have you ever stood beside such a thing and felt a claustrophobia so bad that it squeezed out every last drop of possibility? There are only three openings around Qalqilya: Habla Gate, ostensibly for farmers to have unfettered access to their fields; Jaljulya Gate, for the Israeli army to have unfettered access to Qalqilya; and the checkpoint for all arrivals and departures.

The six of us stand a couple hundred yards from the checkpoint for all arrivals and departures. I peek down the road at the barbed wire, the Armored Personnel Carriers, and the line of Palestinians waiting to enter their city.

Then we trudge forward until we can see the stubble on the faces of the two square-jawed soldiers monitoring the checkpoint. With helmets and semi-automatic weapons, they sit behind a table and decide who passes, who doesn't, and who will be detained. To our left, three stories up, more soldiers watch us from a sniper tower, with khaki netting draped over it like discarded clothes in a dormitory. Behind the soldiers, the sniper tower, and the booth, nestled in coils of barbed wire, a canopied corridor connects Qalqilya to the outside world. It has become the umbilical cord for a whole society.

Andrea, who looks so California dyke she should be the third Indigo Girl, explains to the soldiers who we are, or claim to be anyway. The soldiers don't even stand up. They just shake their heads no. Andrea tries pleading and she tries frustration. The soldiers keep shaking their heads and finally confess that they have orders from above: no foreigners. The rules have changed since the last group snuck in.

We contact our coordinators in the International Solidarity Movement and they contact their contacts. We stand back, keep smiling, and then pounce when the two soldiers guarding the checkpoint leave. Even though other soldiers still crawl up and down the ladder to the sniper tower, and move around the compound behind the trees, if we could just move fast enough—they wouldn't follow us into the city without a sizeable deployment, which takes time. We try to move through the corridor fast enough but end up sandwiched a few steps behind Palestinian families, who we don't want to entangle in our break-in attempt. Sirens blare and jeeps zip to our side. Sorry, sorry, we tell the soldiers. We didn't see anyone, we thought we could go.

Back under the shelter, back to square one, as the sun dips down behind the tough, dry hills. Dust covers our bags and collects in the creases of our clothes; it seeps into our nostrils and slack jaws. A compact soldier with no helmet walks towards us. With his round wire-framed glasses, he looks like he would rather be reading a book in some café.

"Guys, don't do that again," he says. We apologize and then he says, "I am sorry. You cannot come in here. Terrorists might kill you. This is for your safety."

Two navy-blue jeeps slide to a jagged halt, kicking up a cloud of dust. Navy blue is about the worst kind of news 'cause it means Border Patrol. The Israeli army is mostly composed of boys and girls under mandatory draft, but Border Patrol guards are hand-selected for their aggression and inability to question orders. Two men jump out from the first jeep. The guy from the passenger side comes around the back of the vehicle and enters my line of vision and I swoon, just a little, 'cause he is a black-haired hottie with quite a build and his navy-blue shirt is undone, maybe one or two buttons below regulation, but I don't have too much time to look 'cause he swings his rifle in an arc just above our heads and pulls back on the chamber and the bullets lock into place. Soldiers trot toward us. If we don't move fast, I think they might trot through us.

We grab our packs and supplies and stumble backwards. Soldiers point their rifles at our toes.

"You must walk back to the intersection," the spectacled soldier says. We don't see an intersection but we know which direction he means. "Please," he says. "Don't make this more difficult."

The sky turns to darker shades of blue as we retreat down the road, and the branches of the olive trees look like black snakes frozen in space. We keep walking around the gradual bend in the road, even though the convoy of military vehicles has stopped following us.

"Just keep walking. Someone is coming for you," one of our coordinators tells us over the phone. "You're going to sneak in the back way."

Ten minutes later, a van approaches, the headlights snuffed. The man behind the steering wheel waves his hand and we jump in. The rest of the group piles into the back and I jump onto the front passenger seat. He drives into the darkness for twenty seconds before he flashes the headlights on.

We're trying to sort through some concerns about the "back way." Is the gate electric? How much barbed wire? What should we do if we see soldi—

"Here!" the driver says as he stops the van. "We are here. You are going now! *Yalla!*" he yells as he nudges me. We throw our packs over our shoulders and wait till no headlights appear on either horizon. Between us and the gate, a field of boulders slopes slightly downward. *"Yalla!"* the driver says.

We become silhouettes in a field, and we freeze at the crack of a gunshot in the distance. You cannot see passports in darkness. Tonight, we're Palestinians.

"I don't feel comfortable with this," Ady says. Ady. Ady ben Israel. She was born in a town near Haifa but lives in New York City. Her handsome face is frowning.

"If we're going to discuss this," I say, "can we at least duck behind these boulders?" *God, this whole fucking place is rocks. Why does everybody want it so bad?*

We crouch down. The yellow gate is about fifty yards ahead. I peak above the boulders and see the driver waving his arms in overhand strokes. We only have moments and maybe not even these. *Please, please, no Border Patrol.*

We talk logistics: take packs off, toss them through the gate; then, one by one, duck through the gate—don't fucking touch the sides, they may be electric. We don't have full consensus 'cause Ady is not completely sold on our plan, but the quick cadence of blood in our temples drowns her concerns. We scoop up our belongings.

Terry, another dyke from California, looks up at the summer moon, too plump to get all the way above the horizon, and utters a quick prayer to the Goddess. She embraces Andrea and they walk forward, hand in hand. One at a time, we pass through the triangles of space between the yellow beams of the gate and enter the periphery of the city of Qalqilya. When that wall is complete, crossing will never be this easy again.

After we drop our gear at the three-story building with an Internet café and rooftop access, the place I will call home for the next month; after we eat in a shop where you can add carrot chutney, sliced olives, tahini, sautéed onions, or fifteen other toppings to your falafel and pita, I walk down a street with two other activists. It's two in the morning. In the hazy urban orange of night, between the lamplight and shadows of buildings, we see a Special Forces operation in progress. A caravan of at least twenty Humvees, tanks, and APCs rolls down the main boulevard. They only come like this to make arrests and assassinations. The next morning, we find out that they raided a house, beat the teenaged son, and terrified the five-year-old child when they shot bullets into sofas, closets, walls, bags of wheat, dresses, and bathroom tiles. They were looking for a man who had already fled. They settled for his family. For the next two nights, I have nightmares of one of those caravans rolling by my second-story window: the concrete walls are too thin to really keep munitions out, and even if they weren't, maybe the caravan will stop and and batter down our door and shoot—flashes of light and loud bangs of bullets and no place to hide.

During the next month, we meet with farmers at their homes. We pluck grapes from robust vines growing along their porches and pop them into our mouths. The farmers say that the Israeli army often stops them from accessing their fields outside the wall. The next day, when we try to accompany the farmers to their land, soldiers surround us with drawn guns minutes after we exit Habla Gate, the access point to the fields. The soldiers force us to retreat, but not before we see plots overgrown with weeds. And not before we see the boulders that the army has placed at Habla Gate. The boulders prevent farmers from driving tractors and other equipment out of the city, forcing them to harvest by muscle what they once did with technology. The day after our attempted visit, the situation gets worse: the army places another boulder at the gate, perhaps as a form of collective punishment. Now, donkeys and horses can't get through. Even a person must turn sideways to fit between the sides of the narrow gap, but only if a soldier gives his permission first.

Qalqilya is called "the bread basket of the West Bank" because, for decades, farmers have exported food as far away as Iraq. Since construction of the wall began, the farmers can't even feed all the inhabitants of the city.

On July 31, 2003, Israeli officials announce the completion of Stage I of the "security fence," a containment policy unprecedented in scope, composed of a barrier that is longer than 360 kilometers and cuts through the West Bank from Jenin in the north to the Salfit region in the southwest. In Qalqilya, Palestinian, Israeli, and international activists storm this barrier and spatter it with paint balloons the color of the Palestinian flag. We cover it in graffiti and launch a gigantic banner, tethered to helium balloons, above it. The banner reads "No Apartheid Wall!" in Arabic, Hebrew, and English. Media coverage of the action goes global.

But the wall is still standing. In fact, as winter approaches, Israeli contracting firms are rushing to complete the next two stages of construction, laying down the concrete and barbed wire of a barrier that will not only surround the entire West Bank but will also sever it in half. They will erect smaller cages around Palestinian cities and villages located along the periphery of the region, and they will build the barrier to encompass settlements sitting on stolen land. Israel will try to claim this gigantic prison as a new international border, the "necessary" first step to a two-state solution.

While I was in Qalqilya, the Special Forces came every third or fourth night. During one of their deployments, a couple of tanks rolled up and down the main boulevard, right around the corner from our house, and shot bullets that made one-and-a-half-inch holes in street posts and storefronts. They unloaded hundreds of rounds as a distraction, while another unit raided a home on the other side of the city. That night I screamed out WHAT THE FUCK CAN I DO and I still don't know, even as the memories tumble down around me while I drift to sleep on my bed in New York City. But I know this: on every continent, the Grim Reaper wears camouflage and Resistance wears a smile, and maybe this smile is a thin tight line, but sometimes it's a tooth-flashing grin, and that is what keeps us alive.

VITOLIGO VS. THE DRAPETOMANIA SYNDROME*

DR. RALOWE TRINITROTOLUENE AMPU, DDS

*Vitoligo is a skin condition resulting from loss of pigment that produces white patches. Any part of the body may be affected. The word "drapetomania" was created by the noted Louisiana surgeon and psychologist Dr. Samuel A. Carthwright by combining the Greek words for runaway slave and mad or crazy.

GAY.COM MESSENGER   Male | 21 | azusa

superdeformed: a bittersweet coming-out story about white people
superdeformed: a bittersweet coming-out story about white people
superdeformed: there's nothing exciting about being me
superdeformed: there's nothing exciting about being me
superdeformed: that's what suburbia taught me
superdeformed: that's what suburbia taught
superdeformed: los angeles is so erotic
superdeformed: los angeles is so erotic
superdeformed: trapped in the predictable cartoon reality confessional of my ghost shipped out medic staff super hot minority
   reporter vouchsafe to make it stall acoustic obvious there's little upside clinic telling you that your real illness is that you're
   poor
superdeformed: trapped in the predictable cartoon reality confessional of my ghost shipped out medic staff super hot minority
   reporter vouchsafe to make it stall acoustic obvious there's little upside clinic telling you that your real illness is that you're
   poor
superdeformed: piggishly oinks an ice armored boy object patron saint of the sliced penis with patrician precision handling
   and shipping ectoplasmic anchor hoisted chicken taste with the prisoner's jissom on its waist
superdeformed: piggishly oinks an ice armored boy object patron saint of the sliced penis with patrician precision handling
   and shipping ectoplasmic anchor hoisted chicken taste with the prisoner's jissom on its waist
superdeformed: the future shall yield better resolution but no final resolve in the pimp clinic acrylic gluteal fold filled seats
superdeformed: the future shall yield better resolution but no final resolve in the pimp clinic acrylic gluteal fold filled seats
superdeformed: money in my teeth or appetite expressed as a crass vector
superdeformed: money in my teeth or appetite expressed as a crass vector

there were no anthropological aims from the outset. i created michael "superdeformed" for cybersex. it's great. no social econ
tend with. no muss no fuss. over the course of this pursuit of pleasure i discovered a great number of not-so shocking things d
ions with the many lovely gay boys online, of which this is an abridged record. there was plenty of more tea, in fact a field, su-
-n more thorough research. this is an invitation to others that they should experiment on their own. i created this white profile
witness and no doubt relate there exists apparently some gulf between those i deem desirable and these individuals returning
an ordinary fact of living that we all encounter. (guess what i say next.) or is it? i present here ￼ two different chatters. i spoke
with each of these ￼ twice, once as myself and again as my fair alter ego. what follows does not introduce any new carefully
calculated findings, nor do i seek to declare any sweeping social theory. this is merely a record, sadly abridged, of actual exch-
agnes happening in real-time via the internet. and it is also... revenge.

   this is an example of what oppression looks like to me, an oppression of a variety that
   can only inflict damage to the extent that i willfully choose to internalize the oppressive ideology,
   in this instance where value is conferred through one's physical appearance (youth, ethnicity, etc.)
   but as i am often at a loss to rationally understand this behavior...most of this turns into rap...so, ple

SEND

Close   Ignore   Help   Send Private Photos

6. **Vitiligo**
   Vitiligo. Vitiligo is a skin condition resulting from loss of pigment which
   produces white patches. Any part of the body may be affected. ...
   Who Gets Vitiligo? ...
   http://www.aad.org/pamphlets/Vitiligo.html

...one of the "diseases and physical peculiarities of the Negro race." The word drapetomania was created by the noted Louisiana surgeon
and psychologist Dr. Samuel A. Cartwright by combining the Greek words for runaway slave and mad or crazy. It was used to describe

cold, allusive, inbent, hostile

Photos: 1 2 3 4 5

View Full Profile   Bookmark

HIDE PROFILE   HIDE MESSAGE

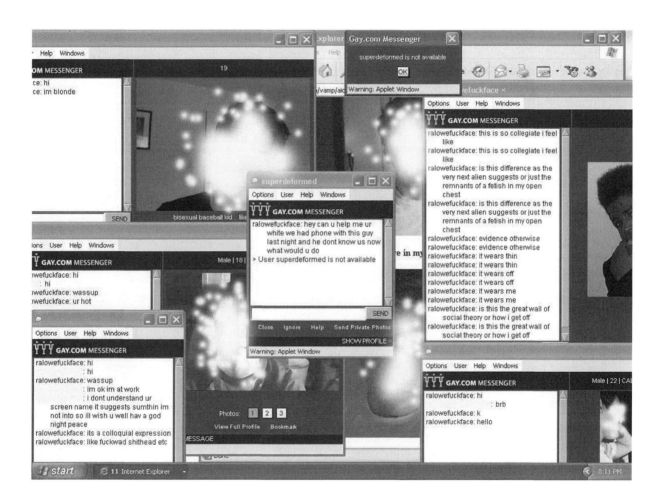

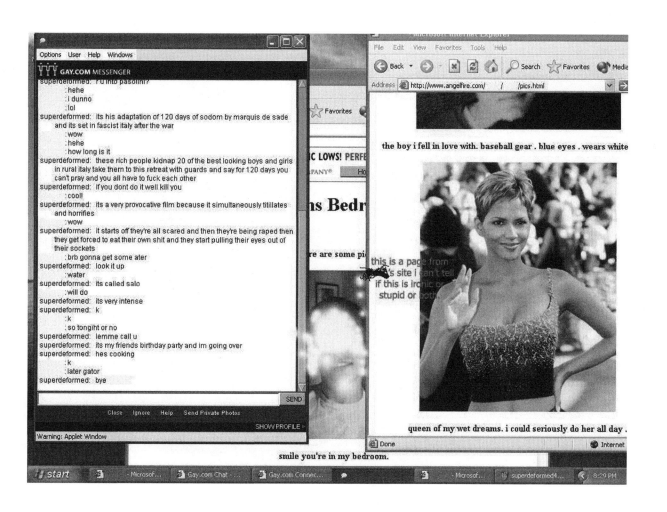

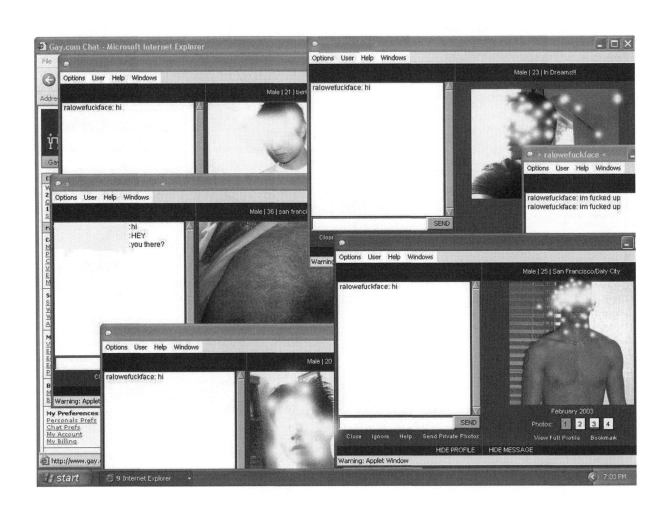

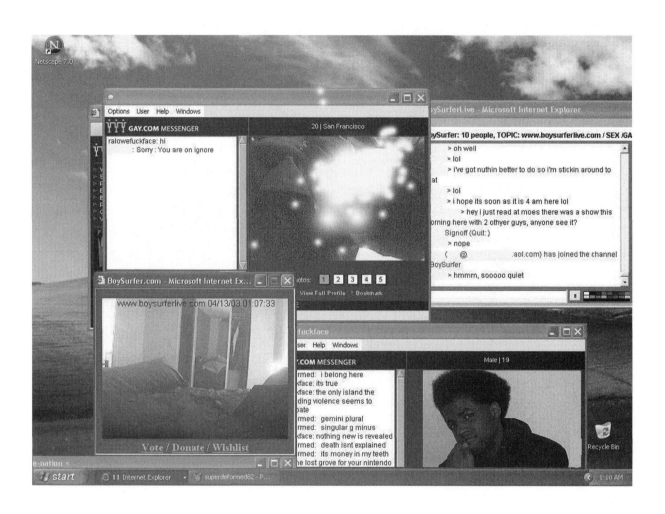

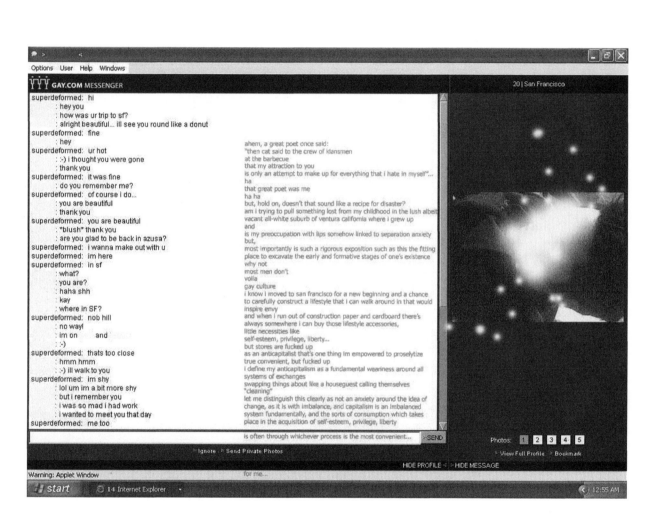

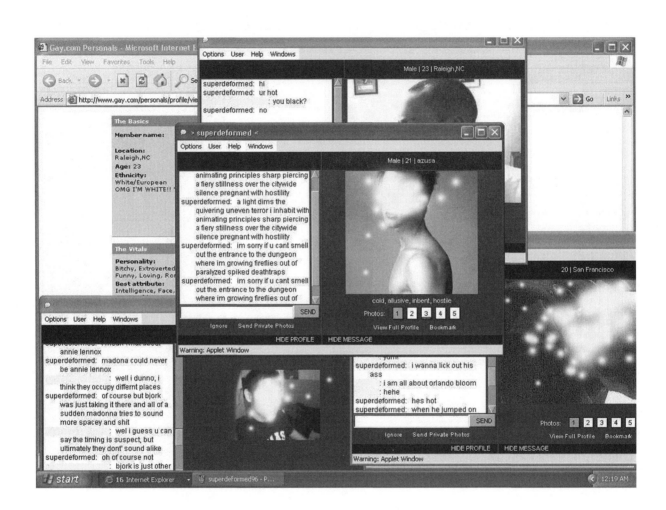

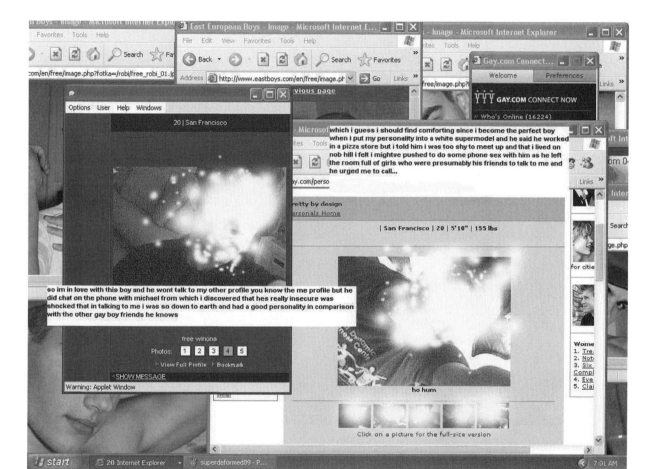

SEX, GENDER, AND LETTERS TO MYSELF

ELIAS SEMBESSAKWINI

> If writing cannot and writing must change things, I thought to myself,
> logically of course, writing will change things magically. Magic operates
> metaphorically. So: I will take one text, New York City, the life of my
> friends, and change this text by placing another text on top of it.
> —Kathy Acker, "A few notes on two of my books,"
> *Bodies of Work Essays* (Serpent's Tail, 1997).

Following are three texts, laid on top of each other: trying to get laid as a political act (I know *I* can function better politically if I'm getting laid); telling who I am and some stories about my body; and making sure you know that's not all, that none of this is simple.

DYKE ON DYKE CRUISING

Can dykes (of all genders) have uncomplicated sexual adventure? Can we get out of the costs, potential complications, and sceniness of bars, clubs, and even sex parties? Can we get out of the pressure to find one decent lay and huddle down with her until we can't be bothered making her tea, let alone making her come? Anyone for variety, free sex?

Our fag brothers cruise parks, alleys, restrooms, clubs, and wherever else they can think of for a nameless fuck, without having to negotiate a dance floor, relationship, or the possibility that the person they're chatting to for over an hour just likes chatting. I didn't think I was the only one peering enviously over the fence at that rougher-edged kind of romance, or maybe the death of romance itself.

So I had this idea. Set up a public space for dykes to cruise each other for sex. And where better to do it than San Francisco? We'd choose a spot, spread the word, and see what happened.

It was beautifully anarchic in that it was using common (public) space, and it was totally free and voluntary—virtually nothing except the idea, the time, and the place was organized. It was up to whomever turned up to make the experience what they wanted.

We lined up the first Dyke on Dyke Cruising "event" as part of (the third) Queeruption—a grassroots, free, queer gathering.

With help and suggestions, my new friend Jaime and I came up with a place (a park in the Mission), a time, and a flyer. And we practiced—pretending to be strangers, rehearsing lines, kissing and fucking amongst the trees.

One of us cut the light near the playground equipment in the park. It was a strategic improvement to the park's ambience, as well as a fun little crime in itself. As night fell, a bunch of adventurers appeared.

I was sitting around on a wooden boat near the playground, sipping tequila with some friends and lovers, feeling like the hostess of a party. I wanted things to happen. I wanted to witness the New Dawn of dyke sexual liberation. But it seemed like the groups of young friends talking and giggling would remain timid. I even tried to pimp lovers and friends to cute dykes I didn't know.

A cop car came and parked fifteen meters away from us, inside the park. The cops sat in their car for a half hour, eating take-out, then left without saying anything. And then it started. First, a pretty, butch girl with a loaded-looking bag got us all watching when she strode brazenly past to stand over near the trees. The people near me seemed interested, too. But before anyone got their shit together to follow her, she strode intently back again, this time stopping way down near the steps. One womyn did follow her then, but apparently not closely enough to keep her interest, and she disappeared.

My hopes and desires rose when a particular small, sexy, slutty, femmey woman I recognized arrived with a friend. Instead of joining the coffee klatch at the playground equipment, Ms. Hope went off and sat alone on a distant bench. Like a gentleman, and a good host, I waited to leave space for someone else, someone totally anonymous, to give her the hot scene she more than deserved. I went back to drinking and talking with my friends and the gathered rabble. Park sprinklers brought Ms. Hope back down to us, but with apparently undampened spirits.

She bravely sat away from us drinkers, waiters, and hesitators. I vaguely noticed her changing clothes. Then I heard the sound of a small stream hitting the playground sand. She was standing on the other side of the wooden boat we were sitting on—her long, black dress pulled up high, no underwear, her legs spread. She was pissing a pretty and tinkling liquid line for the pleasure of us all. "Let the games begin."

When she finished showing off, she approached us and complained in a stranded lady's lilt that she had nothing with which to clean herself. Unable to resist a damsel in distress, I offered my sleeve. Then I offered my mouth. But I wasn't quite sure. I confessed I didn't want piss on my breath all night. No problem: Ms. Hope pulled out a chocolate from her mysterious kit. With that, I turned and gently used my tongue to clean her piss-wet, shaven pussy, taking my sweet time and ignoring the giggles from my friends beside me. Then, true to her word, that slutty priestess offered me a chocolate from between her teeth.

She asked if anyone was wearing a dick, and walked purposefully behind the climbing equipment. "Go on," I said to my eager, sailor-boy friend. But he wouldn't go alone. Maybe he was afraid of losing his erection.

We couldn't leave the lady waiting, so I went with him. Sailor boy had his cock sucked. I felt the pull of my responsibilities as a host, but the lady was squatting in front of him, and I knew she didn't have anything on under her dress. I moved behind that dear, cocksucking lady, pulled up her dress, spanked her ass, and fucked her for a long time. I then kissed her mouth and pinched her nipples while sailor boy worked hard, pushing his dick into her as she requested.

In her true commitment to the cause of encouraging those around us to scatter and fuck, she moaned extra loud.

I'm hoping dyke on dyke cruising will become a more regular, spontaneous phenomenon.

DIALOGUE TRANSCRIPT FOR "INTERSEX EXPOSITION: FULL MONTY"

- It doesn't matter; I'm not that nervous.

- *My name's Shorona. And um, I'm Jewish. I'm . . . my name's a Jewish name, it's a Hebrew name. And um, I was . . . I'm from Melbourne.*

- Are you revealing the construction?

- Yeah.

- Are you being, um, queer . . . queer in text?

- *I'm in the dressing room at the Imperial Hotel, um, before I perform at the Gurlesque lesbian fortnightly strip night in Sydney.*

- My body feels kind of good to me in lots of ways. I use it to do things and I feel really good about that. I feel really comfortable with the fact that it has certain strengths and abilities . . .

- *I'm gonna be doing a spoken work p—a spoken word performance piece that, um—where I'm gonna be kind of talking about my body and my feelings about my body.*

- My body's not like anyone else's body, it's only like my body. Um, I guess that's probably true of everyone's, but mine specifically has certain elements so . . . like, I don't really have much underarm hair. Now that's natural—I don't actually shave, I've never really—I've shaved my underarms at times, but that was to try and encourage some underarm hair. And that's also true about my pubic hair. So I haven't got a lot of pubic hair. And that's not because I shave, or whatever. That's just—that's just my pubic hair.

- *And it's gonna be fairly nonsexual as far as I'm concerned. And um, very persynal, and um—totally improvised.*

- And at six months old my clitoris started to grow to an extent that the—that some kind of health nurse noticed that, and took me—I then went to some kind of medical tests. And the doctors decided—did some other tests—did an exploratory where they opened this part of my body. They cut into here and had a—a look inside. And what they found inside my abdomen was testicles.

- *During that performance, I'm gonna start talking about aspects about my body that refer to, um—my experiences as an intersex persyn, and the way I've been treated and how that's affected my body, and the way that I feel about myself and the way I feel about my body.*

- I had a second operation that also reduced my clitoris in size. Or maybe they cut my penis off—I'm not really clear about that. Um, and at the same time they re-opened this scar and took out my testes. That was at ten years old. So I was, uh—I—I was, I was actually, you know, I was a child. And um, I didn't—I didn't know what was going on. So I—I've been to hospital—they're doing things to my body. And I wasn't really clear about why that was. All I know that—I had a sense that there was something really wrong with me. Something very different about my body. Or about my self. Something even deeper than that.

- *This is basically a strip night so—I'm gonna be taking off my clothes while I speak.*

- My third operation was actually to open the hole of my vagina. They told me that my vagi— I didn't have a vagina, and um, they did an operation when I was fourteen years old.

- *She decided that she was gonna do this, um, performance at Gurlesque and said, "Do you wanna come along and film it?" So I said, "Yep."*

- And it turned out that underneath the—whatever—blocked entrance that I actually did have a vagina, so they cut it open . . .

- *I don't—I probably don't want people to feel particularly sorry for me. And it also just confuses me 'cause I think—I would like to know what people really thought. And there's a sense that if people feel sympathy for you that they—they're not as honest, I think, in the way that they treat you. There's a sense in which that they—ew—like people kind of give you what they think you really need rather than what they actually wanna say or what they actually feel.*

- It's an intersex condition. It's a condition that describes me as a persyn that's less than clearly male or female. That was when this scar was first opened. And my clitoris having grown a little bit—the doctors decided to create me as someone who was gonna look like a female for the rest of my life—and hopefully never question that. So they not only opened this scar and did an exploratory operation to see what was inside. But they also cut my clitoris, or my penis—whatever you might—whatever you wanna call it—to make it more like what they would call a kind of like—an okay looking clitoris. Something that wouldn't be questionable as a clitoris.

- *I was pretty open with my expectations, I think. I was, um, doing it to see what would happen. And um, not even in terms of the audience response, but what—how it would affect me, and I— in terms of that I felt actually remarkably comfortable when I was in—on stage. Like I said— despite the fact that I had no clothes on, and I have had a lot of feelings of shame about my body in the past. Um, and then something, I guess, I considered was possible, but didn't expect. The fact that, you know, I cried quite a bit afterwards and I'm not exactly sure what that was about. I guess maybe that was about, I think, the feeling of loss, that I'd "come out" as an intersex persyn and therefore separated my sense of identity from every—almost everybody else's in the room. Well, probably everybody else's in the room. And really outwardly said—"Even thought you—you thought I was one of you—I kind of am, but you know, I kind of aren't—am not."*

- And it probably wasn't 'til I was about twenty-nine that I had really much sense at all about this. Um, now I identify as an intersex persyn because I really, like, I'm a persyn who grew up with testes—whether they were in my abdomen or in my—whatever you—I don't know labia, scrotum.

- *It was really weird 'cause I was like—"Oh shit, I didn't think of how to end this thing."*

- Hmmm. So, whether—I dunno. I wonder whether it's appropriate for me to strip and talk about myself at a lesbian venue. I don't know whether it is or not—but I have. So, I think I've basically done my thing . . . Thank you very much.

- *Shorona! Well, thank you very much. I dunno if you can hear me but—Thank you so much for performing that, or sharing that at our club. I get very proud that this exists sometimes. And um— it's times like that—*

- You can reveal the mechanisms, but you can't reveal the heartbeat or the—the lungs and the muscles.

SHAMELESS LETTERS

My dearest son and daughter Eli,

I wanted to write and tell you how perfect you are. I've loved you dearly since before you were born. I've been thrilled to watch you grow up and am fascinated by all the things you do. I'm your biggest fan. I call you regularly and e-mail you because I love hearing about your life and all the people in it, because I want you to feel the love and care that I feel for you, and I want to keep up with all your activities. I also want to be there in those moments when things are a bit more dif-ficult, to let you know that I love you, to remind you that you have all the strength, skills, and abilities you need to be happy and successful in everything you do, and that I will help you in any way I can when you need it. I will give you money when you need it, and on your birthdays, so you can treat yourself.

Love always,
Mum.

To Mr./Ms. Elias seMbessakwini,

This letter is to inform you that we have approved your claim for compensation relating to the wrongs and mistreatment you suffered (and continue to suffer from) at the hands of the medical community—specifically that of the Royal Children's Hospital of Melbourne. We would like to offer you a very generous financial compensation payment, as well as our most sincere and heartfelt apologies and the public admission of our guilt beyond doubt.

In addition, we have your testicles and are making arrangements to have them unfrozen, and to replace them in your body. Unfortunately, it may take some time for the sperm to regenerate and mature, but within the next few years you should be able to father children if you so desire. Of course, once your testicles are retransplanted, you will no longer need to take synthetic hormones.

Please get in touch with me with any questions or concerns.

Yours sincerely,

Dr. Garry Warne and the Royal Children's Hospital.

Dear Eli (like your new name by the way),

Thank you for your wonderful story of seeing me in the film *Gendernaughts* in Sydney a few years ago. You mention how important it was to you that I looked so happy and beautiful. And you said I was just about the first intersex persyn you'd known you were seeing, besides yourself. I'm so glad that by just being myself, honest and "out," I had such a profound and positive impact on you (as you said), even if it did make you cry so much. It means a lot to me that seeing me in the film had such a big effect on your life, and I'm proud to see you out there now, creating more possibilities of that happening for other people.

Love,

Hida.

Dear Eli,

I was one of those kids at the hospital you went to when you were young—the ones you'd look at and wonder, "Are they weird like me? Is there something dirty, shameful, and wrong about them too?" You looked kinda scared and in shock and like you wanted to be invisible. I felt the same.

Love,

Tony.

Dear Eli,

You don't know me. I saw your films and a number of your other performances and I want to tell you that I think that you're very talented—creative and skilled, and I eagerly look forward to more work from you. I also admire and appreciate the politics and sacrifice of what you are doing in standing up publicly and telling strange and deep truths about yourself.

But most importantly, I have to say that with all that—I just see you as someone I don't know, who may or may not be nice, who seems kinda cute and sexy but otherwise is just like me and everyone else I know. I don't, in the slightest way, put you on a pedestal, see you as an intersex poster-child, or feel sorry for you.

Yours sincerely,

Everyone in the audience.

To Elias seMbessakwini,

We are very happy to inform you that after looking at your work (without you even submitting it), we would like to publish and distribute a collection of your stories as a book.

Many things have been called literature throughout herstory, and I absolutely champion your persynal accounts of your unusual experiences as very great and highly marketable work.

I think that the story of the glass tube "dilators" that you obediently covered in KY jelly and regularly pushed in and out of your newly surgically opened vagina is reminiscent of Kathy Acker's greater books. The descriptions of locking the bedroom door, taking out the white Tupperware container, pulling down your pants—the smell of the KY—and pushing the glass in enough to hurt a bit while you lay there reading point to a deeper and completely new way of seeing modern society. And when you describe asking your mother after many months how often you should be doing this act that you were barely able to speak of, even to her, and she answers that she thought you knew that you could have stopped months earlier . . . pure Hemingway.

And I persynally love the Kafkaesque story of Dr. Garry Warne getting you, at age ten, to agree to his taking a skin sample from your pubis by telling you it wouldn't hurt or leave a mark, and guilt-tripping you about research to help others. And somehow you keep us guessing until the final moment when you reveal that in fact it "hurt like fuck," and that over twenty years later, you still have the scar, stitch marks, and hairless patch. Not to mention that your mother was there, helping to convince you to agree.

But for me, the most sublime moment was the description of your child knees up in the air, you lying on your back, a disposable sheet across your legs hiding your view of what was going on, and you tightly squeezing your mother's hand while the doctor probed your vagina with his gloved fingers—as lovely as some of Jean Genet's finest and most intricate prose.

I assure you that publishing these stories will not only garner you a living sufficient to set up the urban eco-village of your dreams, but that you are doing a great social and political service, as well as making an important literary contribution. Your views on important social, political, and artistic matters will naturally be in demand henceforth.

In anticipation of your prompt reply,
Instant Success Publishing.

PISS, TRANSNATIONAL CAPITAL,
LICE REMOVER, THE PIERS, MARY,
STUFFED-UP TURKEYS, AND RICKI LAKE

CALLING ALL RESTROOM REVOLUTIONARIES!

SIMONE CHESS, ALISON KAFER, JESSI QUIZAR, AND MATTIE UDORA RICHARDSON

CALLING ALL RESTROOM REVOLUTIONARIES: *People In Search of Safe and Accessible Restrooms (PISSAR) needs you! We are a coalition of queer, genderqueer, and disabled people working toward greater awareness of the need for safe and accessible bathrooms on campus and in the dorms.* BE A RESTROOM REVOLUTIONARY! *Join PISSAR as we develop a checklist for genderqueer safe spaces and create teams to map safe and accessible bathrooms around campus.*[1]

Everyone needs to use bathrooms, but only some of us have to enter into complicated political and architectural negotiations in order to use them. The fact is, bathrooms are easier to access for some of us than for others, and the people who never think about where and how they can pee have a lot of control over how using restrooms feels for the rest of us. What do we need from bathrooms? What elements are necessary to make a bathroom functional for everyone? To make it safe? To make it a private and respectful space? Whose bodies are excluded from the typical restroom? More important, what kind of bodies are assumed in the design of these bathrooms? Who has the privilege (we call it pee-privilege) of never needing to think about these issues, of always knowing that any given bathroom will meet one's needs? Everyone needs to use the bathroom. But not all of us can.

And that's where People in Search of Safe and Accessible Restrooms (PISSAR) comes in. PISSAR, a coalition of UC-Santa Barbara undergrads, grad students, staff, and community members, recognizes that bathrooms are not always accessible for people with disabilities, or safe for people who transgress gender norms. PISSAR was formed at the 2003 University of California Student of Color Conference, held at UC-Santa Barbara. During the lunch break on the second day of the conference, meetings for the disability caucus and the transgender caucus were scheduled in adjacent rooms. When only a few people showed up for both meetings, we decided to hold a joint session. One of the members of the disability caucus mentioned plans to assess bathroom accessibility on the campus, wondering if there was a similar interest in mapping gender-neutral bathrooms. Everyone in the room suddenly began talking about the possibilities of a genderqueer/disability coalition, and PISSAR was born.

For those of us whose appearance or identity does not quite match the "man" or "woman" signs on the door, bathrooms can be the sites of violence and harassment, making it very difficult for us to use them safely or comfortably. Similarly, PISSAR acknowledges that, although most buildings are required by the Americans with Disabilities Act to provide accessible bathrooms, some restrooms are more compliant than others and accessible bathrooms can often be hard to find. PISSAR's mission, then, is threefold: 1) to raise awareness about what safe and accessible bathrooms are and why they are necessary; 2) to map and verify existing accessible and/or gender-neutral bathrooms on the campus; and 3) to advocate for additional bathrooms. We eventually hope to have both web-based and printed maps of all the bathrooms on campus, with each facility coded as to its accessibility and gender-safety.[2] Beyond this initial campaign, PISSAR plans to advocate for the construction or conversion of additional safe and accessible bathrooms on campus. To that end, one of our long-term goals is to push for more gender-neutral bathrooms and showers in the dormitories, and to investigate the feasibility of multistall gender-neutral bathrooms across the campus as a whole.

As it turned out, we weren't the only restroom revolutionaries on campus. We soon joined forces with a student-run initiative to stock all campus tampon and pad machines, a group called, appropriately enough, Aunt Flo and the Plug Patrol. Aunt Flo's goal is to use funds garnered from the sale of tampons and pads in campus bathroom dispensers (blood money, if you will) to support student organizations in a time of tremendous budget cuts. We liked their no-euphemism approach to the bathroom and the body, and joined their effort to make the campus not only a safer and more accessible place to pee, but also to bleed.[3] We also expanded our focus to include issues of childcare, inspired in part by one of our member's experiences as a young mom on campus. PISSAR decided to examine whether campus bathrooms featured changing tables, a move that increased our intersectional analysis of bathroom access and politics.

By specifically including the work of Aunt Flo and concerns about childcare access, PISSAR challenges many of the assumptions that are made about genderqueer and disabled bodies. Why shouldn't every gender-neutral restroom have a tampon/pad machine? Putting tampon/pad machines only in women's rooms, and mounting them high on the wall, restricts the right to menstruate conveniently to those with certain bodies. It suggests that the right to tampons and pads is reserved for people who use gender-specific women's rooms and can reach a lever hanging five feet from the ground. This practice reinscribes ideas about disabled bodies being somehow dysfunctional and asexual (as in, "People in wheelchairs get their periods too?") and perpetuates the idea that genderqueer folks are inherently unbodied (as in, "Only *real* women need tampons, and you don't look like a real woman").

So how exactly does PISSAR work? Picture a team of people taking over a bathroom near you. They're wearing bright yellow T-shirts stenciled with the phrase "free 2 pee" on the back. They're wearing gloves. They're wielding measuring tape and clipboards, and they're looking very disappointed in the height of your toilet. What you've seen is PISSAR in action. We call this a PISSAR patrol, and it's our way of getting the information we need in an unapologetically public way. We gather this information with the help of the PISSAR checklist, a form featuring questions about everything from the height of a tampon dispenser to the signs on the door, from the number of grab bars beside the toilet to the presence of a diaper-changing table.

From the information garnered in the PISSAR patrols, we are in the process of making a map that will assess the safety and accessibility of all the bathrooms on campus. The map is vital to our project because it offers genderqueer and disabled people a survey of all the restrooms on campus so that they can find what they need without the stigma and frustration of telling a possibly uninformed administrator the details of their peeing needs. For people who have never had to think about bathrooms, the map's detailed information suggests the ways in which our everyday bathrooms are restrictive and dangerous. Thus the map also functions as a consciousness-raising tool, educating users about the need for safe and accessible restrooms.

PISSAR patrols aren't simply about getting information. They're also a way to keep our bodies involved in our project. PISSAR is, after all, a project about bodies: about bodily needs, about the size and shape of our bodies, and about our bodily presentation. The very nature of our bathroom needs necessitates this attention to the body. So it makes sense that when we tried to theorize about what a safe, respectful restroom might look like, we realized we needed to meet in the bathroom. Because the bathroom is our site, and the body in search of a bathroom is our motivation, we recognized early on the need to be concerned with body and theory together. PISSAR's work is an attempt at embodying theory, at theorizing from the body.

We do this work partly through our name. The name PISSAR avoids euphemism and gets right down to business. We are here to talk about peeing and shitting, and what people need in order to do these things with comfort and dignity. Both PISSAR's name and the goals of the group come down to one unavoidable fact: when you've got to go, you've got to go. The name endeavors both to avoid abstraction and to highlight the embodied experiences that make bathroom accessibility so pressing when one needs to pee. PISSAR's name isn't an accident, it's a tool. We use our funny name to demand attention to our basic and critical needs. We warn with our name: we're about to talk about something "crude." We take it seriously—you should, too.

Our concern with body/theory is also evident in our insistence that bathroom accessibility is an important issue for a lot of different people. Everyone should be able to find a bathroom that conforms to the needs of their body. Everyone should be able to use a restroom without being accused of being in the "wrong" place. Everyone should have access to tampon dispensers and facilities for changing diapers, regardless of gender or ability. Homeless folks should have access to clean restrooms free of harassment.[4] Bathroom activism is, from the outset, a multi-identity endeavor. It has the potential to bring together feminists, trans folks, people with disabilities, single parents, and a variety of other people whose bathroom needs frequently go unmet. It creates a much needed space for those of us whose identities are more complicated than can be encompassed in a single-issue movement. Viewed in this light, restroom activism is an ideal platform from which to launch broader coalition work. In PISSAR, we tend to think about "queerness" as encompassing more than just sexual orientation; it includes queer bodies, queer politics, and queer coalitions.

ON BODIES IN BATHROOMS: PISSAR POLITICS

There is tremendous social pressure to avoid talking about bodies in bathrooms. First, such talk is not considered polite. We're trained from an early age not to talk publicly about what happens in the bathroom; we don't even have *language* for what happens in there; many of us still rely on the euphemisms our parents used when we were three. Second, the topic is not appropriately academic. For the most part, scholars do not tend to theorize about bathrooms and what bodies do in them.[5] Bathrooms are somehow assumed to be free of the same institutional power dynamics that impact and shape the rest of our lives. Finally, bathroom talk is considered politically dangerous, or at least irrelevant, because of a fear that it will be seen as a trivial issue, prompting the mainstream culture to not take us seriously. Political activism is supposed to be about ideas, the mind, and larger social movements, not about who pees where.

PISSAR is tired of pretending that these polite, academic, political bodies don't have needs. We resist the silencing from mainstream communities that want to ignore our queerness and our disability, while simultaneously challenging the theories that want to pull us away from the toilet seat. We refuse to accept a narrow conception of "queer" that denies the complexities of our bodies.

Keeping this focus on our *particular* bodies is no easy task. Mainstream culture, with its cycles of acceptance and disapproval of homosexuals (and we use this rather limited term intentionally), has always presented a rather narrow view of queer life. In order to be portrayed in the mainstream media, for example, queers must either fit into acceptable stereotypes of gay appearance and behavior, or be visibly indistinguishable from heterosexuals. These positions are highly precarious and strictly patrolled: Mainstream gay characters can only exhibit limited amounts of "gayness," a restriction epitomized in the lack of any sexual contact, even kissing, between gay characters. Those few gay characters that do exist in the mainstream media obey very strict norms of appearance. Unfortunately, this stance is becoming increasingly pervasive within mainstream gay culture as well. One need only glance at the covers of magazines such as the *Advocate* to discover that members of the gay community are supposed to be young, thin, white, nondisabled, and not genderqueer. In fact, mainstream gay media has often contributed to pressure on the gay community, particularly gay men, to be hyper-able and gender conforming. Images of big, beefy, muscle-bound bodies decorate the ads in gay publications and the words "no fats or fems" frequently appear in gay personal ads. We believe that this disavowal of queers that are too *queer*— those of us who are trans identified, genderqueer, too poor to afford the latest fashions, disabled, fat, in-your-face political—is the result of internalized shame.

The gay community has internalized the larger culture's homophobia and transphobia, which has made us ashamed of our visible queerness, especially any signs of genderqueerness. We have internalized the larger culture's ableism, which has made us ashamed of our disabilities and illnesses. This shame has marginalized many trans and genderqueer folks and many people with disabilities, casting them out of the mainstream gay community. Internalized self-hatred, a distancing from the bodies of those who do not fit the idealized norms, an insistence on assimilation: all of these lead to and result from a sense of shame in our bodies—a shame that pervades our conversations, our relationships, and our politics. This tendency to move away from the body, to drop the experiences of bodies out of conversations and politics, is evident in many queer organizations.[6] We lack the language to say what needs to be said; we don't have the tools to carry on this level of conversation.

Because we lack this language, because of our internalized self-hatred and shame in our bodies, the politics of the bathroom—a potentially transgressive and liminal site—have not been given priority within the mainstream gay rights movement. This inattention has particularly strong real-life effects on disabled and genderqueer folks. The need for a safe, dignified, usable place to pee is a vital, but too seldom addressed, issue. It has gone unaddressed because it is so much about the body, particularly the shameful parts and shameful acts of the body. This shame, and the resulting silence, is familiar to many in the disability community. In striving to assimilate to nondisabled norms, many of us gloss over the need for the assistance some of us have in using the bathroom. We are embarrassed to admit that we might need tubes or catheters, leg bags or personal assistants—or that some of us may not use the bathroom at all, preferring bedpans or other alternatives. Particularly in mixed company (that is, in the presence of nondisabled folks), we are reluctant to talk about the odd ways we piss and shit. But this reticence has hindered our bathroom politics, often making it difficult for us to demand bathrooms that meet all of our needs.

Queer bathroom politics have been similarly affected by this kind of ashamed reticence. Our reluctance to talk about bathrooms and bodies, and our sense that discussions about pissing and shitting are shameful, colors our responses to the potential violence facing many genderqueer people in the bathroom. Such acts aren't to be discussed in polite company because they occur in and around the bathroom, itself a taboo topic; because of homophobia and transphobia, these acts aren't seen as worthy of conversation because "those kinds of people" don't really matter; and because they conjure thoughts about public sex in bathrooms.

Indeed, public sex has often been the target of surveillance, and those implicated in such practices have been publicly humiliated, arrested, and abused. In 1998, several local news organizations around the country sent hidden cameras into public restrooms to film men engaged in sexual activities; these tapes were often turned over to local authorities, many of whom used them as the basis for sting operations. A station in San Diego, for example, justified its use of this stealth tactic in campus restrooms at San Diego State University by stressing the need to protect students from these deviant activities. The prevalence of these kinds of news stories, and the presence of surveillance equipment in campus restrooms, serve to police sexual behavior: Threats of public exposure and humiliation are used to enforce "normative" sexuality. At the University of California in Berkeley, this policing was taken a step further when some bathrooms on campus were locked in an effort to eliminate public sex. Only certain people were given keys to these restrooms, literally locking out some bodies and behaviors. These practices—privatizing public spaces and placing them under surveillance—demarcate the boundaries of appropriate and permissible behavior, thereby policing both bodies and bathrooms.

This surveillance of deviant bodies and practices in bathrooms all too often takes the form of brutal physical violence. Genderqueer and trans-identified folks have been attacked in public restrooms simply because their appearance threatens gender norms and expectations. This issue of bathroom violence is consistently delegitimized in both queer and nonqueer spaces as not important or sexy enough to be a "real" issue. In many gay activist circles, there seems to be a pervasive sentiment that no one (read: no straight people) will take us seriously if we start talking about bathrooms. Additionally, there is tremendous cultural shame around the violence itself—either you should have been able to protect yourself, or you must have deserved it, or both.

In the genderqueer community we know how often our bodies cause anxiety and violence. We have been systematically and institutionally discouraged from talking about that violence, or from linking it to these bodies. When a woman in our local community was attacked by strangers because of her androgynous appearance, local police insisted that she was injured in a "lesbian brawl." It was easier for them to talk about (and assume) her sexuality than to admit that it was her queer body, her race, and her confusing gender that led to both her original attack and the subsequent neglect of local law enforcement, who failed to follow protocol in her case. Internalized shame about her body led our friend to take on responsibility for her attack, to allow the police to mistreat her and make false assumptions, and to feel that she had no right to talk about how her attack was based in her refusal of racial, sexual, and gender norms. She was ashamed to talk about her body, about the violence done to it, and about how its needs were ignored. The community felt the impact of our own shame. We stood beside her, outwardly supportive, but unable to gather enough energy to mobilize a collective demand that her story be heard and that the police investigate the crime.

Sadly, as this story illustrates, our shame isn't always directed outward, toward the society and institutions that helped create it. It often drives wedges between communities that might otherwise work together. And it is *precisely* this kind of embodied shame—the shame that we feel in our bodies and the shame that arises out of the experience and appearance of our bodies—that drives the divisions between queer and disability communities. PISSAR initially had trouble bridging this gap, in that some of our straight disabled members worried about the political (read: queer) implications of our bathroom-mapping work. Indeed, many queer disability activists and scholars have drawn attention to the ableism that thrives within queer communities, and the homophobia and heterocentrism that reside within disability circles.

Due to the fact that disabled people are discriminated against on the basis of our disabilities, some of us may want to assert our "normalcy" in other aspects of our lives, including our sex lives. Although this impulse is understandable in a culture that constantly pathologizes our sexuality, this assertion in some cases takes on a homophobic/transphobic quality. Heterosexuals with disabilities may thus distance themselves from disabled queers and trans folk in an attempt to facilitate their assimilation into an ableist and heterocentric culture. Similarly, because of the ways in which queer desires, identities, and practices have been pathologized, cast as unnatural, abnormal, and most importantly, "sick," some LBGTIQ-identified people may want to distance themselves from disabled people in an effort to assert their own normalcy and health. As a result, queers and people with disabilities have been set up by our own communities as diametrically opposed, a move that has been particularly problematic—and painful—for queers with disabilities. For all of us balancing multiple identities, this kind of thinking enacts a dissection, first separating us from the realities of our bodies through shame and a lack of language, then further cutting apart our identities into separate and distant selves.

We suggest, however, that bathroom politics can potentially lift us out of this polarization. Advocating for bathroom access and repeatedly talking openly about people's need for a safe space to pee helps us break through some of this embodied shame and recognize our common needs. It is through the process of going on PISSAR patrol while wearing bright T-shirts and reporting on our findings in loud voices that we begin to move beyond a shamed silence.

Our attention to the body (the pissing and shitting body), and our insistence that we talk about the specificities of people's embodied experiences with humor rather than shame, challenges the normalizing drive found within both queer and disability communities. Rather than mask our differences, or bolster our own claims to "normalcy" by marginalizing others as shameful and embarrassing, we insist on a coalition that attempts to embrace all of our different needs. PISSAR is built around queerness, but a *queer* queerness, a queerness that encompasses both sexually and medically queer bodies, that embraces a diversity of appearances and disabilities and needs. The PISSAR checklist—a manifesto of sorts—models *queer* coalition-building by incorporating disability, genderqueer, childcare, and menstruation issues into one document, refusing single-issue analysis. It entails a refusal to assimilate to the phantasm of the "normal" body by explicitly incorporating the allegedly abnormal, the freakish, the *queer*. The body evoked in the checklist is a real body, a menstruating body, a body that pees and shits, a body that may not match its gender identity, a body subjected too often to violence and ridicule, a body that may have parts missing or parts that don't function "properly," a body that might require assistance. Bathroom politics and organizations such as PISSAR resist the normalization of "queer," striving to acknowledge and embrace all these different bodies, desires, and needs that are too often ignored, obscured, or denied out of shame and internalized self-hatred.

RAISING CONSCIOUSNESS AND DOING THEORY ON THE PISSAR PATROL

The disability access-related activities required by the checklist, such as measuring door widths, counting the number of grab bars, and checking for visual and auditory fire alarms, train PISSAR patrol members in different people's needs, a training that extends far beyond concepts of "tolerance" and "acceptance." In stark contrast to "disability awareness" events that blindfold sighted people so that they can "feel what it is like to be blind" or place people without mobility impairments in wheelchairs so they can "appreciate the difficulties faced by chair users," the PISSAR patrols turn nondisabled people's attention toward the social barriers confronting people with disabilities. Rather than focusing on the alleged failures and hardships of disabled bodies—an inability to see, an inability to walk—PISSAR focuses on the failures and omissions of the built environment—a too-narrow door, a too-high dispenser. The physical realities of these architectural failures emphasize the arbitrary construct of the "normal" body and its needs, and highlight the ability of a disabled body to "function" just fine, if the space would only allow for it. This switch in focus from the inability of the body to the inaccessibility of the space makes room for activism and change in ways that "awareness exercises" may not.

Although disability "awareness" events are touted as ways to make nondisabled people recognize the need for access, we have serious doubts about their political efficacy and appropriateness. Sitting in a wheelchair for a day, let alone an hour, is not going to give someone a full understanding of the complexities and nuances of chair-users' lives. We think such exercises all too often reinforce ableist assumptions about the "difficulty" of living with a disability, perpetuating the notion of disability as a regrettable tragedy. They reduce the lives of people in wheelchairs to the wheelchair itself, distancing the bodies of chair-users from those without mobility disabilities. PISSAR, by virtue of its coalitional politics, focuses attention on the ways that a whole variety of bodies use restrooms and the architectural and attitudinal barriers that hinder their use or render it potentially dangerous.

The educational experience of being in the bathroom on PISSAR patrol, of imagining what different kinds of bodies might need to fully utilize a space, extends beyond the issue of disability access. Just as measuring the width of doors enables nondisabled people to recognize the inaccessibility of the built environment, going on bathroom patrol facilitates an awareness among non-trans and non-genderqueer folk of the safety issues facing genderqueer and trans people. As we began instituting our bathroom patrols, we had to make a variety of decisions in the interest of safety: PISSAR patrols would consist of at least three people; there would be no patrolling after dark; at least one member would wear a yellow PISSAR shirt, thereby identifying the group; and each group would ideally consist of a range of gender identities. Through this decision-making process, all of us—particularly those of us who are not genderqueer or trans-identified—increased our understanding of the potential dangers that lie in not using a restroom "properly." As empowering as our patrols sometimes feel, we have also experienced stares, some hostility, and a general public bewilderment about what our business is in that protected space. Being in groups on "official" business probably mitigated most of those risks, but the experience of entering bathrooms that we might not ordinarily enter helped us recognize the need for safety in these public/private spaces.

Thus, one of the most revolutionary aspects of the checklist is its function as a consciousness-raising tool, particularly within PISSAR's own ranks. It was not until we first began discussing the need for a group like PISSAR that one of our nondisabled members realized that the wider-doored stalls were built for wheelchairs. Another acknowledged that she had never realized how inaccessible campus and community buildings were until she began measuring doors and surveying facilities; going through the PISSAR checklist caused her to view the entire built world through different eyes. Many nondisabled people stopped using accessible stalls, realizing that they might be keeping someone with a disability from safe peeing. By the same token, one of our straight members with disabilities had always ridiculed the push for gender-neutral bathrooms until he began to understand it as an *access* issue. Realizing that gender-specific signs and expectations for single-gender use are barriers to some genderqueer and trans people's use of a space—because of the ever-present threat of harassment, violence, and even arrest—enabled him to make the connection between disability oppression and genderqueer oppression. A space for multiple identity organizing was forged. The PISSAR checklist allowed all of us to understand the bathroom in terms of physical and political access; people with disabilities and trans folk are being denied access because of the ways in which their/our bodies defy the norm.

Now picture this: a boardroom at UC-Santa Barbara, filled with the chancellor and his team of advisors. We're talking about gender and we're taking about bathrooms. We've been talking about gender for quite a while, and no one has asked for any definitions or terms. Now, with the reality of bathrooms on the table, the chancellor needs some clarification about the differences between sex and gender. What he is saying is, "What kinds of *bodies* are we talking about here?" PISSAR and the PISSAR checklists facilitate an open and impolite conversation about pissing, shitting, and the organs that do those things, right there in the boardroom. Because PISSAR is talking about something concrete—bodies, bathrooms, liability—administrators want to understand all the terms. They start to learn the issues: what exactly is preventing this otherwise accessible bathroom from being fully accessible (often something simple—and inexpensive—like moving a trash can or lowering a dispenser); why do genderqueer folks need unisex bathrooms, and what does that even entail (again, often something simple—and inexpensive—like changing the signs or adding a tampon/pad dispenser). And they learn the issues in a way that makes sense to them and that works for us politically. They are being trained by a group of folks devoted to the issue, they are being given specific details and facts, and all the work is being done on a volunteer basis by folks committed to the campus and the causes. What's more, because the realities of bathroom needs and restroom politics forced this table of administrators to ask about gender, sex, disability, barriers, and so forth, the administrators are now better equipped to tackle more abstract issues around trans and disability inclusion on campus and in the larger UC community (for example, when adding gender identity to the nondiscrimination clause happens at the state-wide level, we'd like to think our chancellor will be on board . . .)

Through the PISSAR checklist, we bring both the body and the bathroom into the boardroom. We challenge the normalizing impulse that wants to ignore conversations about attendant care or queer-bashing or inaccessibility. We refuse the expectation that chancellors' offices are places for polite topics of conversation and abstract theorizing, rather than discussions about who does and who does not have the right to pee. We demand a recognition of the body that needs assistance, the body that is denied access, and the body that is harassed and violated. And we insist on remembering the body that shits, the body that pees, the body that bleeds.

Where will you be when the revolution comes? We'll be in the bathroom—come join us there.

PISSAR CHECKLIST

Type of bathroom (circle one):   Men's   Women's   Unisex

Location of Bathroom: Bldg_____ Floor_____ Wing (east, west)_____ Room #_____

Does the bathroom open directly to the outside, or is the entry inside the building?_____

If the bathroom is inside a building, please give the closest entrance or elevator to
the bathroom_____

Your Name & Email Address_____

DISABILITY ACCESSIBILITY

1. Is the door into the bathroom wide enough? Give width. (ADA = 32 in)_____

2. What kind of knob does the door have? Circle one: Lever   Round knob   Handle   Automatic push-button
Other (specify)_____

3. Are there double doors into the bathroom? (i.e., do you have to open one door and then open another door to
enter the bathroom?)   Yes   No

4. Is the stall door wide enough? Give width. (ADA = 32 in)_____

5. What kind of latch is on the stall door?   Sliding Latch   Small turn knob   Large turn knob with lip
Other (specify)_____

6. Does the stall door close by itself?   Yes   No   Is there a handle on the inside of the door to help pull it
closed?   Yes   No

7. Measure the space between the front of the toilet and the front wall_____. If the stall is wide, with open
space next to the toilet, measure the space between the side of the toilet and the farthest side wall_____.
If the stall is a skinny rectangle, measure the width of the stall in front of the toilet.

_____

8. Are there grab bars?   Yes   No   First side bar is _____long, _____high, begins _____ from rear
wall, and extends _____ in front of the toilet. Second side bar is _____ long, _____high, begins _____ from rear
wall, and extends _____ in front of the toilet. Back bar is ___long and ____high.

9. Facing the toilet, is the grab bar on the right side or the left side of the toilet?   Right   Left   Both sides

10. How accessible is the toilet paper holder? Height_____ Is it too far from the toilet to reach without losing one's balance?   Yes   No

11. Describe the flush knob. (Is it a lever? If yes, is it next to the wall or on the open side of the toilet? Is it a center button?)_____

12. How high is the toilet seat? (e.g., is it raised or standard?) (ADA = 17–19 in)_____

13. Is the path to the toilet seat cover dispenser blocked by the toilet?   Yes   No How high is the dispenser?_____

14. How high is the urinal?_____How high is the handle?_____

15. If a multistall bathroom, how many stalls are accessible?_____

16. Is there a roll-under sink? If so, are the hot water pipes wrapped to prevent burns? (ADA = counter top no higher than 34 in)_____

17. What kind of faucet handles does the sink have?   Lever   Automatic   Separate turn knobs Other (specify)_____

18. Is there a soap-dispenser at chair height (ADA = you have to reach no higher than 48 in)?_____ A dryer / paper towel dispenser?_____

19. Is the tampon / pad dispenser at chair height? (ADA = you have to reach no higher than 48 in)

_____

20. Is there a mirror at chair height? (ADA = bottom of mirror no higher than 40 in)_____

21. Is there an audible alarm system?   Yes   No   A visual alarm system (lights)?   Yes   No

22. Is the accessible stall marked as accessible?_____

23. Is the outer bathroom door marked as accessible?_____

24. Are there any obstructions in front of the sink, the various dispensers, the accessible stall, the toilet, etc.? Please specify._____

GENDER SAFETY

25. Is the bathroom marked as unisex? Specify._____

26. Is it in a safe location? (i.e., not in an isolated spot)_____

27. Is it next to a gender-specific restroom so that it serves as a de facto "men's" or "women's" restroom?

_____

28. Does the door lock from the inside? Does the lock work securely?_____

AUNT FLO AND THE PLUG PATROL

29. Type of machine in the bathroom (circle one):   Tampon   Pad   Tampon & Pad

30. Does it have a "this machine is broken" sticker?   Sticker   No sticker

31. Does it look so rusty and disgusting that even if it works, you doubt anyone would use it?   Yes   No

32. Is the machine empty? (look for a little plastic "empty" sign)   Yes   No

33. Does it have a new full-color "Aunt Flo" sticker?   Sticker   No sticker

CHILD-CARE

34. Does the bathroom have a changing table? (Specify location)_____

DISCO QUEEN

RHANI REMEDES

My mom was a disco queen DJ, in sparkly heels, stepping out of an old Corvette. She got down with the ladies around town in San Francisco (or so I'm led to believe). She used to spin records. She met my father, who was spinning records somewhere, maybe at a place called Busby's on Polk Street, in a neighborhood that is soon to be yuppified into bland land. The last hooker bar on Polk Street just got bought out by swanky leeches, and then REALLY the last hooker bar is being turned into a church. Maybe the left-over vibes of high heels and hustling will inspire immoral desperate touching in the confession booth, even though the church won't be Catholic.

My father was probably tearing up the dance floor with one disco hit after another, while twenty-something fags, whose noses were stuffed-up turkeys on a coked-out holiday, bared themselves in un-lucid groping and sweaty handlings of each others' cocks and mouths and holes and things. My dad was probably partaking in most of this, with a Cape Cod in his hand—alcohol fever forever flowing from the bar-heavens, a waterfall. Later he would throw equipment across the DJ booth, as everyone would tell him to calm down.

It was a time when the freedom of sex was worn like a crown. You could lean in for blowjobs and drugs without being told to keep it in the dark. Or so I've been told. It was brief moment in time before the day my parents looked around them from the middle of a sad battle, wondering why all their friends were dying. And not just their friends, but a whole group of people who were hit the hardest: the freaks, the revolutionaries, the artists, the visionaries, a generation of radical queers who were supposed to be my elders.

I was born in a house in West Hollywood, in 1979. I was told that before my birth my dad and our midwife helped themselves to pre-birth drinks, vodka on the rocks. A great reason to celebrate. I can swear that at the time of my birth, the spirit of a fag who died too young jumped into my crying and resistant skin.

As I grew older, I looked for a generation ahead of me still immersed in everything queer and political, loud and bitchy, witchy and trippy. I mean, I read David Wojnarowicz and Cookie Mueller. I saw that Cockettes documentary that recently came out. But only in my head can I have the conversations I want with this generation of lost voices.

At times, in pining away for freakish camaraderie, I reached to my parents for some sort of knowledge. But my mother let the moths build dens in her gold lamé. She put women's lib and queer fun in a photo book under heavy encyclopedias in dusty boxes. She picked, with almost traditional values, muscle men on motorbikes—and weed—over pursuing a perverse life, in an attempt to look at her history as something casual. What I admired in my father, in looking for answers—or at least scouting out my options OTHER than business, college, consumerism, straight-norm hell, hollow eyes, forced smiles, strip malls, bland boring and beige, conversations that never REALLY talk about ANYTHING—is that, well, for one, he wasn't going to sell himself out for a nicer home, nicer clothes, or even nicer drugs. He was still a DJ, albeit in L.A. gaystream clubs, but he loved music and he loved making people dance. I remember him saying it didn't matter, the money, or what people thought, as long as you were true to what you believe in. (I remember him saying this at a time when he hid his queerness from his girlfriend.)

Today my father disowns me over the phone. A cut-all-ties-conversation. He tells me why he is discontented with my life. Averting success is throwing away good talent! Why haven't I finished college!? I should learn how to move myself into the marketplace! It is sad that the reasons I have admired him are the same birds of prey he scorns in me.

A TRAGIC LOVE STORY, OR THE LOVE AFFAIR AS DEFINING MOMENT, OR THE LOVE AFFAIR THAT NEVER HAPPENED

REGINALD LAMAR

I was just a painter when I met her, not a rock star. She was definitely a rock star: a radical, tattooed, motorcycle-riding, gold-teeth-wearing, political, politicized, experimental nonlinear novelist. Oh yeah, she was also a white Jewish woman in her forties. The first time I met her, she was talking about Rimbaud and Burroughs, and how her work was like theirs. I, of course, immediately asked her about drugs.

My roommate has been institutionalized four times in the last three months. He paces and makes erratic, desperate phone calls as I write this. He chooses not to take his drugs. Madness is often a choice against sedation. He was a rock star of the musician sort, moonlighting as a painter when we met in art school. I think it was that painter shit, some kind of Van Gogh complex, that kept him from his medication. Not that I'm pro-medication, but maybe if he were on medication then I wouldn't have lost him to insanity. Though, when he was taking his medication, he wasn't himself. What does it mean to lose someone?

Did I mention that I'm not a writer? I know I mentioned that I wasn't a rock star, but that was then. I was a painter, but not anymore, and definitely not a writer. She was a writer, and the coolest person that I had ever met. Maybe that's why I'm trying to write this now, not being a writer and all. When I first met Kathy, she didn't know I existed and I tried to pretend she didn't exist.

Because she was a rock star—and in case you're not clear, any novelist as badass as Kathy is a rock star. That is, a rock star as representing transgressive cultural possibilities—in art, politics, fashion, and sexuality. But I was pretending, because I'm not a star-fucker. I always wanted to be star-fucked, but I've never been in a popular band. And of course I'm not a writer, and I guess I didn't want to be a groupie. Kathy had plenty of groupies and I somehow wanted to be something more to her.

I wasted so much time pretending she didn't exist. She was so cool and I wasn't. I hadn't read all the high theory and philosophy that she had read. I was just seventeen at the time, and I didn't feel like the kind of down nigga I imagined she would want to kick it with. I didn't even listen to hip-hop. I imagined that the kind of nigga that would kick it with Kathy would be this po-mo high-culture/low-culture mix. Someone who would talk about NWA and Proust in the same sentence. I hadn't yet read Proust or even listened to NWA. I was just this little black boy from Alabama who wanted to be worldly, in San Francisco for the first time.

So I graduated from art school and moved to the East Coast—to become, well, more worldly. In fact, by the time I graduated I had already come a long way toward self-invention. I had read Proust and could quote NWA. I had a blue dreadlocks popping out of the crown of my head. I listened to opera and heavy metal and was obsessed with Hegel, Oscar Wilde, and Judith Butler. On the East Coast, I gave up painting and started a band, became frustrated, and moved back to San Francisco.

When I returned, I felt ready to pursue a relationship with Kathy. The first day I got back, I ran into this punk kid whom I had a crush on. He told me Kathy was dead. I cried, remembering the first time I met her and asked her about drugs. She talked about fucking instead. I knew I was in love.

When I first got back to San Francisco, I thought that I would see Kathy all the time. She was so much of what I thought San Francisco to be. Though she was from New York, she represented a left coast of bohemia, and intellectual, and artistic possibility. With her death, this possibility also seemed to die. The San Francisco that I had known was a romantic memory. The new world order seemed to be yuppies and live/work lofts. For the death of San Francisco, I also mourn.

I often see Kathy walking down the street. I call out her name. The woman who I think is Kathy never responds. I cry—I think in part because I wasted so much time, because she meant and means so much to me. Kathy used to say the main problem with art and politics is a lack of models. Maybe it's because they die and are forgotten. Well I will talk about Kathy and her work and her influence on me until my death, which it often feels like I'm living.

WHAT HAVE I BECOME, OR WHO AM I?

So I'm not a writer, and I used to be a painter, and I'm terrified of being a performer. When I was in art school, I did this artist-in-residency thing one summer in Skowhegan, Maine. This white woman, when she saw the art objects I was making at the time, said that she was surprised, because she'd just assumed I was a performance artist and my static work made no sense to her, because of my performative persona. I was insulted and defensive. I felt I had worked really hard to be taken seriously, intellectually and artistically. At the time, I felt it was limiting to be a Negro performer. How could I escape the white supremacist representations of blackness? How could I fully be myself in this context? How could I not just be cheap entertainment, some "nigga spectacle" for colonized white and black America? I hid from the obvious. I hid from the overwhelming task of creating myself as a performer, hid from having to use my body and all its race and gender implications. It seemed, somehow, much easier to place all that onto an object, something outside of myself. It, in fact, was easier and safer to just displace and hide. But art doesn't happen in a place of safety. Leaving painting behind, I realized that my new work would be about why I ran away from performing and my conflict with the history of African-American entertainers. I realized at some point that by being myself, fully and without compromise, I could, in some small way, disrupt this history.

Does the self exist? One of the questions Kathy would ask of her work concerned the I/eye and this question of vision of sight, "sight by which the self is known."[1] In her '70s work, the I/eye would shift. There was no fixed subject, no identity. Death, or memoriam for identity, was a constant theme. Using my body, my Negroid androgen body, I realized I didn't want to be anything. And being nothing I could embody everything.

WHITE FACE AND DISIDENTIFICATION

When I was on the East Coast, in New York in the late '90s, there was a weekly party called Squeezebox. At Squeezebox, rock music was played in a queer context, which in many ways was a revelation, given the horrific crap played in most gay and queer clubs. Also key to this context was a live band that would perform with various local and national drag queens. Though I wasn't a drag queen and didn't really identify as anything—queer or straight—I felt like I had some right to perform there, that my strange appearance and vocal abilities allowed me some magical entry into this world. Indeed, it was through Squeezebox that I discovered that heavy rock was the appropriate context for me to unleash the performer within. With heavy rock I could manifest a rage and a confrontational persona that seemed to suit me. The history of punk rock—with its political posturing—and glam, with its, well, glamour—were to be the primary tools through which I manifested my new artistic practice.

Eventually, I performed regularly at Squeezebox, but began to feel its artistic limits (very little rehearsal time with the house band, the campy drag standards, etc.). So after a short-lived band in New York, I moved back to San Francisco and started a band with my now-roommate Tracy. He had dropped out of art school and had given up painting years earlier and was in this band called The Deep Throats. When I told him I was starting a band in San Francisco, he begged me to be a part of it. What I didn't fully understand at the time was that his mental illness broke up our band. But through all of this I had found a voice as a performer. I had found a clear relationship (though often conflicted) with the audience. Longing and contempt would come to define this codependent connection between performer and audience. It was performing in white face that would highlight my critical reflections to myself and to the audience.

I picture people asking themselves questions about my motives. Is he just some weird goth? Is it a corpse-paint black metal thing? Does he want to be white? I often make jokes about wanting to look more like everyone else in my band. They're all white. But I think performing in white-face is ultimately about refusing to be a "black performer" and all the expectations that come with that label. Kathy used to say that because she was a woman, she was outside of the history of writing; that history being a dick thang where women are always subjugated. Similarly, I feel that in order to embrace my blackness as a performer, I have to disavow, to some extent, the long history of the black performers in the American and European traditions. Though there are examples of radical black performers throughout American history, they are mostly in blues and jazz, and that radicality always becomes more complicated, and often compromised, when the audience becomes predominantly white. Indeed, it is white supremacy and white spectatorship under capitalism that overdetermine the course of so much potentially radical cultural production. Certainly expectations around the performance of race and other identities continue to uphold and maintain the status quo.

Kathy use to say jokingly, "I'm Jewish and that means I'm not white." And in many ways she was right. Although no one can escape the stigma of white skin privilege or the mark of negritude, Kathy made her body a site of contestation, through body piercing, tattooing and bodybuilding. Her text was in many ways written on her body. For Kathy, and now for me, practices of the self and aesthetic practices are one in the same. Art is life and politics art. Identity is a prison.

For Kathy Acker and Tracy, with love always.

PUNCH LINE OR PUNCHING BAG?

RICHARD E. BUMP

The queer punk listserv has been a-buzz lately with folks debating the topic of bands like Turbonegro, who pose as gay, even to the point of encouraging straight guys in the audience to perform fellatio on them during their shows. See, they can "afford" to play gay 'cause it's all a sham. It's all a joke. A sure-fire laugh. A way to make your band stand out among the other all-too-similar-sounding three-chord-playing white heterosexual male punk bands. "Yeah dude, I'll go to that Turbonegro show. Ain't they the ones that let guys suck their dicks? That's fuckin' crazy shit!" The very act of pretending to be queer, in fact, underscores their hyper-heterosexuality. "I'm so straight that I can let another guy blow me." Whereas bands with actual queer performers are often mocked, ridiculed, ignored, or only booked to play queer venues or queer fests, which ultimately forces them to play to smaller audiences. This is not a new trend. Historically, "playing gay" when you're not has been the easy punch line in modern pop culture and mainstream entertainment.

I recently produced a show featuring five acts. Juha consists of two mixed-race queer guys who rap about the plight of the Palestinians, animal rights, and butt-fucking. Nomy Lamm is a queer woman who sings cabaret songs about love, revolution, and body image while playing the concertina. Ninja Death Squad is a grind/noise duo composed of a straight guy and a bi boy (both of whom are engaged to be married to women) who released a song on an earlier album called, "If God Hates Fags/I Hate God." Myles of Destruction includes one queer guy and a straight man and woman who perform a dark gut-wrenching gypsy violin song about male-on-male rape called "Mourning Sickness." I don't know the sexual identity of the three crusty kids who are in Crush.Bastard.System. All that matters is that they are good musicians. Two boys and a gurl. Definite allies.

And like the performers, the sexuality of the audience was diverse. Straight boys, bi anarcho boys, bi womyn, baby dykes, fags, etc. So I guess my point is that we can create the kind of diverse pansexual community that we want. If we don't like the scene we find, we can get off our butts and create the one we desire.

But before the show in Providence, an acquaintance of mine approached me to show me some stickers he had made that he was extremely proud of. They featured an image of two guys with their arms around each other's shoulders with the headline "JOE IS OUT OF THE CLOSET - SUPPORT GAY LIBERATION" or something like that. He had Photoshopped a picture of the guy running sound for the show that night into the cover art from a 1970s book on gay liberation. Probably a book I had read when I was a queer teen in the years right after the Stonewall Rebellion.

So at first I thought, cool. Paying homage to those who paved the way. But then he told me that it's a big joke 'cause the sound guy is really straight and the two of them were engaged in a sticker war and this, apparently, was the ultimate joke/insult/put down. Oh yeah, that's so funny. He's not really gay. It's such an old joke, and would my "friend" have thought it was as funny to put an image of me on a "Celebrate Heterosexuality" pamphlet? Probably not, 'cause what's funny about that? I mean, don't we all aspire to pass as straight?

Okay, history lesson: Perhaps the first time the word "gay" was used in a Hollywood movie . . . Cary Grant in *Bringing Up Baby* (1938), wearing a lace nightgown, is asked if he dresses like that all the time. He shouts, "No! I've just gone gay . . . all of a sudden!" See, the joke is that his character is completely het, it's just that someone mistook him as gay 'cause of what he was wearing. Side-splitting humor, right? But the ironic thing is that at the time, Cary Grant was probably involved in a loving sexual relationship with another Hollywood celebrity, Randolph Scott. Gay playing straight playing gay—very Victor-Victoria-esque. But it wasn't only a movie. It was the closeted life Cary Grant was forced to live if he wanted to be a star.

And how is it any different in the indie music scene today? If you want to make it big, then keep your mouth shut about who you sleep with. Unless, that is, you are a boy who sleeps with girls and then that's all you sing about. Go ahead, name one openly queer guy who's achieved any real lasting mass-appeal fame in punk, hardcore, or hip-hop. Sure, we can name plenty of small indie bands on indie labels that are queer or that include openly queer folks. But I'm talking about fame on the level that white hetero punk boys have achieved like those in Green Day, Blink 182, or Sum 41.

So gays have played straight for years, and that's not funny, it's sad. But when straights play gay, it's supposedly hysterical. It goes all the way back to Shakespeare and his confused gender comedies where a guy falls in love with a guy who's masquerading as a girl, or falls in love with a girl who's masquerading as a guy.

There's a commercial currently running on TV about some malt beverage or something and this dude kisses someone in the dark and he has to identify which woman kissed him by the taste of what she was drinking. Then he realizes that a bunch of women are all drinking the same beverage and they're all "beautiful" so he's confused (haha, little joke), but then he realizes that another guy is also drinking the same thing (wink wink). HAHAHA!!! Maybe he kissed a guy! The commercial closes with a wide-angle shot and everyone is cracking up. Maybe he kissed a guy—funny stuff indeed. Actually, it's just an old worn-out joke that might provoke a chuckle or two if queer people, and those perceived as queer, weren't still getting gay-bashed and killed every single day.

Punch line or punching bag? Are you laughing yet?

Back in the early days of punk there were acts like Jayne County and Divine who fucked shit up. Now we've got bands like Turbonegro playing gay.

So, while it's interesting to discuss the ramifications and cultural significance of straights "playing gay," it really boils down to how we choose to live our lives on a daily basis. We can either be part of the audience and allow others to define us, or we can take the stage and star in our own revolutionary punk rock operas. That's what my bisexual boyfriend Neil and I do every time we kiss and hold hands in a prison visiting room surrounded by armed guards, electric fences, and homophobic inmates. Sure, some folks in the room snicker and guffaw at the sight of us refusing to play straight even in that most queer-unfriendly locale, but it's simply who we are, it's not about the audience. Resisting societal expectations can be that simple. And that liberating.

Punch line or punching bag? You decide.

FED UP QUEERS

JENNIFER FLYNN AND EUSTACIA SMITH

Fed Up Queers (FUQ) was a direct action group that existed from 1998 to1999. In that time, the group engaged in close to fifty direct actions. Fed Up Queers sought to stem the tide of normalization and acceptance of the queer community, in order to make the point that our acceptance was not freedom. In fact, our acceptance was often at the expense of someone else's freedom.

This began as a dialogue between Eustacia Smith and Jennifer Flynn, two former members of Fed Up Queers. Mattilda later joined the conversation.

FUQ WHO?

Eustacia Smith: Fed Up Queers sought to up the ante of the status quo of activism by pushing the limits whenever possible, wherever possible, through acts of civil disobedience and covert actions. FUQ took action over queer issues and brought a queer voice to any other social conflicts that members were interested in addressing. Our intention was to be powerful, edgy, sexy, and subversive, pushing the gay cultural norms wherever possible, and to do this through actions, not through dialogue and process.

Jennifer Flynn: I'd have a hard time explaining the mission of Fed Up Queers. I do think there were values that we all shared—which makes sense, since we were a pretty homogenous group. The group was interesting in activist circles because, while we were mostly white, we were also mostly lower middle class. Few of us were raised particularly wealthy, but most of us went to college. We never actually discussed our shared (or not shared) values, but looking back, they were there. There were about twenty members of the group. The group was definitely not open—you had to be voted in by the whole group. Since that was one aspect of FUQ that I was definitely not comfortable with, I still find it heartwarming, and even a little subversive, when I meet people who say they were a part of FUQ. Who beyond the twenty of us actually know who was really on the official membership list? For that matter, maybe there was another official membership list altogether.

FUQ U: A BRIEF HISTORY OF FUQ

JF: You can't talk about FUQ without talking about the Matthew Shepard Political Funeral, which happened on October 19, 1998. FUQ technically started as an affinity group of the October 19 Coalition, the group that came together following the attack by the New York Police Department on eight thousand protestors who formed to march and mourn after the brutal murder of Matthew Shepard, a young gay man. A few of the organizers of the Matthew Shepard Political Funeral were also involved in the formation of FUQ. After he was brutally beaten, Matthew Shepard was tied to a ranch post and left to freeze to death. Matthew, a young, white gay man, tugged at the heart strings of many other young white gay men, who happened to have some power. Matthew's story flooded the media airwaves, and his senseless murder became fodder for the harsh reality that most of America still really hates gays. It really didn't matter if you were white, cute, and going to college. The organizers of the political funeral, whether intentionally or not, saw through Matthew's death that gay assimilation would not only hurt others, it might even backfire. Power that is handed over, conceded without demand, is always a gift that can be taken back at will.

Many veteran activists and organizers felt that the planners of the march, which drew eight thousand people with less than one week to organize, were ill-prepared for the police response. Of course, no one could have known that the police would launch a full-scale attack on the marchers. Many of the protestors hadn't been to a protest under the regime of the New York City's new Mayor, Rudy Giuliani, and they certainly weren't used to the irrational police force that he employed and encouraged.

Mattilda: It was insane how the cops did everything they could to make the march as disorganized as possible in order to make the point that the streets didn't belong to us. We'd expected maybe one thousand people and here we had ten thousand, and ten thousand people can't march on the sidewalk. But it wasn't necessarily a politicized crowd. It took the arrest of over one hundred marshals to get people into the street, then once we were in the street, the cops started arresting everyone with a red arm band (which meant you were a marshal). I remember the few marshals left hiding our armbands, and then still trying to organize the crowd. I was the one person in charge of front-to-back communication, trying to avoid arrest at all cost, and then the cops were clubbing people in the face and trampling protesters while on horseback. It was scary, though what was amazing was seeing people, who at the beginning were holding candles on the sidewalk, screaming at the cops by the end. It was a moment where mainstream gay people were politicized against police violence. I think the critiques of our lack of planning don't really speak to the action or our state of mind—we felt it was an emergency and we needed to act immediately. The activists voicing their concerns after the event were people whom the organizers had contacted, but who had chosen not to participate. There were also veteran activists saying this was the second Stonewall. It certainly was a time of extremes, and also a time when younger activists like us were coming into our own.

JF: Whether the organizers of the Matthew Shepard Political Funeral should have known better, the fact remains that the march carried baggage that the organizers wouldn't be able to shed throughout FUQ's existence.

ES: While FUQ didn't actually come to be until after the very large Matthew Shepard Political Funeral, the name had already been thought of, and there are several earlier actions that are often associated with the group. A lot of us were involved in the planned civil disobedience action where we chained ourselves across Fifth Avenue in New York City to block then-Mayor Rudy Giuliani from marching in the Gay Pride Parade. In order to infiltrate, we wore stolen T-shirts from Heritage of Pride, the organizers of the Parade, who'd invited the Mayor to march. Underneath, we wore other T-shirts highlighting the Mayor's proposals to get rid of safer sex education in New York City public schools and his policy of de-sexualizing the City by shutting down sex clubs.

JF: In August, 1998, some members/leaders in FUQ led a march in Brooklyn to protest an attack on a lesbian leaving a bar in Park Slope. This wasn't a FUQ action—in fact, it was several months before the official genesis of FUQ—but it is often called a FUQ action, and because of the racial and class tension that was growing in that area due to rapid gentrification, the anger surrounding it plagued FUQ.

Many of us were involved in ACT UP and had gotten involved in the mid-'90s. This, of course, was a little bit after that group's time in the spotlight.

In ACT UP, I remember always feeling worn down by the long meetings. I was worn down by the slowness that surrounded the process. I look back now and I realize that's what made, and continues to make, ACT UP great. But, I think that frustration was shared by many people. We got into ACT UP looking for energy, looking for sex and power, and instead we were handed the reigns of a group we didn't create, a history we didn't intimately know, and a bunch of people heavily weighted by enormous, unfathomable grief that we could never fully understand. I think I can say the frustration felt by some of us at this process, at this slowness, and frankly, while I say it guiltily, at this disappointment, actually led us to one of the shared values of FUQ: action over discussion. Unlike in ACT UP, there was no staying up all night going over the press release word by word. Instead, if FUQers were staying up all night, we were at least going to be wheatpasting flyers, spray-painting graffiti, or maybe driving all night to New Hampshire for an action.

Mattilda: Or waiting outside jail.

JF: It was the late 1990s and we kind of had that dot-com, Nike ethos of fuck planning, just do it.

Mattilda: It's funny that you talk about dot-com ethos. I don't remember being very aware of that. What I do remember is that many of the people in FUQ were professional activists working for nonprofits, who brought an in-depth knowledge of New York politics and a frenzied drive to act. I always felt that people in the group had really radical politics when it came to activism, but when it came to their personal choices outside of activism, I wasn't so sure. Some people even had corporate jobs. We all make compromises in order to survive on a daily basis, but it always disturbed me how people in FUQ didn't really integrate their radical politics into how they treated one another. FUQ always felt really competitive and hierarchical.

JF: I was a professional community organizer, and I chose that position specifically because of my radical politics. I felt then, and I actually feel even more so now, that the only way towards profound change in our society is to consistently and regularly—even through day jobs—work to transfer power into the hands of the powerless in seemingly small ways. But I, too, really question our comrades toiling for the man in the corporate elite . . . even if I was happy to meet in their conference rooms and spend their money.

We were expressing what a lot of people in society seemed to be feeling: the world was about to get a whole lot more fucked up than it was at any point in our sheltered lives. I remember when an AIDS housing activist asked me why I participated in one of our more chaotic actions. She shared a story about her experiences in the 1960s with the Weather Underground, and she tried to warn me against getting involved in something that was over my head, like so many of her friends did. I was really struggling to explain the reason for my actions, the rationale for my thinking, and all I could think was—I have to do something. Things were getting worse and maybe I didn't have the historical perspective to fully understand that things have always been bad, but I felt like it was happening on my watch. I mean, I work as an AIDS organizer. I know the incredible victories that thousands of people with AIDS, who are now dead, once fought for, and I saw the victories being dismantled and the weight of that responsibility felt enormous. And, even now, looking back, I think it was right to feel that way. Even if the tactics and organizational structure of FUQ are something about which I feel very conflicted.

ES: I think that one thing that was good about FUQ was the fast-paced turnaround. If something came up that we wanted to act on, we pretty much acted immediately, without a lot of process. This is only possible when acting in a group where you already know each other's values, strengths, beliefs, and ways of working. Even though we did not discuss and process, there was a definite understanding of our shared values. Basically, a core group of us lived, breathed, and slept FUQ.

Mattilda: In the beginning of FUQ, we were very clear about wanting to focus our energy on actions, and not trying to create an organizational structure. Some of us had gone to months of October 19 Coalition meetings to create an activist group after the Matthew Shepard Political Funeral; these meetings ultimately stalled over process. With FUQ, we tried to avoid this problem by only meeting when someone wanted to plan an action.

JUSTICE FOR DIALLO

FedUpQueers

GIULIANI OUT OF MY ASS

FedUpQueers

THERE ARE NO GOOD COPS

FedUpQueers

AN AIDS MONSTER
IS ON THE LOOSE

BEWARE OF NETTIE
MAYERSOHN

Assemblymember Mayersohn has made a political career out of feeding public hysteria about AIDS. She's behind legislation that seriously compromises the health care and confidentiality of people with HIV. Mayersohn would rather find out who has HIV than get people educated and into treatment.

FedUp Queers

BILLY JACK GAITHER
1960-1999

BEATEN to death with an axe handle.
BURNED on a pyre of tires.
MURDERED for being a gay man.
Coosa County, Alabama.

HATE & BIGOTRY KILL AGAIN

AND AGAIN	Amadou Diallo	NYPD/NYC
AND AGAIN	Matthew Shepard	Laramie, Wyoming
AND AGAIN	Patrick Bailey	Brooklyn, New York
AND AGAIN	James Byrd, Jr.	Jasper, Texas
AND AGAIN	Julio Rivera	Queens, New York
AND AGAIN	Troy Hoskins	Inwood, NYC, New York
AND AGAIN	Steve Dwayne Garcia	Houston, TX
AND AGAIN	D. Fuller/Lauryn Fuller Page	Austin, TX
AND AGAIN	unknown male in women's clothing	Houston, TX
AND AGAIN	Brandon Teena	Nebraska

POLITICAL FUNERAL BILLY JACK GAITHER

MARCH: Monday, March 15 at 6pm at Columbus Circle/59th St.
FOR INFO: call 212-618-7411 or e-mail respondtohate@hotmail.com
RESPOND TO HATE: african-americans, latinos, lesbians, gay men, and transgenders are under attack.

FedUp Queers

STOP THE HATE **STOP THE KILLINGS**

The first known AIDS memorial read "for Bobby," and existed on this block for over fifteen years. Then, the Jane Street Neighborhood Association decided to cover it up.

We will not be erased.

Fed Up Queers

ES: One thing we definitely valued was not assimilating into the mainstream of homogenous culture. We felt that most of the lesbian/gay community was headed in that direction. One of our actions that represented was our action in Provincetown, Massachusetts, against HRC, the Human Rights Campaign. HRC is a mainstream lesbian and gay political advocacy organization. They tend to advocate for things like gay marriage. We certainly did not feel like they represented us as queers or the values that we felt were important. So, we did a little redecoration of their store, both inside and out, with paint, stickers, and banners. Perhaps our stickers carry the message best of all. HRC DOESN'T SPEAK FOR ME! HRC = HOMOGENOUS RULING CLASS! HRC = HELPING RIGHT-WINGERS COPE. This action was in keeping with our original idea of covert street-art actions, where we remained anonymous as individuals.

JF: We were anonymous media whores.

ES: This action also represented the fast-paced movement that was so different than the ACT UP we had been schooled in. About half of FUQ was on vacation in Provincetown.

JF: Living large off those professional activist salaries.

ES: There was no time to wait for the next meeting to process, discuss, or get some type of approval by the whole group.

JF: Our house rental was about to run out!

ES: If you weren't there, in the moment, then you just didn't matter for that moment. You had to be there to keep up with the group, or else the group itself was not going to take the time or energy to make sure you didn't get left behind. Of course, that didn't mean that a few people weren't upset that they hadn't been consulted!

JF: I think we sort of assumed that we had more values in common than we really did. We weren't all comfortable identifying as anarchists. We said we were sex radical, but we all had radically different definitions of what that meant. We all believed that sex clubs should be open, that Giuliani's crackdown on sex shops was really just a way to get rid of queers and a way to free up the land so that the rents could be jacked up. We knew that the crackdown was just another way to get the poor out of Manhattan. But we had differences when it came to sex and gender.

Mattilda: I remember Susan Tipograph, our lawyer who'd been active since the '60s, asked us if we were anarchists, and everyone except me and one other person shook their heads no. I think we were resistant to ideology, and that was healthy, but I also think people were resistant to living outside the status quo workaday careerist world. Like what you said about identifying as sex radicals, I don't think I would have credited that to the group at all. As someone who made my living as a whore, I definitely felt separate from the rest of the group—I was certainly accepted, but that's because I didn't give people an option. When someone else—a dyke—started working at a brothel, it was a scandal.

JF: As an organizer, I should have remembered that you can't just assume that people come with a detailed political analysis. One of our first "official" FUQ actions was "Wake Up Nettie Meyersohn," who was a New York State assemblymember. She was passionate about requiring health officials to report the names of people who tested HIV+ to a State registry. Her campaign was fueled when Nushaun Williams, a young black man from upstate New York, allegedly infected over thirteen young white women. FUQ felt that names reporting was not real public health, but rather public hysteria. FUQ went to Meyersohn's home in suburban Queens at Midnight on the eve of World AIDS Day and tried to "wake her up to the issues."

Mattilda: We posted the neighborhood with flyers that said, "An AIDS Monster Is on the Loose," and showed a picture of Nettie Meyersohn.

JF: We all shared a commitment to holding on to our anger—to seeing the injustice around us. Being a mostly white group, we were aware that we could choose not to focus on certain issues.

Mattilda: I think that was one of our strengths, that we recognized our privileges as mostly white, mostly middle-class, mostly college-educated queers, and yet we decided to do things with our privilege that maybe other people might not be able to risk. After Amadou Diallo, an unarmed West African immigrant, was murdered by the NYPD [in February 1999], we had nine people who were willing to get arrested and we thought, fuck it, we're gonna take the Brooklyn Bridge anyway. We're just going to chain ourselves across and lock down. That was extremely empowering, to think that there was a state of emergency—unarmed people of color were being gunned down by the NYPD—and we had to do something, and even if there weren't many people willing or able to take the same risks as us, we were going to go with it anyway. We were going to raise the stakes. And when we ended up getting arrested—not at the Bridge, which was foiled, but after chaining ourselves across Broadway in rush hour—we did raise the stakes. Here we were, a small, mostly white queer affinity group to a larger, mostly straight and more mainstream action organized by people of color—lying down in the middle of the street because a black man had been gunned down by the NYPD, and I remember reporters looking at us completely baffled, asking why? White people weren't supposed to care. Our action really raised the stakes, pretty soon Al Sharpton was calling for mass civil disobedience.

JF: One crucial thing that we didn't agree on was our image. When FUQ was created, at least in my mind, it was supposed to act as an affinity group with its members never being known to the outside world. I thought we'd create spoof publications like *Splayed* [a satire of the *New York Blade*, which fired a reporter for being an "activist" when challenging ex-gay ministries on *Ricki Lake*], or do billboard modification or graffiti, like the Jane Street Pink Triangle Action [where we recreated the first AIDS memorial, a spray-painted pink triangle that said "For Bobby," which had been erased as part of neighborhood "beautification."] But a lot of the experience that we had in the group was actually around organizing large scale demonstrations and doing arrest scenario civil disobedience. We didn't think of it, but those actions actually went against our original idea that none of us would be exposed.

Mattilda: Originally, we decided to be a closed group so we could trust each other with covert, high-risk actions, but then we moved away from those actions—and I'm not sure we ever trusted one another.

JF: I envisioned people all over the country starting to use the FUQ logo and saying, "I'm a Fed Up Queer!" like Al Sharpton did. But somehow we didn't change with the new demands of being a group that was half exposed/half secret. We didn't change our structure from only allowing people "in" who were known to a few of us. We didn't suddenly start holding open meetings at a regularly scheduled time. I think it was this half-in-the-closet behavior, as it were, half-out, that really led to the destruction of FUQ.

WHAT WAS GOOD/WHAT WAS FUQED

JF: While FUQ had a formal start and even end, it really felt completely organic—it felt charged with sex, power, ideals, and even acceptance. I think that for some of us, FUQ was our version of queer high school. Even today, FUQ seems like the movie *Foxfire,* or one of those end-of-the-world movies where a small group of underdogs representing "good" ban together and battle evil. FUQ gave me the feeling of freedom—how fucking liberating to have a few minutes where finally we could be queer and we could be powerful.

Mattilda: FUQ was the first time when I realized how much just a few people willing to take a lot of risks could actually get done. I think it was also a turning point for me, where I transitioned from being an activist who got involved in various struggles, to an organizer who saw myself as an instigator, willing to create my own activism.

ES: The name itself is edgy. There's something about just saying FUQ loudly that feels powerful. One of our chants, I'd say our favorite was, "Fuck, fuck, fuck with us and we'll FUQ, FUQ, FUQ with you!" and we had a banner that said the same. My favorite action was the Roosevelt Hotel [where FUQ crashed the Log Cabin Republicans' conference]. It was my favorite because it was fun and represented the sheer determination to "fuck things up," so to speak. There was so much intense planning and anticipation that when things didn't work out as they were supposed to, it *was* just kind of like an explosion. And it got very sensationalized in the media. It was sensational.

The Roosevelt Hotel really exemplified the loyalty of the group. Not one of us went home that night. As people returned from the hospital [due to police and hotel security violence] were released from jail, saw the action on TV, we all came together and did jail support. At all FUQ actions, if you got arrested, you could always count on other FUQers to be waiting on the outside with coffee and cigarettes.

JF: Loyalty was definitely a shared value of FUQ. When one of our original members refused to do jail support for the Roosevelt Hotel action, that person was really moved out of the group.

ES: I would have to say that going to Tennessee to attack Al Gore and the whole campaign that followed, to expose the relationship between the U.S. Government International Trade Office and affordable access to global medicines, was our most effective series of actions. A group of us went to Tennessee and managed to be up front in a crowd of thousands in Al Gore's hometown. All of the media was already there waiting for him to announce his presidential candidacy. So it was the perfect setup, ripe for an action. Later that same day, Gore flew to New Hampshire to make his second candidacy announcement and we had a second group hold a banner right behind him in the media spotlight.

The very next morning he appeared in New York City, and we had traveled back from Tennessee and New Hampshire, and there we were, again, right in front with our placards.

We continued to follow him on his campaign trail. Then, along with ACT UP New York and ACT UP Philadelphia, we did an office takeover of the United States Trade Representative's office. Half of us climbed up the outside of the building and chained ourselves to a balcony while the other half managed to go past the and security guards and into the offices. This was a well-planned, fierce action, where the plan worked.

This entire campaign put the issue of the U.S. government's involvement with access to medicine in poor and developing countries on the global agenda and actually sparked global political change.

FED UP WITH POWER?

ES: FUQ was a group clearly powered by dykes. Although there were men actively involved in the group, the energy and force behind planning, producing, and carrying out an action was largely the women. In some ways, we all had power. It was a very powerful feeling to just act when you wanted to act—to be bold, flashy, and provocative without really thinking it through.

Mattilda: I'd spent most of my formative years surrounded by dykes, and so it made sense that there weren't many fags in a radical queer activist group, since most fags haven't even gotten to Feminism 101. Still, it was a bit alienating at times, being in a group where most of the dykes had long histories with each other, and there were constantly these insane power struggles. It was definitely some serious, dyke drama. Sometimes there'd be these crazy arguments in the meetings, and later I'd find out that the argument had more to do with who was sleeping with whom and less to do with the issues.

JF: While we were a collective, with no formal leadership, there were actually leaders who took power and even used it in really dysfunctional ways. For me, it was the first time I was free to be queer, and I hadn't learned that with that freedom comes consequences. At times, I know that I used my power in dysfunctional ways. But there was no room in FUQ to develop leadership skills, to call people out in a supportive way, to give us a safe space to talk about the ways that our group was and wasn't working. Our antiprocess process was kind of a kill-or-be-killed ethic. You either stood up, stood out, took power, or you were unimportant. We didn't exactly switch around our leadership roles so that people could learn new skills. I think some of us thought that we had been activists for so long that there were no new skills to learn. Since I've been a professional organizer for close to ten years and I'm still learning huge, enormous, new things, I guess that line of thinking was not only shortsighted and probably destructive to the group, but it was also stupid.

ES: Leadership development was something that we talked about and wanted to do, but we just moved at too fast a pace.

JF: It was that dot-com thing. It's really sad how capitalism soaks into all of our psyches, even those of us who thought we were resisting it. People have criticized FUQ by saying that we were addicted to actions. To which I say, we'd be crazy not to be addicted—the whole point of living is to be able to accept who you are and to live free—and we were getting a taste of that. So yeah, I wanted to taste that freedom over and over again.

Mattilda: I actually think people were addicted to *arrest*; I mean, I think we all recognized that arrests were crucial in order to get press, but we didn't really explore many other options. And sometimes people went overboard, like they had to get that high.

JF: I wanted to be able to feel different from everyone else—special but still safe. Another of FUQ's shared values was our intense loyalty to each other. We were loyal to each other because of that feeling of being out and proud and not in the gay card store way. In the very real and honest way that as a dyke, I never got anywhere else. Certainly not when I'm walking home with short hair or with a girlfriend. Loving that freedom is normal, and it should be part of what we are struggling towards.

IN THE END, FUQ GOT FUQED

JF: I think everyone who was involved in Fed Up Queers would agree that it wasn't a process-oriented group, to say the least. In fact, I can't even remember having a political conversation.

Mattilda: Actually, I remember that at the beginning, we had a lot of process conversations: First, over the question of whether to be an open or closed group. Then, over whether to focus on covert or mass actions. And we had several meetings about whether to consider property destruction.

JF: Also, as an almost entirely white group with increasingly tense relationships with some of the organizations that were led by queer people of color, there was a real question about whether we should even exist. Since we didn't talk to each other, we couldn't work on ways that we should be committed to being antiracist. We all were committed to being antiracist, but being white, we acted in some racist ways and there was no room within the group to help people unlearn some of those behaviors.

ES: The lack of process left us ill equipped to deal with some difficult issues that came across our plate, like what to do with money (which we got from lawsuits and even a small grant) and issues around sex and sexuality. We were faced with difficult decisions about how we defined queer. For example, there was some real tension over whether certain people were actually queer or just pretending. We were all different people with different definitions of what is radical and what is queer.

Mattilda: My breaking point was over the cliquishness of the group, how it started to feel like a dyke cult.

ES: The group was cliquish. It was a little bit like a bunch of girls in high school. At one of our last meetings, we went around the room and almost every single person said they felt like the rest of us were all friends, except for them. At the end, someone realized that if everyone had that same feeling, it couldn't be true, but people's feelings were hurt, and it was too late to really try to fix it. Also, many of us were much more interested in working on an ongoing campaign, rather than just doing flash-in-the-pan actions. So, many of us started working on the issue of trying to get medications for AIDS and other diseases to Africa and other developing nations.

JF: One of our last actions, the takeover of the U.S. Trade Representative's office, was a tough arrest. It also carried a stiffer penalty than we were used to. We had to grapple with the very real possibility that one of our members might go to prison for one year. I don't know if it was because I was getting older or if it was sinking in, but I really didn't want to do something that might cause me to go to prison. Many people in our society can't make that choice. I felt terrible—and I still feel like I am giving up, accepting the status quo—but I was and continue to be really afraid.

Many of the former FUQers keep in touch and continue to fight for social justice; they are all really committed and great people. I hope that my fear leads me to be thoughtful about how I express my anger, but that I use it to continue fighting. Staci sure does. Staci's friends have a theory that she has been arrested for political civil disobedience more then anyone else in New York City.

If you don't want whores in your neighborhood.... **THEN LEAVE.** We were here first.

GAY SHAME: FROM QUEER AUTONOMOUS SPACE TO DIRECT ACTION EXTRAVAGANZA

MATTILDA, AKA MATT BERNSTEIN SYCAMORE

Activism disappears from the public record almost as quickly as activists burn out and disappear from struggle. At the tender age of thirty, after twelve years of considering activism a central part of my life, I now find myself telling friends about actions and activist groups of which they've never heard. Sometimes there will be a shared remembrance, but all too often, I find myself struggling to remember the details of a particular action, struggling to remember my own history.

My initial drive to write about Gay Shame comes from a desire to enter it into the public record. Rarely does a participant in a particular struggle get to write his/her own history (and have her/himself as an editor), though this is an opportunity we should all enjoy. My initial impulse was to keep myself outside of this history as much as possible for fear of claiming ownership of events—though who was I kidding? "Objective" history is a cruel lie, and I'm not interested in perpetuating such viciousness.

Nevertheless, by choosing to write an abbreviated impression of each Gay Shame action rather than an in-depth analysis of a few, I do resist a stronger point of view and instead focus on generalizing statements that cannot help but hold some inconsistencies. I mean for this history to be a beginning rather than an end, an invitation for others to write their own versions of the madness and the mayhem. An invitation for others to instigate their own Gay Shame.

WHOSE QUALITY OF LIFE?

Gay Shame emerged at a very specific moment in New York City history. It was June 1998, the height of Mayor Giuliani's reign of terror known officially as the "Quality of Life" campaign, during which rampant police brutality against unarmed people of color was the norm, community gardens were regularly bulldozed to make way for luxury housing, and homeless people were losing services and shelter faster than Disney could buy up Times Square. Giuliani's crackdown also meant the policing of public sex spaces, both indoors and outdoors, and the closure of sex shops to make neighborhoods safer for gentrification, as well as the mass arrest of youth of color, sex workers, and transgendered women to make the streets "safer" for tourists and yuppies. Neighborhoods historically associated with outcasts, artists, and immigrants (Times Square, the Lower East Side, and the Meatpacking district) became destinations for cool lawyers and partying suburbanites.

Guiliani's attempts to dismantle virtually everything creative and unique about New York City took place with the direct support of many New Yorkers, including gay property owners and businesspeople in gentrification battleground neighborhoods. This was not surprising, considering the direct role gay people have long played as "pioneers" in fringe areas who ultimately make neighborhoods safer for development. Gay Shame emerged to create a radical alternative to the conformity of gay neighborhoods, bars, and institutions—most clearly symbolized by Gay Pride.

By 1998, New York's Gay Pride had become little more than a giant opportunity for multinational corporations to target market gay consumers. The goal of Gay Shame was to create a free, all-ages space where queers could make culture and share skills and strategies for resistance, rather than just buy a bunch of crap. We held Gay Shame in June of 1998, at a collective living/performance space in Brooklyn known as dumba, and it consisted of performances, activist speeches and tabling, free vegan food, and dancing. Several hundred people showed up for the festivities.

A large part of the first Gay Shame was the free 'zine that we created, called *Swallow Your Pride: A Do-It-Yourself Guide to Hands-On Activism*. *Swallow Your Pride* contained advice for stickering, wheatpasting, civil disobedience, and stenciling, as well as samples of propaganda and stories, rants and articles about sweatshops, union organizing, the crackdown on public sex, Megan's Law (mandating "sex-offender" registries), welfare "reform," fat activism, AIDS profiteering, and needle exchange.

In a New York City where a visible culture of radical queers barely existed, Gay Shame was essential in building ties between queers who might otherwise have been isolated from one another. That being said, Gay Shame was always a project that included a very specific segment of queer New York: diverse in terms of class and gender but definitely dyke centered, largely middle class, white, under thirty-five, and mostly anarchist leaning.

Gay Shame in New York inspired people to do similar types of events in other cities, many of them also using the name *Gay Shame*. Gay Shame in Toronto started one year after New York, and Gay Shame in Sweden started shortly after that. I will spend most of this piece discussing Gay Shame in San Francisco, which started in 2001, shortly after I fled New York.

SAN FRANCISCO

I returned to San Francisco because late-nineties New York offered me little more than a rabidly consumerist, commodified, careerist monoculture that drained and disgusted me. I returned to a San Francisco that mimicked all the worst aspects of New York. Entire neighborhoods had been bulldozed to make way for giant new lofts, and the radical outsider queer culture that I craved had been virtually demolished and replaced by high-fashion hipsters looking for the coolest parties.

Helping to instigate Gay Shame in San Francisco holds a central place in my struggle to create a cultural home and to find maybe a little bit of hope in a world of rot. For me, Gay Shame has been an opportunity to help build something transformative, deviant, and dangerous out of alienation and desperation.

TIRE BEACH

In San Francisco we decided to hold Gay Shame in an outdoor public space. We chose Tire Beach, a rotting industrial park on the San Francisco Bay where discarded MUNI streetcars are dumped and a concrete factory borders a small grassy area. One of our flyers sums our goals up best: "Are you choking on the vomit of consumerist 'gay pride?'—DARLING spit that shit out—GAY SHAME is the answer." We encouraged people to "dress to absolutely mesmerizing ragged terrifying glamorous excess" and to "create the world you dream of." We turned Tire Beach into our

GAY PRIDE, MY ASS

it's all **GAY** **SHAME**

about a queer autonomous space

Saturday June 16th 2pm to sunset

Tire Beach @ 24th St & the bay in sf

politics & play *food* a carnival

a freakshow performances bands

kidspace

installations djs art-making

dress to terrifying ragged excess

FREE

info & directions @ (415) 820-1411

queer autonomous space for the day, which included free food, T-shirts and various other gifts, bands, spoken word, DJs and dancing, a kidspace for children, and speakers on issues including San Francisco gentrification and the U.S. colonization of the Puerto Rican island of Vieques, as well as prison, youth, and trans activism. We encouraged people to participate in creating their own radical queer space, and people argued about political issues, painted, poured concrete and made a mosaic, dyed hair, and mudwrestled naked. We organized the event in less than a month, and several hundred people trekked out to Tire Beach to join in the festivities.

In San Francisco, we structured Gay Shame in a similar way to New York, though we had two stages and an insane number of bands. Like in New York, people tabled for political causes on the outside of the stage areas, and speakers addressed the crowd in between performers and bands. We were able to attract several hundred participants in a few weeks time because San Francisco, unlike New York, harbors a large number of queers (mostly dykes and trannyboys) who are drawn to outsider culture. The downside is that there exists a trendiness to a radical queer aesthetic and a scene of apathetic queer hipsters. What happened at Gay Shame is that, in spite of our efforts to create a politicized space, many participants were rude to the speakers and seemed uninterested in anything beyond partying and socializing with their friends. We realized that, as organizers, by separating the "politics" from the "partying," we unwittingly helped participants ignore our radical intentions. We resolved to be more confrontational in the future, to ensure that our political agenda would remain clear.

Here is where writing "history" becomes difficult. When I say we resolved to be more confrontational in the future, I created a false sense of unity. Though Gay Shame reached consensus to develop more confrontational actions in the future, there has always been a tension between the party and the politics.

THE GAY SHAME AWARDS

In 2002, the San Francisco Pride Committee adapted Budweiser's advertising motto for the official Pride theme. "Be Yourself—Make It A Bud" became "Be Yourself—Change The World." After intense discussion among Gay Shame organizers, we decided to directly confront the Pride Parade. We started planning early—over two months beforehand—and were looking for a way to get people excited. We created the Gay Shame Awards, where we would reward the most hypocritical gays for their service to the "community." We sought to expose both the lie of a homogenous gay/queer "community" and the ways in which the myth of community is used as a screen behind which gay people with power oppress others and get away with it.

We decided to hold the Gay Shame Awards one month before Pride at Harvey Milk Plaza, the symbolic heart of the whitewashed gayborhood that is San Francisco's Castro district. We bestowed awards in eight categories: Exploiting Our Youth, Helping Right-Wingers Cope, Making More Queers Homeless, Best Target Marketing, Best Gender Fundamentalism, Best Racist-Ass Whites-Only Space, the "In" Awards (Celebrities Who Should Have Never Come Out of the Closet), and the Legends Award (Straight Allies of Reactionary Gays). As with any awards ceremony, we created an official program (complete with a smiling Elton John on the cover) that listed the nominees in each category and also contained a glimpse into some of our discussions as organizers.

For the official Gay Shame Awards ceremony, we built a wooden stage so that attendees could see the ceremony better, and also so we would have leverage in case we were attacked by angry gays. By the time we started, Harvey Milk Plaza was packed with attendees, and people were soon spilling into the street. Gay Shame participants served free food and gave out homemade patches and artwork, Gay Shame buttons with the image of Rosie O'Donnell or George Michael, and various other delicacies. As requested, people dressed to excess, in exaggerated, smeared makeup and glitter, torn ball gowns, and crumpled dress shirts. One participant wore a dress made entirely out of shopping bags—the Gap, Starbucks, Abercrombie & Fitch, and other gay mainstays—and stilt walkers dressed in garbage bags added to the festivities.

A different person announced each category and award winner, and at the drumroll, we burned a rainbow flag. This was the point when we were worried that we'd be attacked by angry gays, but instead the crowd reacted in jubilation, yelling, "Burn baby burn." As the award ceremony came to a close, people discreetly moved sofas and the sound system into the middle of the street, and the crowd followed. On went the music as people danced, pranced, and romanced in the streets. This was a fiery moment—I think we were a little in disbelief that it had all gone so smoothly. As police negotiators handled the cops, we held Castro and Market streets for several hours before packing up, with no arrests.

The Gay Shame Awards marked a turning point for Gay Shame, where we morphed from a once-a-year festival of resistance to a year-round, direct action extravaganza. But we didn't yet know this. What we did know is that we had succeeded in inseparably connecting the spectacle with the politics. The crowd included many queers, both a generation older and a generation younger than us, and even straight tourists gaped in disbelief and wondered, Is it always like this?

BUDWEISER PRIDE

San Francisco's Pride Parade, perhaps the largest in the world, consists of a gated, endless procession of floats and close to a million bystanders. In preparation for our Pride confrontation, we discussed the feasibility and effectiveness of attempting to block the Parade and eventually decided, instead, to set up our festival of resistance in the middle of the Parade and from there bestow awards upon various contingents. We collected sofas, tables, and other discarded furniture to install in the middle of the Parade so that we could not be easily removed. We also created a seven-foot-tall, cardboard Budweiser can that read "Vomit Out Budweiser Pride and the Selling of Queer Identities" and a large closet, so that people could put their patriotism back where it belonged. Just in case people wouldn't have time to reach the official Budweiser Vomitorium, we also created official Gay Shame vomit bags, which described our three primary targets: the consumerism, blind patriotism, and assimilationist agenda of the Pride Parade.

Our plan was to meet at the very end of the Parade route, where the floats disembarked (the only part without police barricades around it), and to enter the Pride Parade and install ourselves within. Gay Shame organizers met early on the morning of the Pride Parade and prepared to move all of our props, which required two vans. We arrived at Ninth and Mission streets, a block from our destination, to a cheering crowd standing confused on the side of the road. As the festivities commenced, the people in charge of scouting made a last-minute decision to change our route, and we arrived at the end of the Pride Parade on the wrong side of the barricades. To our surprise, volunteer Parade Marshals began to shove Gay Shame participants and even instigated the police against us. In the resulting commotion, one participant accidentally spilled coffee on a police officer and was targeted by the cops, grabbed, and restrained. After the crowd rallied to her side, she was handcuffed, dragged half a block, and thrown into a Burger King, which the police

commandeered as an impromptu headquarters. In the course of this person's arrest, another Gay Shame protester was thrown into a waiting police van.

As these two participants were dragged off to jail, Gay Shame organizers realized that we had failed to plan for the worst-case scenario. In fact, we had specifically assumed that the Pride Committee would not want to have us arrested. How would it look, queers being dragged off for attempting to "join" the Pride Parade? We soon found out that this concern was not high on the Pride Committee's list of priorities. Several organizers went with a lawyer to the jail, and the rest of us installed ourselves outside the Parade barricades. Our festivities continued, but we lost our momentum as a group and were confused as to how we should proceed in order to maximize confrontation. We attempted to bestow awards upon various contingents—a rainbow nightstick for the gay cops, a Greyhound ticket for Mayor Willie Brown (his famous quote was "If you can't afford to live in San Francisco, you should leave"), and a closet for the Human Rights Campaign (HRC), an elite gay lobbying group.

PROP N STANDS FOR NIGHTMARE: GAVIN NEWSOM'S QUALITY OF LIFE CAMPAIGN

As Halloween approached, a scary monster spread its tentacles to target the most vulnerable San Franciscans. This monster was Supervisor Gavin Newsom, the city council member representing San Francisco's richest district, including the posh neighborhoods of Pacific Heights and the Marina. Gavin Newsom proposed a ballot measure for the 2002 election, Proposition N, cynically known as Care Not Cash, which aimed to slash homeless people's General Assistance checks from the already paltry amount of $322 to the preposterous amount of $59 a month. The missing $300 would be replaced with "care."

As the election approached, several groups prepared actions in opposition to Gavin Newsom's brutal Proposition N, and Gay Shame originally intended to create a spectacle that would enhance the effectiveness of these actions. As it turned out, we ended up with our own event, which we called "Prop N Stands For Nightmare: A Pre-Halloween Festival of Resistance." This marked a broadening of the Gay Shame agenda, from focusing primarily on the rabid assimilationist monster of Gay Pride to challenging all hypocrites and, specifically, to confronting the racist policies of a "gay friendly" politician.

We decided to install ourselves on the stretch of Fillmore Street where Newsom ran five businesses at the time: his campaign office, two restaurants, a bar, and a wine store. We planned to build a Haunted Shantytown and hold the Exploitation Runway, where past, present, and future greats of local, national, and international exploitation would . . . take it to the runway. In order to avoid the problems of our Pride action, we planned for the Marina action in anticipation of arrests, with a civil disobedience structure that included front, back, and side marshals, police liaison, communications people, emergency decisionmakers, and emcees. We gathered in a park a short distance from Gavin Newsom's campaign headquarters and planned to march en masse, taking the street and blocking the intersection in front of the campaign headquarters. We wheat-pasted and flyered for a month in advance of the action and anticipated a large crowd.

When we arrived in the Marina, the crowd was not as large as we had expected, but people were spirited. Though cops forbade us from taking the street, we nonetheless did so smoothly and without incident once we neared our destination. We then rolled out a "bloody" carpet and held the Exploitation Runway in the middle of bustling Fillmore Street. This was a scripted event in which impersonators of key exploiters walked the runway in several categories, including Gentrification Realness (Old School and New School), More Blood For Oil, Displacement Divas, Gavin Authenticity, Luxurious Liberals, and Eviction Couture.

The Marina action was another example of how our spectacle served to draw people in rather than alienate them, which became apparent when Marina yuppies gathered around to observe our glamour, and we distributed a pamphlet that exposed the lack of care in "Care Not Cash." Nonetheless, the cops consistently harassed us, and we made an emergency decision to take the runway up to Pacific Heights and confront Newsom at a nearby campaign function. In retrospect, we probably could have held the street much longer, but our frantic decision turned out to be the most beautiful and symbolic moment of the evening, as one hundred fifty or so of us pushed the sound system and our shantytown up a steep incline and marched up to Pacific Heights, the richest part of San Francisco.

When we arrived at our destination, a temple where Gavin Newsom was holding a public forum, we were told that he was not, in fact, speaking. As the cops began to shove people, we retreated to the other side of the street, realizing only later that this had been the exact moment

Prepare for

The

Exploitation

Runway

Dress to absolutely terrifying,
devastating ragged excess

In the spooky Marina District

Friday October 25ᵗʰ at 5:30 pm sharp

Webster x Chestnut Streets

415-540-2947

gayshamesf@yahoo.com

PROP N STANDS
FOR NIGHTMARE:
A PRE-HALLOWEEN
FESTIVAL OF
RESISTANCE

GAY SHAME
THE VIRUS IN THE SYSTEM
ALL ARE WELCOME!!!

when Newsom had arrived. When we returned to the temple side of the street, police informed us that we were too late to attend the forum.

POLITICAL FUNERAL

Just one week after the Marina action, Gay Shame scrambled together a "Political Funeral For Murdered Queers: Gwen Araujo and Jihad Alim Akbar." Araujo, a seventeen-year-old trans-gendered Latina, was bludgeoned and then strangled to death by four men at a party in Newark, California, after they discovered she was transgendered. Akbar, a twenty-three-year-old gay black Muslim man was shot dead at point blank range by SFPD officers after he reportedly bran-dished two butcher knives he'd removed from the kitchen at Bagdad Café, a popular Castro dis-trict restaurant. Gay Shame held our political funeral outside Bagdad Café, one month after Araujo's murder. We felt that a percussion protest was necessary because most protests of Araujo's murder had been quiet, and no protests of Akbar's murder had taken place. We wanted to call attention to both the extreme transphobia that still exists in the Bay Area and to the blatant racism of the SFPD.

About a hundred people gathered at 5 PM on November 3, 2002, with drums, whistles, home-made instruments, air-raid sirens, and other noisemaking devices. We marched down Eighteenth Street with torches, all the way to the Valencia police station. Though we were prepared for potential conflict with the cops, we encountered no police whatsoever until we reached the sta-tion. This was clearly a conscious decision on the part of the SFPD, due to nervousness regarding public scrutiny of their murderous behavior. Though we had little time to plan the action, the act of noisemaking worked to make the action angry, confrontational, and even festive. When we reached the police station, we made as much noise as possible for thirty minutes or so, which rat-tled the five or ten police officers who had been ordered to stand outside the police station entrance without riot gear.

Though we lacked a closing ritual, the political funeral felt powerful. The sad thing, howev-er, was that several people at the protest voiced their concerns about our outrage at the murder of Akbar. They echoed the media argument—he was armed and black, and therefore he deserved to die. This tacit racism was precisely what we were attempting to illuminate by linking the murders of Araujo and Akbar.

THE WAR

As the U.S. drew closer and closer to war with Iraq, Gay Shame found ourselves necessarily drawn to antiwar organizing. Mostly, our participation as a group involved collaborating with organizers—or disorganizers—of the breakaway marches that occurred at each large mainstream antiwar demo. Though we were appalled by the impending war, what seemed just as appalling was the spectacle of 100,000 people marching down the street and doing nothing to destabilize or confront the actually machinery of war or the ways in which the war serves U.S. consumerist needs.

Participation in the breakaway marches carried with it both a sense of empowerment and powerlessness. The large mainstream antiwar demos served as a cover for a little bit of mayhem and property destruction, of which most of us wholeheartedly approved. Nonetheless, the mostly straight white male organizers of these marches often carried with them a certain militaristic fetishism and didn't mind putting other participants at unnecessary risk. This was most apparent when so-called Black Bloc participants would throw rocks at stores from the back of a crowd of over a thousand people, and the police would charge those in front.

For the February 16, 2003, breakaway march, Gay Shame was ostensibly collaborating with antiwar organizers, and initially this march proceeded along its planned route, but soon it devolved into a police riot against peaceful protesters as we were surrounded by the cops, and many of us were beaten, strangled, or trampled by police on horseback. Dozens of protesters were arrested and nine, including several Gay Shame participants, were held in jail for three days to two weeks. In a city overwhelmingly against the war, why was the supposedly progressive district attorney holding nine antiwar protesters on inflated felony charges? Clearly, this was an intimidation tactic geared toward silencing any opposition more radical than a permitted march through an abandoned downtown.

There was some disagreement within the group regarding the amount of energy we were expending trying to secure people's release from jail. We had never met many of the arrestees, but we found ourselves doing most of the work to get them out of jail. In addition, since one Gay

Shame protester's nine-day stay in jail resulted from police surveillance at a previous demo, many questioned our association with the so-called Black Bloc, media demon and FBI darling.

THE EAGLE

The manager of the Eagle, a San Francisco bar traditionally catering to white leathermen (though reinventing itself on certain nights as a space for bands to perform and fans of all genders and sexualities to attend), approached one Gay Shame organizer with the offer of a benefit. This was controversial since, for many, the Eagle—a gay white male space that was notoriously misogynist and racist (like virtually any gay bar)—represented exactly what Gay Shame was formed to critique. Nevertheless, we agreed to hold the benefit, since many of us had spent money on various costs associated with demos (photocopying, van rental, paint, etc.).

Though financially successful (Gay Shame raised $1,200), the Eagle benefit brought up deep divisions within the group. At the benefit, it came to our attention that our good friend Gavin Newsom was having his own benefit one week later at the LGBT Center. While I attempted to announce this illustrious occasion, called "Hot Pink," over the sound system, Eagle staff turned off the microphone, telling me that I was too loud, my queeny voice was too irritating. Louder and more irritating, apparently, than three bands. I explained that this benefit was more than just an opportunity to make money for their bar—we wanted to promote our actions. I was told, "You need to stop prancing around in here." Later in the night, the manager of the bar came up to me and explained that they did not allow people to announce outside events. When I expressed my disagreement with this fictitious policy, he picked me up and pushed me out the door.

For many of us, the Eagle incident was a blatant example of why Gay Shame needed to be challenging discriminatory policies at bars instead of throwing parties there. Nevertheless, many regular patrons of the Eagle within Gay Shame were extremely resistant to confronting the long history of misogyny and femme-phobia at leather bars, claiming, "They're part of our community." Since we had formed Gay Shame specifically to critique those within our so-called "community," hearing such rhetoric was particularly disconcerting. This issue became extremely volatile, and it was clear that we would not reach a satisfying consensus. Three people went to the Eagle to talk to the manager, and he seemed to lack any understanding of the bar's history of exclusionary and hostile policies toward queens, women, and people of color. Though he did express some vague regret, he seemed to think that he was just a big guy and that was how big guys behaved.

HOT PINK

A week after the Eagle festivities, we held a small protest outside of Gavin Newsom's benefit for the LGBT Center. Newsom's fundraiser was nothing more than a straight politician's attempt to pander to San Francisco's gay elite in order to bolster his looming mayoral campaign against several gay candidates. Our flyers read, "Gavin Newsom Comes Out Of The Closet—As A Fascist!" We gathered not only to protest Newsom's closeted right-wing agenda but also to call attention to the hypocrisy of the Center for welcoming Newsom's dirty money instead of taking a stand against his blatantly racist and classist politics.

With about forty people in attendance, the Hot Pink protest was perhaps our tamest. To be sure, we dressed for the occasion in numerous hot pink atrocities, but we had little time to plan much more than a banner drop and flyer, though one flourish included handing out hot pink bags of garbage to smiling patrons. Attendees, thinking perhaps we were a part of the festivities, even agreed to pose for pictures while holding the delicately arranged trash.

In spite of the tame nature of our protest, police officers—called by "our" Center—were there to greet us when we arrived, over an hour before the start of the fundraiser. Perhaps this protest would have gone unnoticed by the San Francisco public if not for the brutality of the SFPD. As soon as Gavin Newsom arrived and was escorted inside, the police started to get rough with us. I was thrown face first into the middle of oncoming traffic and was saved only by another Gay Shame participant (my first boyfriend) who caught me; we tumbled into the middle of the street. After the two of us were dragged into a police van, one of the same police officers who originally hit me from behind swung his police baton at another Gay Shame participant, shattering one of her teeth and bloodying her entire face. Four of us were arrested; one arrestee was put into a chokehold until he passed out.

The press loves blood, and the spectacle of the SFPD bashing queers outside of San Francisco's LGBT Center was not lost on local media. Pictures of the police violence became cover stories in both gay papers, and even corporate newspapers, as well as on network news channels. With the arrests of antiwar protesters ten days later, we were unable nonetheless to use this public outcry much to our advantage in indicting either the police or the Center. Those arrested at the Center were held in jail for up to three days and faced charges as ridiculous as assault on a police officer (four counts for me) and felony "lynching," an antiquated term for removing someone from arrest. Our court cases lasted eight months and charges were only reduced to infractions after our publicized subpoena of Gavin Newsom.

WAITER, THERE'S A WAR IN MY SOUP

Gay Shame participated as an affinity group in the mass direct action organized for the day the war against Iraq began. Our goal was to block a specific exit ramp from the highway, and on March 20, 2003, we gathered furniture, a refrigerator, huge pieces of metal, and construction barricades for this purpose. Nonetheless, we were unable to secure the ramp for long and, instead, turned into a roving band of marauders, supporting various affinity groups throughout the city, including one outside the notorious Bechtel corporation, which had just won a $680,000,000 contract to rebuild the Iraqi oil fields after the war. This day of civil disobedience was successful in shutting down the city, but clearly it came too late to have any effect on the war. The next several days, however, were a volatile time of public protest and the mass arrest of over 2,000 protesters—though, perhaps, these arrests could have been more effective if they'd occurred earlier. The crackdown was shocking; police helicopters flew overhead all night and protesters were thrown into police vans for marching *on the sidewalk*. It seemed that the war had broken out in San Francisco as well.

GAY SHAM

Just days after the war broke out, a few Gay Shame organizers from San Francisco and another few from New York participated in a conference held at the University of Michigan calling itself "Gay Shame." Though the conference used the name of our activist group, we were the only activist-specific panel. It was obvious to us that we were a fetish object called on for a few realness points, and we arrived at the conference ready to stimulate a debate on this blatant appropriation.

At our panel, titled for us "Gay Shame Activism," we proposed a critique of the conference that involved an invocation of the Reagan-era doctrine of trickle-down economics, which professed that when the rich got richer, eventually the money would trickle down; the poor would pick up the pennies on the sidewalk and buy houses with them. Of course, trickle-down economics really meant that the rich got richer by looting the poor and seizing anything of value that they could get their hands on. The Gay Shame conference, we explained, was *trickle-down academia*, by which academics appropriate anything that they can get their hands on—mostly people's lived struggles, activism, and identities—and claim to have invented them.

We pointed out that part of our group process is to critique every flyer and to make sure that our political agenda is represented, and we questioned whether the conference's publicity for the Gay Shame Conference was purely sensational. We also pointed out that there was a typo on the conference literature, resulting in an extra *e* in the second word: "Gay Shame" should read "Gay Sham." We spent most of our panel talking about the history of Gay Shame, both in New York and San Francisco.

Immediately following our panel began a panel called "Fuck Activism?" Clearly, the conference was organized in such a way that one activist panel in an entire weekend was still too threatening without immediately questioning the validity of activism altogether. After this panel, there was a surprise question-and-answer section during which famous academics literally stood up and started screaming at us. Much of this screaming was unintelligible, but one person likened us to Dick Cheney, implying that by critiquing the academy we were furthering the work of the Christian Right. Clearly, this was a flimsy attempt to shut us up. Another person said that this conversation about appropriation had happened thirty years ago, a not-so-subtly ageist remark to "put the kids in their place."

Disciplines like queer theory and cultural studies emerged to address the wrongs of earlier disciplines like anthropology and sociology, specifically the eurocentric model of educating "savages" and "discovering" their cultures. What is frightening is the ways in which these new disciplines have become edge-trendy, elitist ways to continue the same questionable practices. By critiquing the ways in which the Gay Shame Conference appropriated the idea of Gay Shame without the politicized activist content, we expected to engage critically with academics. Personally, I expected everyone to nod their heads in agreement, maybe write a few clever papers and then fail to apply what we were saying on any level. Instead, we were met with shouting and blatant attempts to immediately silence us. The level to which academics seemed unwilling to engage in critical thinking was somewhat shocking. Sometimes, I compare the experience of the Gay Shame Conference to getting bashed outside of the LGBT Center. No one at the University of Michigan physically attacked us, yet the unwillingness of conference organizers to hold themselves accountable for their appropriation felt eerily similar to the Center's unwillingness to take responsibility for allowing queers to get bashed on its doorstep.

THE WALK OF SHAME

For the second Gay Shame Awards, we wanted to take the ceremony further and actually confront some of the award winners. Originally, the idea was to organize a "Walk of Shame" through the South of Market (SOMA) district to confront gay leather bars and sex businesses on their blatant racism, misogyny, and transphobia. This became controversial for some who thought that we shouldn't be focusing our attention on establishments where we were supposedly welcome, but should instead shift our attention once again to the Castro. Furthermore, we wanted to ensure that there would be a crowd of people in our path, since SOMA streets are generally empty, whereas the Castro is packed.

For the Second Annual Gay Shame Awards we added numerous categories: the Commodification of the Male Gays, Propagation of Lesbian Bed-Death, Wargasm Award, Our Favorite Lofts, Best Front Row Seat to Watch Police Brutality, Model Minority Award, Gay for Pay Award, Racial Profiling Award, and the Auntie Tom Award (For Gay Allies of Reactionary Straights). The 2003 theme for the Pride Parade was the inspirational "You Gotta Give Them Hope," a patriotic call to arms masquerading as a Harvey Milk quote, and so we added the Hope Award. Our ceremony began in front of the beautiful LGBT Center, winner of the Lifetime Achievement Award for succeeding in bashing queers in one short year of existence. Putting together the Gay Shame Awards was somewhat of a struggle due to lack of organizer initiative, and so we were surprised to see our largest crowd since the first Gay Shame Awards.

For the Walk of Shame, we created actual awards, such as a rainbow chastity belt for the Propagation of Lesbian Bed-Death, a rainbow phallus as the Gender Fundamentalism Award, and a framed picture of Dan White, the murderer of Harvey Milk, as the Auntie Tom Award. We were surprised to find that we were actually able to negotiate with the cops to march down an entire side of Market Street, San Francisco's main thoroughfare. Along the way, we bestowed awards upon deserving businesses. As expected, onlookers stared at us with a combination of bemusement and dismay as we made our way to Eighteenth and Castro streets, to the front of Harvey's, the bar named after Harvey Milk and owned by a staunch supporter of Gavin Newsom. The highlight of the ceremony was when we burned an effigy of Newsom in the middle of Eighteenth Street and people danced in jubilation as the effigy burned all the way to the ground, and a fire truck arrived to disperse us.

Though some of us were initially upset at our decision to choose the easier targets in the Castro over the more complicated targets South of Market, the Walk of Shame, similar to the first Gay Shame Awards, was the action where we were most successful in blending the energy of the crowd with our spectacle as organizers. Perhaps this was because radical queers, ironically, found themselves more comfortable in the gayborhood.

PRIDE

At one point during our planning of the Gay Shame Awards, it seemed likely that we as a group did not have the energy or commitment to create something as grand as the Walk of Shame, and we agreed on doing a smaller action at the Pride Parade, a judging booth for floats. This was a hasty choice and did, in fact, contradict an earlier decision to avoid an action at Pride. Nevertheless, after the success of the Gay Shame Awards, several people were motivated to do a second action two days later. The plan called for people to meet near the end of the Parade route, though the meeting place stretched an entire block and people had difficulty finding one another. At the last minute, when participants learned that Gavin Newsom was actually marching in the Parade, several activists jumped over the barricade, ahead of Newsom's contingent. This resulted in Newsom supporters attacking Gay Shame activists and ensuring the arrest of eight people, who were then held several days on ludicrous felony charges. Those of us not participating in this action immediately scrambled to gather legal support for an action that we had not planned. Luckily, we were able to create enough of a scandal that charges were dropped against all arrestees upon their release from jail.

PROCESS, PROCESS, PROCESS

In the first two years of Gay Shame's existence in San Francisco, we managed to operate on a loose consensus structure without engaging in endless conversations as to who we were or what we stood for. To be sure, many actions involved intense disagreement and even bitterness, but somehow we lasted two years without experiencing a stall in process. During our antiwar actions, Gay Shame meetings swelled from about five to fifteen participants to thirty or forty. At times, we would arrive at meetings and there would be fifteen people whom no one had ever met before. In order to run the meetings more smoothly, we initiated a more formal consensus process and a more organized system of facilitation. Though this failed to please everyone, we were still able to continue our weekly, open meetings without major incident.

We also decided, both for security reasons and in order that no one be identified as a "leader" of Gay Shame, to call ourselves "Mary" when speaking with the press. This was one example of the creativity and sense of humor that Gay Shame lent to serious concerns of security and accountability. By calling ourselves Mary, not only were we invoking a camp queer history and spoofing media concerns about authenticity, but we also developed a way to endlessly amuse ourselves with new Mary names: Mary Poppers, Mary Calendar, Mary Nigger, Mary Tyler Mutiny . . .

Like the arrestees at antiwar demos, most of the arrestees at the Pride Parade were people whom Gay Shame organizers had never met, and many were even from out of town. Upon release from jail, one Gay Shame organizer decided to call a press conference for the following day. This was a departure from Gay Shame process, since in the past we had only conducted press conferences in order to get people out of jail.

The press release stated, "Queer Community Unites Against Newsom," and at the press conference arrestees and the Pride Committee President spoke of their anger at Newsom's policies of targeting poor and homeless San Franciscans. One participant repeatedly identified his legal name for the press. To many Gay Shame organizers, the message of "queer unity" at this press conference directly contradicted everything we sought to represent—the resulting controversy exposed fundamental disagreements within the group about issues of accountability and even arguments over the core values of Gay Shame. Though we started Gay Shame to expose the idea of a queer community as a lie that serves only those with the most privilege, increasingly it seemed that many within Gay Shame were questioning this confrontational stance.

Over the next two months, virtually every Saturday meeting was spent arguing over process. After much discussion, and the first block of consensus in our entire two years, we agreed not to hold emergency press conferences unless someone was in jail, and we clarified our commitment to identify ourselves as "Mary" to the press. We also came up with a list of "Points of Unity," though many of these were so contentious that in the resulting document, it was unclear whether we were saying anything at all.

Another concern that arose during our process period involved one of the nominees in the Model Minority Award category of the Gay Shame Awards, the black gay hip-hop group Deep Dickollective (D/DC). The nomination stated, "[we nominate] Deep Dickollective for being radical enough to stay trendy but not enough to question their own masculinity or resist marketing themselves to a largely white audience." This was the only nominee at the Awards to solicit boos from the audience. The audience critique centered around the fact that Gay Shame, a mostly white group, was criticizing an independent (and popular) queer black artist collective. The irony, of course, was that the most vehement proponents of this nomination were two black Gay Shame organizers, one of whom had been part of D/DC.

Several questions emerged: Is a Gay Shame Award successful if people within our social circles are upset? How can a mostly white group responsibly critique the hypocrisies of "progressive" queers of color? Are Gay Shame Awards a measure of infamy or an invitation to discussion? Within a mostly white radical queer activist group, what space exists for people of color to critique other people of color? Would rejecting the nomination of Deep Dickollective have silenced people of color, specifically black males, within Gay Shame? And, of course, an old favorite, one that had plagued us since the very beginning of Gay Shame: Who is "our community?" Is there a contradiction between creating a culture of resistance and allowing some queers to be exempt from criticism?

MARY FOR MAYOR

As part of Gavin Newsom's mayoral campaign in 2003, he introduced Proposition M, which sought to ban all forms of panhandling (except, of course his own panhandling to the rich). As the election loomed, and Newsom held an enormous lead in public opinion polls, Gay Shame came up with the Mary for Mayor Campaign, in which a new candidate—Mary—entered the mayoral race and delivered a truly radical platform that included converting all members of the SFPD to nutritious compost, supporting terrorism in all forms, and advocating forced relocation of loft condominium owners into the San Francisco Bay. In addition to a fictitious candidate with grandiose plans, we created numerous organizations who wholeheartedly supported Mary in her campaign: Terrorists Against Gavin (TAG), Fashionistas Against Gavin (FAG) and Riffraff Against Gavin (RAG). TAG resurrected the image of Patty Hearst, a.k.a Tania, in the 1970s Symbionese Liberation Army, gun in hand, and FAG pronounced: "Gavin Newsom is *so* last season."

The Mary for Mayor action included all of the Gay Shame hallmarks. First, a festival of resistance, this time outside a Gavin Newsom fundraiser in the heart of the theater district. Second, a ceremony, in this case the delivery of Mary's platform, including a campy theme song resurrected from mid-1990s club culture ("Tyler Moore/Mary"). Third, elaborate and disastrous costumes that included construction site material, bloody underwear, and a stuffed snake. Fourth, a 'zine that detailed both the vicious platform of Gruesome Newsom and the liberatory absurdity of Mary's largesse. Fifth, the usual assortment of hand-painted signs, free food, and banners and buttons. And sixth, an event that markedly differed both in scale and scope from our original intentions.

The Mary for Mayor Campaign Kick Off commenced down the block from the Newsom fundraiser. The police had already arrived in order to prevent us from moving closer, and immediately threatened confiscation of the sound system and the arrest of anyone who disobeyed their orders. Of course, we quickly took to the street, blocking traffic in front of the gala, and then when cops began to surround us we moved a block away, in front of the luxurious and fashionable Clift Hotel. We finished our ceremony in the middle of the street, occupying the whole block for over an hour while burning effigies, delivering Mary's platform, attempting to enter the Clift Hotel, and—of course—dancing, prancing, and romancing.

The Mary for Mayor Campaign Kick Off was both more and less participatory than any of our previous events. We recruited people on the spot to improvise Mary's campaign pronouncements,

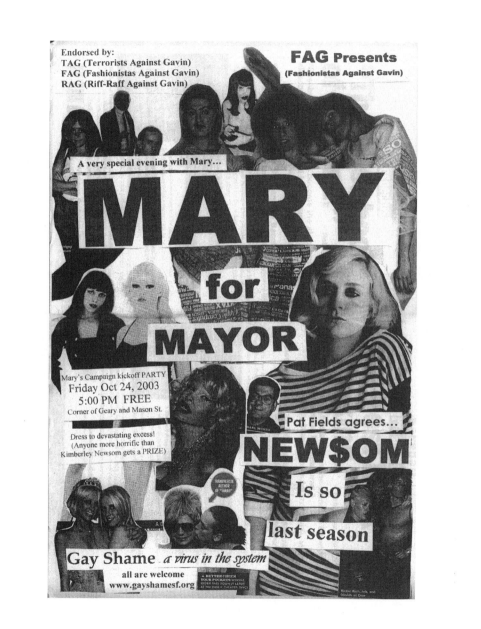

Endorsed by:
TAG (Terrorists Against Gavin)
FAG (Fashionistas Against Gavin)
RAG (Riff-Raff Against Gavin)

FAG Presents
(Fashionistas Against Gavin)

A very special evening with Mary...

MARY
for
MAYOR

Mary's Campaign kickoff PARTY
Friday Oct 24, 2003
5:00 PM FREE
Corner of Geary and Mason St.

Dress to devastating excess!
(Anyone more horrific than
Kimberley Newsom gets a PRIZE)

Pat Fields agrees...

NEW$OM
Is so
last season

Gay Shame *a virus in the system*
all are welcome
www.gayshamesf.org

and encouraged the crowd to join us in everything from blocking the street to doing runway outside the Clift Hotel. Nonetheless, most members of the crowd seemed more resistant than ever to joining the festivities and preferred to watch from the sidewalk. We struggled, as organizers, to empower the crowd to engage in the same level of risk taking as we did. By the time we marched through the Tenderloin to City Hall, our numbers had dwindled from about one hundred fifty to forty. The Mary for Mayor Campaign nonetheless arrived at City Hall and was rudely rebuffed by members of the sheriff's department. Of course, Mary had plenty to do outside.

FREEDOM TO BURY

Three months after Gavin Newsom's narrow win in the mayoral election, he pulled the ultimate risk-free political stunt and "legalized" gay marriage. Throngs of gay people from across the country descended upon City Hall at all hours of the day and night, camping out, sharing snacks and wine, and toasting Gavin Newsom as the vanguard leader of the gay and lesbian movement. If Gay Shame organizers already felt marginalized for protesting Newsom, now we felt like pariahs. It was obvious to us that if gay marriage proponents wanted real progress, they'd be fighting for the abolition of marriage (duh), and universal access to the services that marriage can sometimes help procure: housing, healthcare, citizenship, etc. Instead, gay marriage proponents want to fundamentally redefine what it means to be queer and erase decades of radical queer struggle in favor of a sanitized, "we're-just-like-you" normalcy (with marriage as the central institution, hmm . . . sounds familiar). Just the fact that challenging the gay marriage bandwagon became immediate heresy exposes the silencing agenda of gay marriage proponents as they move steadily towards assimilation into the imperialist, bloodthirsty status quo.

Soon after Gavin Newsom's marriage stunt, a forum took place to thank "Saint Newsom" for his hard work (the Sisters of Perpetual Indulgence, a drag troupe who dress up as nuns, later performed a canonization ceremony at their annual Easter celebration). The gay press was uniformly fawning. Even more embarrassing was a cover series on gay marriage in the March 17, 2004, issue of the *San Francisco Bay Guardian*, San Francisco's progressive weekly. The subheading of *Bay Guardian* editor Tim Redmond's article read, "Newsom, Gay Marriage, and the Politics of the

Revolutionary Gesture." In the article, Redmond compares Gavin Newsom's decision to direct city officials to grant same-sex marriage licenses with "AIDS activists who crashed meetings to demand action [and] pacifists who tried to shut down the war machine." At the time of Redmond's article, AIDS services were being gutted due to a state budget that slashed healthcare to the most vulnerable, and Newsom had made no attempt to save these services. Nor has Newsom ever made any statement condemning the U.S. war in Iraq; in a city overwhelmingly against the war, we can only assume that Newsom's silence means he supports it.

Newsom's marriage charade is anything but a "revolutionary gesture." It's a risk-free give-back to the gays who got him elected and a ploy by a power-hungry, ruling class politician to get national attention. The rush by the straight left to jump headfirst onto the marriage bandwagon exposes a lack of understanding about progressive or radical queer politics, and even a lack of commitment to left "values." Marriage is still a central institution of patriarchy, right?

The fight between pro-marriage and anti-marriage queers is not a disagreement between two segments of a "community," but a fight over the fundamental nature of queer struggle. When Newsom weighed in on one side, he gained not only the loyalty of assimilationist gays, but the support of liberals across the sex-and-gender spectrum. As former foes of Newsom capitulate to this newfound "unity," resistance can seem all the more futile.

Gay Shame has struggled to respond to the shifting political allegiances in San Francisco. We made a flyer proclaiming, GAY SHAME OPPOSES MARRIAGE IN ANY FORM. We also wrote an op-ed in one of San Francisco gay papers, the *San Francisco Bay Times*. Our latest effort is a sticker that imitates the ubiquitous red, white, and blue heart-shaped "Freedom to Marry" sticker. Our sticker proclaims, "We All Deserve the FREEDOM TO BURY," and continues, "How many Iraqis were murdered while you were getting married?" These stickers are hastily removed by angry gays.

The level to which gay marriage proponents will go to obscure queer anti-marriage messages was especially evident when the *Bay Area Reporter* ran a cover photo of a banner hanging from the LGBT Center, which originally thanked Newsom for his "Leadership, Courage and Commitment to Equality," but had been covered with dripping red-paint. The *Bay Area Reporter* failed to address this obvious critique of Newsom's gay marriage stunt, instead choosing to quote Center Director Thom Lynch as saying, "it shows that even in San Francisco, we can be attacked."

It is no coincidence that queers who oppose gay marriage are shut out of the picture, since we expose the gay marriage "movement" as a grab for privilege, rather than a civil rights issue. While not all gay marriage proponents may want the freedom to slaughter Iraqis, the gay marriage "debate" allows straight, white, male, ruling-class politicians like Newsom, George Bush, and John Kerry to fight over a fake issue while the real goods stay in their pasty palms, and the U.S. government bombs away. While not all gay marriage proponents may advocate rampant police brutality against people of color, their blind support for Newsom allows him to go ahead with his real agenda: the displacement of anyone who gets in the way of property development. And while not all proponents of gay marriage may favor a rabidly assimilationist gay identity, their prioritization of gay marriage as the central issue for queer struggle narrows the options for everyone else.

What will Gay Shame do next? It's up to you.

THE POLLINATORS' TOOLBOX

CLEO WOELFLE-ERSKINE AND ANDREA MAYBELLINE DANGER

Thank you for your interest in this toolbox!

> Included:
> A strong set of hands: good for lifting, tinkering, and touch (a unique feature specific to the human species)
> A bridge: excellent for unity of a wide range of different forms
> An altar: necessary for sacrificing unruly idiosyncrasies
> A heart: too many uses to list here
> An ear: useful organ for listening
> Two empty drawers: left open for further tools my brain forgot to conjure up or design
> — Blake Nemec

Pol•lin•a•tor: 1. any insect or animal that deposits pollen gathered from the stamen of a plant to the pistil (often of another plant), fertilizing the flower in the process; 2. any person, of the queer variety, who travels from place to place depositing information gathered from previous locales, fertilizing ideas as it goes.

How to identify a Pollinator:
An affinity for honey
Queer, probable gender deviant
Love of language and linguistic subversion
A geek fetish
Tinkery hands and/or mandibles
Carries many tools, probably used or homemade

The Pollinators is a transgressive collective loosely based in the Bay Area. We have worked on projects ranging from billboard alteration to pirate radio, urban gardening to gender intervention. The types and numbers of Pollinators have changed, and the tools we carry around are constantly evolving. Sometimes our target is the mainstream. At other times we attempt to transform perspectives within activist circles or build infrastructure within radical queer movements. This exchange is the essence of what we do: We pollinate cultures, moving between different social movements, communities, cities, and campaigns, bringing tools and skills—both social and tangible—between groups who normally would not interact with or learn from one another. We hail from anarchist, do-it-yourself (DIY), poor, queer, and trans communities; these communities give us strength, a sense of belonging, and a rich history of resistance. We exist on the economic fringe as handypeople, artists, sex workers, writers, and tattooists, and we have also worked in schools, in health clinics, and for nonprofit organizations focused on youth and environmental justice. We choose to enter the mainstream to share survival skills that we have learned in our own communities—we know other people need these skills as well. We stand with one foot in our home cultures and one foot in the normal world. But as we straddle that divide, the precarious nature of our situation is ever present: Will we lose ourselves as we try to reach out to others?

Our houses are full of Pollinators' memorabilia: stickers, old posters, flyers, and T-shirts. When trying to come up with a central metaphor for this piece, one scrap of paper caught our attention. Across the top it read, "Black 'n' Better Trust Toolbox." Blake Nemec created it. In it are tools we have found useful in transforming our interpersonal dynamics as we fight for a better world. In this article, we have expanded the toolbox to include tools for strategic intervention in the mainstream, as well as for building infrastructure—both social and physical—in communities engaging in resistance. We picked up these tools in various cities and situations, and offer the stories of their acquisition as well as the tools themselves for your use.

When the WTO came to Seattle in 1999, the rumble of stomping feet shook the towers of finance, and fleet-footed rock-throwers busted a crack in the seamless wall of media monopoly. Our faces flashed across TV screens; sound bites of our resistance to global capitalism made it into millions of blue-glowing living rooms. Among the 50,000 protestors—drum corps, marchers and chanters, those gassed while locked down, stroller brigades, Teamsters, and turtles—was a small band of queers dressed as pollinating insects, complete with goggles and hard hats.[1] A dragonfly and a blister beetle buzzed in the streets, engaging in conversations with passersby, un-arresting other protesters, overturning dumpsters, and generally assisting with the creation of a citywide autonomous zone.

Other Pollinators were spotted at a large, squatted warehouse that housed three hundred protestors during the week of action. We were taking care of security, barricade maintenance and plumbing, and designating a room where queer sex was the norm. The day after the squat got evicted—as the last of the six hundred arrested in the streets were being released via jail solidarity—squatters, protesters, and street fighters got together in late-night back rooms, secret squats, public parks, and bars. From the darkness, the voices said: "Next time the city is ours, and we again occupy some of the buildings—we'll open them up to the public—and the cops will be kept out by the sheer numbers of people. Then we'll have our radio station, we'll have our shows, and we'll hook up the plumbing again; but the water will come from the rooftop and end up in the garden, and if there is no garden nearby, we'll tear up the streets and make one." As each person spoke, an apparition rose up in the space between us—an understanding that we were a part of a new world growing through the cracks in the system we were fighting to destroy.

Over the next two years, Pollinators in various outfits and configurations tapped into networks energized by antiglobalization street protests, in order to conjure this apparition. We organized the Mobilization Radio and guerrilla gardening actions at the 2000 IMF/World Bank protests in D.C. and contributed organizing and teaching skills to DIY Skillshare conferences in the Bay Area. With our "megaphone"[2] we broadcasted the RadioActive Queers radio station over the Oakland airwaves and live from a baby stroller in the protest march when the National Association of Broadcasters came to San Francisco. We published an anthology of stories about

urban gardens and land struggles in cities across North America. We did a lot of traveling. Many people came in contact with our ideas, participated in our projects, taught alongside us, or learned from our workshops. We were simultaneously inspired by the skills and ingenuity that our community possessed and frustrated that the Skillshare workshops rarely reached beyond the boundaries of the anarchist-activist scene. The gatherings and mobilizations demanded a tremendous amount of energy yet failed to generate the momentum or create the infrastructure to keep projects alive without burning us out.

The Pollinators Skills and Sweat Road Show and Barn Raising Tour was one "blueprint"[3] for creating radical infrastructure while building alliances between different groups working for social change. We sent pamphlets describing the skills we could offer to collectives, projects, and partners in crime and describing the exchange we had in mind—we knew we had a lot to learn. It read, in part, "In the past year, the mass protest movement's quarterly protests against corporate globalization and the unsustainable status quo have been brought into the average ammerikkan's living room. But the dynamics of opposition are different from those of creation. What are people gonna do once the Nike sloths are gone? Like many folx who fucked shit up in the streets of Seattle, D.C., Philly, and L.A., the Pollinators were excited by the energy generated by these actions and frustrated at the lack of concrete local change that followed . . . People everywhere who are fighting to reclaim public space, for land to grow food on, and for control over their daily lives can offer tools they've used against the powers that destroy and make use of others' strategies . . . We believe that by working together towards common goals, by learning from our peers in a free-skool setting, and by confronting differences face to face, we build solidarity and understanding that can lead to powerful alliances down the road."

After months of correspondence, we decided to travel to Arcata, CA; Olympia, WA; Seattle, WA; Minneapolis, MN; Detroit, MI; and Montreal, QC. On our way we taught low/no-cost methods of reusing household wastewater, water conservation, urban gardening, DIY sex toys, knots (useful in a number of instances), screen printing, radio broadcasting, carpentry and greenhouse construction, plumbing, gender interventions, watering gardens with saved-up rainwater, solar cooking, and bike-powered laundry machine construction. Some projects came closer to the mark than others; at the Trumbullplex in Detroit, we hit the nail on the head. Despite problems within our collective—such as communication breakdowns and lack of preparation, money, or a vehicle to transport tools and supplies—we built a greenhouse, diverted an entire house's gray-water to their garden, dug a pond, and brought appropriate technology diagrams and our sometimes slipshod, do-it-yourself ethos to high school kids from Detroit Summer, a local youth empowerment arts and urban gardening program.

Two of our hosts asked us to lead an intervention because relations between the house and one of its genderqueer members had driven that member to the breaking point. We put down our screw guns and picked up our "ratchets"[4] for a day to torque the gender expectations of the mostly straight Trumbullplex collective. As anarchist genderqueers from outside this scene, we were able to buzz between the two factions to search out common ground. As the night wore on, we were reminded that this work was just as important as the physical structures we had been building outside.

While we worked in Detroit, many of our friends and co-conspirators were fighting against global capital at the meeting of the G8 in Genoa. Seventy protestors were beaten bloody while they slept and a young Italian anarchist, Carlo Guilani, was murdered in the streets by police. Back in Detroit, a small group of anarchists—young and old, local and pollinator—marched through the streets carrying hand-painted banners and quickly made signs. Instead of a eulogy, our voices rose up in a collective scream that held our grief, our rage, and our determination to continue our struggle.

After the tour we realized that building greenhouses and water systems was possible with a little ingenuity. Though we had not broken out of the anarcho-punk circle as much as we would have liked, we had infused a healthy dose of Bay Area gender transgression into the mostly straight Detroit scene. But we realized that breaking out of our subculture and creating alternative structures that actually undermined the dominant system was going to take a lot more work. We were excited to take our Oakland-based media and urban sustainability and education projects to the next level. We were broke, yet we felt inspired to try and acquire a space to house ourselves and our projects. But that fall, the social and political contexts of the country changed completely, and we had to add some new tools to our box.

After September 11, the D.C. protests against the International Monetary Fund—billed as the most confrontational yet—were abandoned. Activists began to fight against a new era of repression, and tactics that had seemed tame could now land you a lengthy sentence under the

PATRIOT Act. The economy crashed. In the eerie space that opened up between September 11 and the attack on Afghanistan, we took our "torches"[5] to the flagpoles of media-sponsored patriotism that we encountered on every block. We led nightly attacks on the walls, bus stops, and billboards of Oakland and San Francisco, posing the questions "Why war?" and "Just when does war benefit anyone?"

At the end of September, wondering where rent was going to come from, one Pollinator speculated about what ce would do if someone handed hir eight grand—put it toward a down payment on our dream community center or give it to some surgeon to cut hir tits off. All too often, we all faced such irreconcilable choices. We tried various ways of making a living: sex work, odd jobs, insurance settlements from bike accidents (which had almost wrecked our bodies), or getting a haircut in order to score a nonprofit job.

Using our "trowels,"[6] we transplanted DIY skills and ideas into the straight world. We brought "pipe wrenches"[7] to college students and environmentalists. We taught them how to build graywater systems and to re-direct the flow of the waste stream into sustainable processes. People in the straight world were often confused by our transgressive genders and skeptical of our DIY methods but always came away excited about the information. In the "machine shops"[8] of public schools we taught kids about the ecology of their cities. We helped them to craft tools to break down the problems in their communities and rebuild the communities in new ways. They constantly asked us, "Are you a boy or a girl?" At times there was barely enough space to breathe; sometimes we carved more room, and sometimes we just had to hold our breath and stick it out. We'd always come back to our "sawzalls"[9] and chop away again. It's always a battle to enter the straight world, but we've got an ever-expanding toolbox at the ready.

Meanwhile, inspired by Gay Shame's fierce commitment to street actions, we got involved in—then brought our "hammers"[10] to—their struggles. We were frightened by their lack of security consciousness or tactical foresight, and we connected them to legal, tactical, communications, and facilitation workshops within the anarchist community. Through all of this we formed a greater affinity with Gay Shame. One fall night we again found ourselves mourning our dead. After a young transwoman, Gwen Araujo, was murdered, we carried flaming torches through the streets of the Castro with Gay Shame, banging wildly on buckets. In an echo of Carlo Guilani's memorial, we again screamed our grief and rage into the night.

The last time the whole Pollinators crew met up, we led a spontaneous ten-thousand-bike charge at the Bay Bridge on the tenth anniversary of Critical Mass. Gathering strength from our affinity for each other and our shared history through past projects, we turned the endlessly circling ride into a determined mob in a matter of minutes. Sometimes, though, our projects can be as amorphous as late-night reminiscences of past exploits or schemes for future plans. Pollinators are available at the drop of a hat for late-night plumbing or the next big action that needs some juice. Rather than just a onetime project, Pollination has become a way of life.

Berthold Brecht, revolutionary playwright of the late nineteenth century wrote in "To those born later":

> Truly I live in dark times! . . .
> Anyone who laughs has not yet heard the terrible news
> What kind of times are these
> When it's almost a crime to talk about trees
> because it means keeping silent about so many monstrous deeds.[11]

More than one hundred years later, the Pollinators insist on not only talking about trees but also planting them in public places where they inspire people to see more possibilities in the world. We talk about war, gender, water, and corrupt politics, and we put out different versions of reality against the terrible news that fills the airwaves daily. We battle cops in the streets of San Francisco in retaliation for the latest invasion of Iraq. We tear down the fence around a Sacramento community garden slated for development, and we lead five hundred anti-WTO protesters from the Millennium round of meetings to plant trees in the streets. These battles require a fierce culture of resistance, both in order to keep ourselves going and to cross-pollinate solidarity between different people engaged in the same struggles. In these dark times, we struggle to keep hold of ourselves while still reaching out to others. As Pollinators, we are able to do this because we've come to realize that our most useful tools lie not at our fingertips but in our hearts.

GETTING TO THE ROOT

JESSE HEIWA

A wave of in-your-face, direct action, queer protest groups came on strong from the late 1980s to the mid-1990s, starting with ACT UP (AIDS Coalition To Unleash Power) and continuing with Queer Nation and the Lesbian Avengers. ACT UP changed the trajectory of the AIDS crisis by demanding that all people with AIDS have full access to treatment, and (in the case of some chapters) linking the struggle against AIDS with struggles against homophobia, classism, misogyny, and racism. Queer Nation challenged the notion that queer people should stay in gay ghettos and announced that wherever we were, we should be out and loud about it. Lesbian Avengers spotlighted the challenges queer women faced and created a space for lesbians in the larger queer community through the Dyke March.

At the same time as this wave of activism, queer people of color organizations were growing and strengthening all over: organizations for Latino/a, African descent, Asian/Pacific, Native American, Arab/Middle Eastern, and pan-Third World queers as well as for all other types of queers. In New York City, the Lesbian and Gay People Of Color Steering Committee was formed in 1989 in response to the need for increased representation of people of color in the NYC LGBT Center. This helped birth other new organizations and publications such as *Color Life!*, a magazine by/for progressive lesbian, gay, bisexual, transgender, and two-spirit people of color. Out of these networks came institutions such as the Audre Lorde Project, the nation's first community organizing center for queer people of color communities. Queer people of color were an integral part of larger struggles for social justice, ranging from fighting police brutality to fighting for economic justice as well as challenging discrimination against people of color. While facing some of the same issues of homophobia that white queers faced, queers of color were also more likely to face issues affecting the communities that they came from: violence, poverty, incarceration, unemployment, and even racism from other queer people.

In 1994, queer radicals who were disgusted with the commercialization of the Stonewall 25 celebrations of that year organized alternate events as well as protests of official events. We held an unpermitted march on the night before the official march (and after the Dyke March) where all were welcome (some groups were not allowed to march in the official Stonewall 25 celebration). At the unpermitted march, we were committed to the original spirit of the Stonewall rebellion—linking struggles against oppression and war and against assimilation into a racist, capitalist, imperialist system. We held a forum looking at the intersection of radical and queer issues, and we joined with ACT UP and others in marching up the original route of the 1970 march, which went out of the gay ghetto and up Fifth Avenue (against traffic) to Central Park. On First Avenue, the official march included the world's largest rainbow flag. It seemed that this flag, which was "created" by a white man in 1978, had quite a resemblance to the long-existing flags of indigenous peoples in Latin America. By 1994, it had become the design used to sell every gay product under the sun.

AIDS activism, which continued after its peak in popularity in the early nineties, took a nosedive domestically with the introduction of retrovirals in the mid-1990s. Conservative pundits Andrew Sullivan and dissident activists declared the "end of AIDS." Now that the epidemic was in communities darker and poorer than many of the gay men who were originally hardest hit, attention flagged. Some U.S. chapters of ACT UP joined with new activists around the world to focus on the global pandemic. Queer Nation was long gone, burnt out by infighting and a lack of radical analysis to match its militant visibility actions. The Dyke March was the main thing remaining from the Lesbian Avengers (although chapters continue in some areas). Queer people of color organizations were trying to sustain themselves, since often they were the only places where queer people of color could go for a support system not provided either in people of color or queer communities.

In 1998, many queer folks attended the predominately straight, anarchist-oriented Active Resistance conference, and out of that came interest in holding a queer-oriented radical gathering. At around this time, Mayor Ghouliani (sic) was busy trying to take all the sin away from Sin City. A group called Sex Panic came together to challenge Giuliani's crackdown. Out of this came the Fuck the Mayor Collective, which formed when concerns about the intersections of race, class, and gender were not dealt with in Sex Panic, which focused primarily on white gay men's access to public and private sex spaces. Fuck the Mayor organized Gay Shame as a response to the commercialization and apathy that existed in many Pride events and related LGBT entities. Gay Shame occurred at dumba, a radical queer cultural and political space, and attracted a heady mix of queers.

Some of the people involved in organizing Gay Shame decided to organize a larger radical queer gathering, which took its name from a gathering in London, England, in 1998 called Queeruption. Ours took place in October 1999. We figured that even though our event was its own creation, it would be good to keep a concept going, and so we called our gathering Queeruption also. We wanted it to be very participatory, accessible financially, and attract folks from all over North America (and the world). We succeeded at these goals. Where we failed was in creating a diversity beyond the overall whiteness of the punk/alternative scene from which Queeruption arose. At the same time, the event was transformative to many participants, particularly for those who didn't have access to the choices available to many of us in larger, more expensive cities. Queeruption organizers did work on involving people of color, but most of the organizers were white. To many participants, whether the gathering was predominately white was less of an issue to folks than whether there was vegan food. The core organizers were aware of this contradiction, but did not succeed in shifting the vision of the gathering.

Some of us organized a people of color caucus at Queeruption, which met on the the roof of dumba. The sheer invisibility of people of color and the unwillingness of white attendees to focus on this issue were our main concerns, especially in a city where the majority of residents were people of color. Some people in the caucus wanted to leave in disgust. Others wanted another option, since if we just left then people might not even know why. We decided on a "consciousness-raising" exercise. With the support of some of the core organizers, we put up big wall posters with questions geared to provoke awareness and discussion. These ranged from "Did you wonder why this gathering is so white?" to "Why aren't there more workshops that are dealing with challenging racism?" and from "Why vegan food but not people of color?" to "Why so many different colors of hair but not people?" The posters did the trick—some people were angry with us for bringing up these issues! Others were confused and not sure what to do.

A few people took up the challenge and organized a discussion open to all but geared toward white queers on the issues raised by the wall posters and the people of color caucus. While this discussion did not change the makeup of the gathering, it did result in people incorporating these concerns in other organizing projects. It networked queer people of color who were active in predominately white activist scenes into projects that were organized around people of color. In addition, many people of color gained the confidence to bring up the concerns they had in predominately white spaces.

Queeruption continues as a gathering in different areas of the world (so far in the "developed" world: London, New York, San Francisco, Berlin, and Amsterdam). A major concern is the continued marginalization of people of color and minorities in these gatherings. It seems that making this pattern visible at Queeruption in NYC didn't seem to change this dynamic at the future ones. Partially it was because of the model used, which didn't structurally guarantee the participation of people of color as equal partners at the very beginning, thus creating a cycle that resulted in predominately white gatherings. But it was also because of a widespread attitude that this wasn't a priority issue. Those who brought up these concerns out of a commitment to change were often treated with contempt and ire. There's never a nice way to say it when folks keep ignoring the problem.

In Europe, the QEKON (Queer and Ethnicity) conference was organized in 2003. It focused on queers who were also minorities, immigrants, and others marginalized in Europe. In the United States, the PRISM conference provided a place for queer people of color to gather where their concerns were front and center. My question is, how can one create an integrated space? One idea might be to organize two gatherings that are separate but overlap—one specifically for people of color, the other open to all but most likely predominately white. We could organize some joint workshops, plenaries that examine issues around racism but also acknowledge that people come from different places depending on their life situation, which is often about much more than being queer.

An opposition to a mainstream, commercialized gay community does not automatically result in a radical current not replicating some oppressive patterns. How to oppose the mainstream in a way that demands change and accountability while still allowing folks to continue organizing what often are transformative events is the key. It might mean some of us have to be willing to be the curmudgeons. It might mean some of us need to organize people of color–specific events so as to come to the table for future events as a collective instead of just as individuals—in order to ensure there is equanimity in how something develops from the beginning. It might mean white queers need to organize their own gatherings to focus on the issues of white supremacy and challenging racism. White queers and queers of color need to examine what divides us and what brings us together, while continuing to challenge the oppressive values of the mainstream.

STAYIN' ALIVE: TRANS SURVIVAL AND STRUGGLE ON THE STREETS OF PHILADELPHIA

MICHELLE O'BRIEN

Trans people in Philadelphia have fought for decades for our survival and liberation. Many trans people in Philadelphia face penury, racism, street violence, and harassment. Completely excluded from the wage economy through job discrimination and poverty, many of the city's poor trans people and trans people of color are left with few options but sex work to make ends meet. Until recently, trans people have had no access to affordable and respectful health care. Trans women find hormones on the street when doctors' offices are too hateful or too expensive. Excluded from homeless shelters, brutalized by police, unjustly held in prison, and faced with high rates of HIV and Hep C, trans people have had to rely on each other for our survival.

Gender variant communities across the city have spent years developing networks of mutual aid and support. These networks have taken many forms. Some trans people, particularly black trans women, have found support and care in the infrastructure of House families within the Ball Scene, an underground dance subculture. House families provide literal surrogate families and regional systems of support. House families assist each other in housing and medical and emotional care. This network is invaluable for many trans women with nowhere else to turn. Trans people in Philadelphia have also developed an interconnected collection of support groups, where we provide each other with advice and dignity through difficult times.

Informal systems of mutual support for trans people have begun to provide the beginnings of political movements for justice. Trans community and health activists recently organized a successful trans health conference, bringing together diverse communities to fight for affordable, accessible, and respectful health care. We are beginning to plan a trans-run emergency housing facility for gender minorities. Marginalized trans people are defining and leading these innovative social service and health projects. We are redefining the world of social service agencies, both gay and straight, that have long excluded trans people.

Philadelphia trans politics have long been hampered by extreme racial and class division—deep, insurmountable splits between suburban white heterosexual cross-dressers and center city African-American trans sex workers, between young white punk transmen and femme queen vogue dancers, between successful professionals and trans people in prisons, in inpatient facilities or on the streets. Much of the successes of recent organizing comes from beginning to build respectful connections across these many divides of race and class.

As a trans woman with white and middle-class privilege, I've been working with a few other white or middle-class trans people to establish relationships of accountability and respect with other trans communities. Working out these relationships is complex and requires understanding, patience, and dedication. By recognizing the differences of privilege, access, and experience within our communities, we are laying the groundwork for standing with each other as allies in ways that are lasting and real. As white or economically privileged trans people, challenging our own racism and classism is crucial in order to be effective and sincere participants in a movement that addresses the needs of all trans people.

These new cross-racial connections among trans people are powerful and exciting. They are possible because of relationships we formed in organizing a memorial for Nizah Morris in February of 2003. Just before Christmas 2002, in center city Philadelphia, Nizah Morris was mysteriously murdered. Nizah was well known as a performer, a loved member of her family, and as a mentor for other African-American trans women. While the circumstances are far from clear, the police stories from that night are extremely dubious. Suspicions of police culpability are buttressed by less deniable truths: the media and police response to Nizah's death reflected extreme racism, transphobia, negligence, and hatred.

For weeks, the police refused to investigate Nizah's death or to classify it as a murder. Media coverage horribly misidentified Nizah as a male prostitute and made repeated unsubstantiated accusations of illegal drug use. Nizah's family, and many throughout trans and gay black communities in Philadelphia, were offended and outraged by the media and police. Many mainstream gay organizations failed to respond to her murder. The *Philadelphia Gay News* ran a horrible and offensive article on her death that parroted police lies, clearly indicating the reporter's failure to actually talk to Nizah's friends or family.

We put together a coalition of individuals and groups to organize a large memorial for Nizah. The organizing was extraordinary. Trans people managed to maintain consistent leadership, and a working-class black trans woman from Nizah's community took the main leadership role. It was the first time anyone remembers black and white trans people working effectively together in Philadelphia. With the participation of Nizah's family, we drew from the support of many communities and organizations around Philadelphia and put together a widely publicized and powerful memorial, drawing over three hundred people. We managed to define and solicit the support of gay- and lesbian-run organizations, like the community center or legal activist center, without letting them take charge. Instead, the needs of Philadelphia's marginalized trans people defined the agenda.

The event had a major impact on the police and media response to her death. Police finally began an investigation of sorts, and classified the death (six weeks later) as a homicide. The district attorney conducted an investigation. News coverage improved dramatically. The *Philadelphia Gay News*, in particular, did a dramatic turnaround. In subsequent months, they ran a penetrating series of articles on the issue, exposing police misconduct and institutional negligence, and spotlighting Nizah's extraordinary life.

Nizah's death was far from an isolated instance. In beginning to build mass movements that link justice for trans people to other movements for social justice and survival, we must locate our work and oppression within a broader context. The organizing in honor of Nizah was powerful not only because of the relationships built between diverse trans communities but also because of the ways her death linked to larger issues of racism, capitalism, and state violence. Looking at this history can contribute to building the effective, strategic, and powerful movements we need in order to defend the survival and freedom of trans people. Philadelphia has a long history of extreme police brutality focused against the city's poor people of color. The more publicized police terror against black liberationists Mumia Abu-Jamal and the MOVE family are just a part of the larger violent war that has been waged over decades against poor black Philadelphians by the police department.

This war is particularly vicious for poor trans and gay people of color in Philadelphia. Nizah Morris is one in a long, long list of trans and gay black people who have died either at the hands of police or under circumstances that the police have been unable or unwilling to effectively respond to. In a well-known gay neighborhood, police harassment of poor black gay and trans people—especially sex workers—is constant. As a social service worker and support group facilitator, I've heard more than my fair share of stories of trans people raped repeatedly and otherwise brutalized by police.

Two Philadelphia organizations have consistently linked the racist wars within our city to a broader regional and global context: the International Concerned Family and Friends of Mumia and ACT UP Philadelphia. While neither has placed trans issues centrally, both provide the breadth of analysis and work that is invaluable in understanding the relevance of trans organizing for health care and against violence.

International Concerned Family and Friends of Mumia has spearheaded a global movement to free death row political prisoner and activist Mumia Abu-Jamal. They've been successful at linking Mumia's struggle for freedom and survival to a broader context of white supremacist violence and to a wide range of other social justice struggles and oppressed communities. They've drawn together an extraordinary, diverse, and global movement to stand against Mumia's execution. From French government officials to Los Angeles neighborhood groups, Italian Communists to Mexico City prison abolitionists, Mumia's case and Philadelphia-based organizing have networked a remarkable coalition against white supremacy, state violence, and capitalism.

The organizing around Mumia's case can be an inspiration for trans activists in Philadelphia. Despite the homophobia and transphobia of key leadership in International Concerned Family and Friends of Mumia, queer and trans people have been central to Mumia solidarity groups across the country. Trans people, particularly trans people of color, have been on the forefront of challenging the state violence and white supremacy coming to bear against Mumia. Groups such as Rainbow Flags for Mumia and Queers for Mumia have fought against homophobia and transphobia within Free Mumia campaigns by establishing a visible presence of trans people across the movement. Trans people working to free Mumia have opened up new possibilities in developing relationships of solidarity and support between trans people and other, interconnected liberation movements.

Philadelphia ACT UP has successfully linked the struggles of poor people living with AIDS in Philadelphia, especially African Americans and people in prison, to the global struggle over access to AIDS drugs in developing countries. With protests on the streets of Philadelphia and by sending activists to international trade conferences in Qatar, ACT UP Philly has made it clear that what is happening on the ground here is part of a much deeper, much bigger global struggle over health, power, race, and sexuality.

Nizah's murder and the police and media response to her death are manifestations of a global pattern showing the interconnections of white supremacy and transphobia. The current United States right-wing, corporate-run puppet governments in post-invasion Afghanistan and Iraq and the U.S.-funded wars in the Philippines, Colombia, and Palestine are just the more visible manifestations of a much deeper war. We are witnessing a massive consolidation of global wealth linked to a dramatic intensification of U.S. white-supremacist imperial violence across the world. The economic, cultural, and social survival of hundreds of millions of poor people of color around the globe is in crisis as the empire of global capital is restructuring economies, governments, and societies with rapid ferocity. This global violence is systematically obscured by the rhetoric and strategies of mainstream gay movements.

The needs of transnational capital and profit have placed high demands on the organization of governments throughout the world. The neoliberal states formed through IMF restructuring have actively pushed racist and classist policies, including mass incarceration, forced consolidation of peasant land, crushing of labor and social justice movements, and a hypermilitarization of society. These policies also have especially profound and terrifying consequences for transgender and gender variant people. Trans people are among the most swiftly displaced and terrorized in the economic disintegration and political brutalization of neoliberal society in many countries across the globe.

In Guatemala in the mid-1990s, for instance, the U.S. began to de-escalate the war it had been waging with the help of a military dictatorship against the country's social justice movements and indigenous peasant populations. After decades of scorched earth, death squads, and mass concentration camps, it became politically expedient to make Guatemala into a more stable society that could support the construction of *maquiladoras*—ultraexploitative industrial manufacturing centers for clothing—in a predominantly agrarian economy. So the government signed a few peace treaties, disarmed the guerrilla groups, and hired most of its army as security guards. Meanwhile, the only death squads that continue to operate in Guatemala City are not targeting social justice activists or ex-guerrilla *politicos* (although both could face such violence if there were again political movements threatening capital in the country); instead, these death squads are primarily targeting trans sex workers. Like several other Central American cities—San Cristobal de Las Casas, San Salvador, Panama City—the last few years have been marked by a dramatic escalation of paramilitary violence against the city's poor trans people.

Here in the United States such links are obvious to anyone looking. In the agendas of the New Right, whether we are talking about Ronald Reagan or George W. Bush, transphobia, homophobia, and racism are intimately linked. Extreme sexual and gender normativity, enforced throughout the state's policies, are deeply interwoven with the intensification of white supremacy through the prison system, in exclusions from higher education, or in the gutting of social services. Immigration policy offers one example of the institutional interconnection of racism and transphobia. Trans immigrants face serious discrimination: bans against immigrants living with HIV, wide personal discretion given to transphobic immigration officials, inadequate asylum rights for trans people, and systematic violence against trans people in INS detention facilities. These forms of violence are embedded in a profoundly racist structure designed to terrorize immigrants of color. Here in Pennsylvania, one Guatemalan trans woman is fighting deportation while being held by the INS. The racism and transphobia of the INS here is intimately linked to the violence on the streets of Guatemala City.

Our organizing for the survival and health of our trans communities is deeply wrapped up in this ongoing reality of racist and transphobic violence institutionalized on all levels of state and corporate policy. State violence doesn't just take the form of death squads and police helicopters dropping C4 bombs, but it also manifests as institutional neglect, poverty, and poor health care.

While many trans women have died at the hands of Philadelphia police, more have died of AIDS in a city with grossly inadequate resources to address the health crises in poor trans communities. Our work for health care, housing, and against violence sets us against racist capitalism.

By linking these issues in our analyses and work, we can all begin to do what mainstream gay movements won't: build movements committed to justice for all people, movements committed to challenging capitalism and white supremacy alongside fighting homophobia. The survival of trans people, poor queers, and many others across the globe urgently depends on these movements.

CORRODING OUR QUALITY OF LIFE

JUSTIN ANTON ROSADO

*We fight against the absurdity of social politics, which do not include us. We
take radical action through the development of youth leadership, skills transfer, campaign building, and the practice of healing. We subscribe to the ethic
of organizing for us by us. Now that's FIERCE!!!*

Growing up poor, Latino, and always knowing that I was attracted to boys but not always
knowing what to call it, I never had any space to explore or find myself. Family, the projects, school, the boys club, and the streets I grew up on—none of these spaces welcomed me.
Public spaces in the Village were the only places where I could find a community, where I could
find myself. My first stop was Washington Square Park, where at age fourteen I joined with outcasts from the rest of the city and became part of the rave scene, which was not only a party scene
but also a community for the freaks to get away and attempt to create families (places of PLUR—
peace, love, unity, and respect). The park and the rave scene didn't teach me to fight back or how
to make change, but they did teach me to think on my own, to defy the mainstream, and to nour-
ish my own dreams for a different world.

At the age of fifteen, I dropped out of Seward Park High School, a public school in the Lower
East Side (LES). I was sick of being harassed by straight boy after straight boy as well as by the
police, who had recently (under Mayor Giuliani) taken over school security in all NYC public

schools. After that, I spent my days with friends, walking up and down St. Marks Place hanging out at the Cube (an "island" in the middle of the Astor Place intersection where cars and people whizzed by, and where skateboarders, ravers, and kids from the LES would chill), and at Washington Square Park. Still, among the freaks, I had to hide that I was queer; there were only a few of us, and we secretly found refuge with each other.

A twist of fate brought me to the Hetrick Martin Institute, the nation's oldest and largest LGBT youth center—which happened to be down the street from the Cube. Most of the kids at the Cube were homeless, none of us had any money, and all of us were hungry. Ironically, a couple of the straight girls in our crew regularly ate at the Hetrick Martin Café, and they told me to come with them. I became a regular at the Hetrick Martin Institute, where I found my first queer community. There, I was exposed to all different varieties of queerness; unfortunately, though, everyone was separated into cliques. Even though the youth at Hetrick were every day experiencing police harassment and gay bashing and being discarded like trash by the city, we were being taught to be quiet, not to make a ruckus.

I was raised to view the world through a radical lens, to see the police as the enemy of poor people of color and homeless people. My family, along with all the other people in the Lower East Side, was always harassed by the police. We saw the city's politics as a design to keep people of color poor. I believed that the only way for people of color to succeed was by working together and watching each others' backs. However, because of the cliquishness of Hetrick, I started thinking only of myself and the shade I could throw at other queer youth. Even though at Hetrick I was becoming comfortable with being queer, I was also learning how to participate in dividing queer youth from one another—to do exactly what the city wanted.

While I was being taught to "sit down and shut up," only a mile away a group of trans and queer youth (who were mostly of color) came together to create a radical youth-run organizing project. They were responding to the total absence of any organization in NYC whose mission was to organize LGBT youth for revolutionary social change. In this world built by and for wealthy, straight white men, where—even within most LBGT organizations—white male wealth still sets the agenda, these youth were fighting to build their own power. They were motivated by their vision of a world free of homophobia, transphobia, sexism, racism, classism, and capitalism; free from police brutality, violence, and homelessness. This vision came out of their individual life struggles, their experiences, and their needs.. They were forming their political and organizing knowledge and skills, while I was more concerned with the color of my hair and sharpening my shade tactics.

From Hetrick, I became part of the Christopher Street Piers community. Life was good for a while. The Piers were the one place in the city where we could find ourselves and be ourselves without embarrassment or fear. We would laugh, scream, kiss, vogue, have fun, and hold hands, without having to hide our queerness. On any relatively warm night, there would be hundreds, sometimes over a thousand, youth—partying, chilling, living. Homeless youth and youth who had been thrown out of their homes would sleep there, knowing that their friends were watching them and that they were safe. (Out of the 22,000 and growing homeless youth population in NYC, over 35 percent are estimated to be out lesbian, gay, bisexual, or transgender—it is these youth that depended on the Piers the most).

As great as the Piers were, there was no one set of morals or mission because it was a public space for all of us—the voguers and the ballroom children, the MSMs (men who have sex with men but don't identify as gay or bi), the ravers, the Hetrick kids, the Center kids, older queer people of color, and even the older gay white men looking for a trick. Our purpose was to be free and wild, but when our way of life became endangered, we did not know what to do. First, we noticed the increase of police surveillance and arrests—random arrests, often a whole sweep of five to fifteen youth at a time who were doing nothing illegal. After that, we began to notice other changes at the Piers. Our connections to the services we needed were disappearing.

The Piers were a chill spot, but also a networking mania, where large outreach vans, equipped with bathrooms and portable clinics would perch right next to us at the last blue planter on the pier. They provided us with condoms, food, juice, a restroom to use, HIV testing, checkups, and counseling, as well as referrals to queer shelters and Transitional Living Programs. This was the only public place in the city where we could get the basic services that we needed. These programs and vans were no longer coming in such large numbers or as often and our chances to get help were dwindling. The police, resident vigilante groups, as well as the "Guardian Angels" had been intimidating, threatening, and pushing out these vans. It had gotten so bad that the police were even arresting some of the outreach workers who were providing us with services.

That was the beginning of the end of the Piers as my friends and I knew them. Without guidance or knowledge, we did not how to stop our world from being taken from under our feet. We were left without services, while the police would arrest us for everything they could think of—from public urination to soliciting with the intent to prostitute to loitering—in other words, for just existing. One of my friends was arrested on the pier for "playing her radio too loud." My friends and I watched the arrest and asked the police why they singled her out of the crowded pier of people playing radios. Of course, we got no response. She had a small old radio, with one speaker, and the giant boom boxes surrounding us drowned out the volume on hers. Yet they only arrested her. The only reason we could come up with was that it was because she was of color, and most of the other radios were being played by white folks (this happened during the daytime hours when the Piers were mostly white people and people from the neighborhood; but in the early evening until dawn of the next day, the Piers were mostly queer youth of color). To this day, that event still makes me furious. We knew things would only get worse.

What we didn't know was that Mayor Giuliani had enacted a set of "quality of life" policies that reinforced laws dealing with petty nonviolent crimes as well as adding "crimes" such as loitering to the list of offenses. We also didn't know that the "quality of life" measure began as a pilot project within the Sixth Precinct, the precinct that has jurisdiction over the West Village. Soon, I myself had fallen victim to the Sixth Precinct's effort to protect the quality of life of residents and tourists at our expense. After a day of trainings at another youth center, me and my friends made our way to the West Village, like we did every day. The police, pushed by the city to increase the number of arrests, had set up shop on West Fourth Street posing as marijuana dealers. This was part of the "quality of life" policies, to arrest as many people as possible for petty crimes like marijuana possession. At the time, I was only sixteen years old and had no idea what I had stepped into. I wound up buying from a police officer posing as a dealer, which led to my arrest one minute after the purchase.

This was when I began to understand how severe things had gotten in the Village. My friends all witnessed my entrapment. After the police cuffed me and put me in the police van, I had to sit and wait, for around three hours, while the police continued to trick people into getting arrested for the sake of numbers. My friends (who were future FIERCE! members but had not yet been politicized or trained by FIERCE!) didn't really know what to do. So they sat in front of the unmarked police van and held makeshift signs reading "Let Justin Go." While I sat chained to the floor of the van as the officer puffed on his cigar, I could hear one of my friends playing his guitar as the rest sang songs of freedom. The whole situation was too much for me to process at the time. But the experience of getting arrested and spending two-and-one-half days in Central Booking helped me to understand from a personal perspective how the "quality of life" policies really were actively *corroding our quality of life.*

After I was released from jail, I returned to the Piers to find that a section had been fenced off. We were distressed because our space was being eroded; I was personally distressed because the area they had fenced off was the spot where my first love asked me to marry him. None of us knew why this happened because no one thought to inform us, the people who depended on the Piers. So we chilled as usual and tried to pretend like things were okay, but we knew that they weren't. The Piers were being changed without any consideration of our needs. Our friends were getting arrested in record numbers by uniformed and undercover police alike. The police even had a surveillance tape watching the Piers from across the street—they told my friend this as they arrested her.

We knew the police were watching us, so why did they not help us when we were gay bashed? My best friend JayDee Melendez and I witnessed a gay bashing on the pier, in the same spot where my friend was arrested from the police watching on camera. We were sitting against the water, and we heard screams. Then we saw a young gay black male running from a black straight male (the straight male was a regular drug dealer on Christopher Street, and we suspected that the gay male had hit on him, causing the straight male to flip). There was a chase and the straight male was screaming homophobic remarks and threats of violence. We were scared for our friend as well as for ourselves, and we didn't know what to do. So we hid behind a structure on the pier and waited. A half hour later, when we returned, we found out that the gay man had been stabbed. I wasn't sure of all the details, but I do know that there was a lot of chasing and fighting before the stabbing. Yet during this time there was no police intervention or help, even though the police would in a heartbeat to arrest us for nonviolent crimes or for doing nothing at all. This proved to us that we were being targeted and pushed out of the West Village. This was the area of the city where we were pushed into, on the edge of the island, and now they wanted us to leave.

The next day, my friend JayDee and I went to the New Neutral Zone ("New" because the original neutral zone was created to give the LGBT youth on Christopher Street a safe place to

Protest gentrification and police brutality in the West Village

1:00pm - Midnight Saturday

Oct 5, Sheridan Square

We are sick and tired of watching the police, wealthy resident associations, and Big Business take over the West Village as part of their 'Quality of Life' Campaign.

We Demand an end to the curfew laws, misdemeanor arrests, and physical violence targeting transpeople, queer youth of color, sex workers, and the homeless!

Revolt! Reclaim! Resist!
Come Out To Protest On October the 5th!

FIERCE, an organization for TLGB Youth   (646) 336-6789   Please do not post this flyer

Queer youth of color, Trannies, sex workers and the homeless are being 'cleaned out' of the west village.

But we are NOT trash!

WHO PAY$ FOR YOUR QUALITY OF LIFE?

go at night and was then "evicted" by the resident groups that wanted the youth out of the Village). The New Neutral Zone (at this time located right above the Village) was our second home, where we chilled, ate, slept, and sometimes worked. The Neutral Zone had offered to house FIERCE! until FIERCE! could get their own space. So, of course, we were influenced by these amazing activists planning to change the city for the benefit of queer youth. We came to them with our worries and fears for the West Village. As JayDee was describing the displacement of the services and vans, the growing number of arrests, the fences, we realized the need to organize ourselves and the community around these issues. This was the beginning of the Save Our Space campaign, which would grow and expand, leading and developing FIERCE! as well as the queer youth of color community in the Village.

We decided that we needed to document the events that were happening—to get our story down for all to see. That's when we started the *Fenced Out* video. This video was a collaboration between FIERCE!, Paper Tiger Television (a video activist organization), and the Neutral Zone. The video was formed, filmed, directed, and edited by a group of queer youth of color who were directly affected by the events we were documenting. *Fenced Out* was a big step for FIERCE! as well as for me. Throughout the production, I learned more and more of the world of politics, queer issues, and history, as well as how to be an activist and make change. I am the person I am today because of this education and skills exchange.

While learning about the history of the pier, I even got to meet older queer activists who had formed the original queer movement in New York City. Learning from and working with legendary activists like Sylvia Rivera, Bob Kohler, and Regina Shavers is an experience I will never forget. Sylvia Rivera gave us a walking tour of her old, squatted home on the pier, where she lived among and fought for a community of queer and HIV-positive homeless people until they were evicted by the city (under Giuliani) in 1996. I discovered from Sylvia that she, along with a group of young queer street kids (not so different from me and my friends), was one of the instigators of the 1969 Stonewall rebellion against the police. The intergenerational work that FIERCE! does really helps youth to find a path to victory, by giving us a frame to work with, and showing us that we as queer people do have a history that *we created* by resisting assimilation!

While researching *Fenced Out*, we learned that the city had sold the Piers to a state-owned corporation called the Hudson River Park Trust, which planned to redo all the piers from Fifty-ninth Street down to the southern tip of the Manhattan island. Their plans included restaurants, parks, boating activities, and green lawns. These plans were developed to attract white families with money and to create a tourist spot in the Village. Along with the redevelopment of the Piers, the city is supporting private real estate companies in building expensive apartment complexes right across the street from the Piers.

As a way to develop the Save Our Space campaign, we did regular outreach at the pier with the goal of building community and developing consciousness. We created a survey to gather information about people's experiences of police harassment and profiling in the Village as a means to document concrete instances of police abuse and pursue potential legal action. We produced a petition and began to inform and educate youth about the current situation, and we gathered hundreds of signatures for our cause. This petition demanded the following things:

1. The LGBTST youth community must have input into the Hudson River Park Trust development of the Christopher Street Piers.

2. The repeal of the imposed 1 A.M. curfew on the Piers.

3. The end to racial and gender profiling and harassment by the Sixth Precinct and Midtown South vice and narcotics squads.

4. The end to resident vigilantism within the West Village that targets these marginalized communities and the social service agencies that outreach to us.

5. Put halt on the city spending towards policing in the West Village, and instead provide funding for community-based programs.

6. In particular, we demand an all-night LGBTST youth drop-in center located in the heart of the Village.

We took these demands to City Council member Christine Quinn and State Senator Tom Duane, gay elected officials representing the Village district, who were known for their relative-

Saturday 1pm
October 5th
Sheridan Square
7th Avenue & Christopher Street
FIERCE! (646) 336-6789

RECLAIM our **SPACE**

Saturday 1pm
October 5th
Sheridan Square
7th Avenue & Christopher Street
FIERCE! (646) 336-6789

RECLAIM our **SPACE**

Saturday 1pm
October 5th
Sheridan Square
7th Avenue & Christopher Street
FIERCE! (646) 336-6789

RECLAIM our **SPACE**

Saturday 1pm
October 5th
Sheridan Square
7th Avenue & Christopher Street
FIERCE! (646) 336-6789

RECLAIM our **SPACE**

ly progressive stances. Although they expressed to us that they personally were on our side, they also made it very clear that they could not always publicly stand with us, due to the fact that their voting constituents are the very residents who want us out of the Village. Under Giuliani's rule, it was even more difficult to get these officials to create change in the city's policies.

While Giuliani reigned, he created a police state where poor people of color across the city were displaced. When his term ended, we thought it would be a great opportunity to make our demands clear to the new mayor. We helped initiate—along with other community organizations from across the city, such as the Prison Moratorium Project, the Black Radical Congress, the Coalition Against Police Brutality, and Jews for Racial and Economic Justice—the Peoples' Agenda for a New Beginning. We integrated all of our organizations' demands and held a rally on Mayor Bloomberg's first day of office, calling on him to turn our demands into reality.

Instead, Bloomberg delivered us the "West Village Initiative," an attempt to further crack down on "quality of life" crimes, only a month after his term began. The West Village initiative was ushered in on February 12, 2002, through a "community forum" entitled "Is Quality of Life in the West Village Spiraling out of Control? Yes!!!!" organized by the Community Board 2, the Sixth Precinct Community Council, and RID (Residents in Distress—named after the lice remover—a group of West Village residents formed to push the queer youth of color out of the Village).

We knew that this meeting would basically be a space for wealthy residents to complain and talk shit about queer youth of color and homeless youth, who may not own property but still claim the Village as our home. We needed to have a presence at this meeting, since *we were* part of the community in the West Village, whether they liked it or not. So we mobilized for the meeting in mass numbers, and we made up almost half of the three hundred or so people there. We sat quietly, holding back our fury, as the residents hysterically screamed as if our very presence was an attack on their quality of life. We endured their claim that they were getting community input for their "West Village Initiative," which focused on petty "quality of life" crimes, through unnecessarily adding police in so-called high crime areas in the West Village (despite their own claim that crime was already down in the West Village, which would make one think that you wouldn't need to put more resources into policing).

We held signs that read: "Whose Quality of Life?"; "Whose Streets? Our Streets Too!"; "Clean up your streets? We are not trash!!!"; and "You say police protection, we say police brutality."

Community Board Two, the residents, and the police were all unhappy with our presence, claiming that we had no right to attend "their meeting." Even though we were right there, they talked about us like we weren't. "My daughter shouldn't have to see those people as she comes home from school" and similar shady remarks are embedded in our memory. When they asked if anyone wanted to say something, they always overlooked our raised hands. When we did finally get a chance to speak, they ended the meeting early.

It was clear to us that this was not an actual community meeting when they did not hesitate to move forward with the West Village Initiative, even though more than half of the room clearly expressed that it would severely decrease our quality of life.

We attended several other Community Board 2 and Sixth Precinct meetings, making our presence and issues known, as well as gathering information on what they were planning to do. We also organized against RID, who continued to organize against us. They lobbied to pass a "three strikes you're out" law for nonviolent "quality of life" offenses, which would put the offenders in jail for years and get them off of "their" streets. RID even went as far as to hold a rally in Sheridan Square—our historical spot, the very place where Stonewall took place—called "Summer is coming! Take Back our streets!" They called for mass arrests of "prostitutes, hoodlums, and panhandlers," which is coded language for queer kids of color and homeless people. FIERCE! organized a counter-rally to make our perspective clear to the residents, the politicians, the police, and the TV and print media who were swarming around this West Village scandal. Once we made our message clear and received coverage from every news station, we decided to separate ourselves from the RID rally and marched down Christopher Street to the Piers, crying out, "Whose streets! Our streets!", startling the West Village residents who were returning home from work. We then hung our signs on the fence that kept us off the Christopher Street pier, as a symbolic way to reclaim our space.

As part of reclaiming our space, we decided that it was time for us to hold an independent action, for us and by us. In order for this to be an event truly for the youth at the Piers, we needed to get input from youth. We held a huge meeting where about seventy to eighty queer youth came. They came from the Piers, the Neutral Zone, the Hetrick Martin Institute, and elsewhere. This meeting, along with many others, shaped the October 5 rally.

Our rally, which we called "Reclaim Our Space: a Festival of Resistance," began at Sheridan Square at the foot of Christopher Street. We gathered there with our signs, our dreams, and our demands. We set up a mike and youth spoke and read poems. We then marched up Christopher Street, declaring our self-empowerment, screaming our pains, and demanding justice. We held many different signs made by our members that expressed our demands: "You say police protection, we say police brutality" and " Where is the quality of life for the homeless youth of color in the Village?"

We gathered again at the corner of Christopher and West streets. There we sang, read poetry, and vented. This was our chance to fight against the Hudson River Park Trust, the residents, the city, and, of course, the police, who stood around us in intimidation. We celebrated our pride, our community, and our power. We played music, danced, and played card games. We were taking back the space that was being stolen from us. We chilled in the West Village, like any other day at the Piers. Yet we knew that this day was different, though of course the city and the police showed how much power they do have to control us by shutting down our rally. I remember when the police came and approached the tactical team and told us, "YOU HAVE TO GO NOW." The police were not open to reason or even listening to what we had to say.

Another one of our major events was the Sakia Gunn Memorial, which we held together with The Audre Lorde Project. Sakia Gunn was a young queer youth of color who found safety, fun, and community in the West Village and at the Piers. She was murdered on her way home to Jersey after a night at the Piers with her friends. This type of bias crime is committed against our community time and time again, and goes unnoticed by the rest of the world. There was a short news report on the TV, an article in the papers, and that was pretty much it. But Sakia Gunn fell victim to a bias crime, and she fell victim to the racism, classism, ageism, and homophobia of the media and of this city.

We gathered at Sheridan Square. We once again held our signs and made our voices heard; even the pouring rain, which fell relentlessly, could not stop us from marching to the Christopher Street Piers. When we got to the Piers, we held a memorial and candlelight vigil for Sakia Gunn. Friends of Sakia and other members of the community read poetry for her, sang, and cried for her. We brought Sakia back to the pier where she felt most safe, where she felt she could be herself.

FIERCE! not only empowers youth to create change in the world but also helps us to find our way in life. FIERCE! is a sanctuary from the oppression we face, for being of color, for being young, and for being queer. I would not be in the place I am these days if it wasn't for FIERCE! While the "mainstream" queer movement might be concentrating on marriage, we are concerned with more important things, like being able to hang out in the Village without getting harassed or arrested and getting the condoms, food, medical, mental health, housing, and jobs we need. We're fighting for our right to exist, now that's FIERCE!

DEALING DISCOURSE: DRUGS AND THE (RE)INVENTION OF RESISTANCE

ERIC STANLEY

DAYTIME TV AND THE DEATH OF DIFFERENCE

17, 18, 19, floor after floor, the elevator climbs through the glowing Boston night skyline. By the time we reach the penthouse floor, my palms are soaked, the lump in my throat makes it hard for me to breathe, and my knees are shaking. The elevator doors slide open, and we exit into the hall. I can't resist the temptation to drag my finger through the hotel insignia stamped into the freshly changed ashtray sand. The long hall empties into room 20-03, the destination we'd confirmed from a health-food store's pay phone hours earlier. I check for stairwells and second doors throughout the halls—making mental notes of each way in and, more important, each way out.

Billows of cigarette smoke push from the room, which is lit by the aura of the TV. It's too dark to register the number of people in the room. Once inside, we're checked for wires and forced through nervous small talk. Drug dealers are, surprisingly, some of the most boring people I know. The seductive notion of *New Jack City* more often than not gives way to the reality of middle-aged junkies or, even worse, suburban white kids "gone bad."

Matt and I take the chairs with our backs to the wall-sized Marriott windows, and Phillip sits on the edge of one of the beds. The cash is piled in the middle of the other bed for recounting and packaging. Trafficking money is almost as sketchy as the drugs; sixty thousand dollars in cash is harder to hide than a few sheets of LSD, or whatever it may be. A hundred pounds of mushrooms is a bit more complicated, but we would hide them in the false walls of the van and in compartments under the seats. This time, two other people had driven the van of mushrooms to the East Coast, and now we're retrieving the van and picking up the bag of cash. It's more or less a simple deal.

Someone flicks the light on, exposing three others in the room. There is a body flipping around on a third mattress. His glassy eyes, sweaty moans, and violent jerks speak in the language of heroin, a fluency I always try to escape. He must be trying to kick or something; all the junkies I know would grab a handful of cash from the pile lying on the bed and score dope before the first scratch of the arm.

The man counting the money looks a bit out of place—more like a bridge-and-tunnel Jersey club guy than a mushroom dealer, but then again I'm a seventeen-year-old straight-edge fag.

The guy is combining twenties into piles of a thousand dollars each. There are sixty of these stacks lined up across the bed. As Phillip recounts each stack, the third boy in the room nervously flips the channels. He's much younger than the other two—and cute, at least in comparison. His lips pull smoke from cigarette after cigarette, and he exhales through his teeth while ashing on the floor. *Go Rickie—Go Rickie—Go Rickie*—this familiar early to mid-nineties sound reminds me to breathe.

The rainbow flags adorning Rickie's set for the day pull me in deeper . . . gays. Rickie welcomes her guests to the show, "Gay Teens Speak Out." Each guest files across the stage and sits in a prearranged chair. Battles are waged between gay sons and homophobic parents, butch daughters and their ex-boyfriends, and fathers trying desperately to de-fag their cocksucking sons. The boy sitting across from me nervously comments on how "no one would choose that life so it must be genetic." This plea for salvation confirms my theories of his sexual desires.

"Why would anyone choose to be gay? It's such a hard life." He's talking more to himself than to us, crossing his legs in the other direction as ash hits the carpet.

The money is bundled and thrown into a green book bag we brought up with us. They offer us the room for the night, since it was rented for this meeting, but after only a few hours in Boston, California is calling us back. As we fling token good byes through the air, my Rickie is cut devastatingly short. What is to become of the gays?

EXILE

It was neither the rainbow-soaked economy of gay visibility that fed and clothed me, nor was it the Human Rights Campaign that protected me from being strung up on a Wyoming fence post. Selling drugs saved my life. I found my shelter where I could, usually under cars and in fields, and not inside the purple walls of LGBTIQ centers. Having dropped out of school by the age of fifteen, Gay Straight Alliances did me little good.

I want to challenge the ideology that the "gay community" is nonfiction. The violence of such an assumption has beaten me almost as bloody as the batons gripped by gay cops and has scarred me deeper than a childhood spent in the Confederate South. "Community" is a mirage used by those in power to secure their own places while also creating exploitable margins. But life in the margins has placed me in a culture of resistance and has inspired me to protect these same margins from co-optive destruction.

ASSIMILATION AND OTHER FORMS OF FASCISM

When *the love that dare not speak its name* started speaking out on *Rickie Lake*, I knew all hope for deviance within mainstream culture must be abandoned. This realization was not a longing for some kind of queer-inclusive representation on daytime television. It was, paradoxically, born of the reality that the sex I had always held onto as a safety net against the oppression of heterosexual culture was being sold and traded for a homonormative lithograph of the dominate culture I despised.

It was not then—nor is it now—simply my punk rock rebellion that refused assimilation. It was the material reality that assimilation is a systematic web of power that would have never let me in, even if I had chosen to try everything possible. Selling drugs was neither a pastime I engaged in with the hopes of gaining some kind of subcultural respect, nor was it simply a way for me to supplement the luxuries of a suburban adolescence. Those realities were only available in the two dimensions of the media.

Homelessness, though far from a glamorous existence, helped expose the ways capitalism and the gay "community" were co-conspirators in my death and the death of all remotely like me. The layers of dirt often covering my body seemed to help keep normalcy at bay, giving me a space to study its trappings and mechanisms.

I was lucky, but most homeless people are not so lucky. I lived in a social subculture that had access to large amounts of drugs and clients who could afford them. I had always been too scared to be involved; prison was a less desirable living situation than the concrete of a highway rest stop (my summer home). But I knew I did not want to "get a job and make something out of myself." I also had no realistic avenue for such a rags-to-riches story to unfold. Sixteen-year-old homeless queers are not exactly desirable job candidates within the boundaries of late capitalism. I had two options. The first was sex work, and the second was dealing drugs. I opted for the second.

I am not suggesting that either selling drugs or sex work are specifically outside of capitalism or intrinsically anti-assimilation. Yet there is a way in which both occupations operate outside the boundaries of normalcy and produce ways of knowing and ways of resisting that are not always visible. Selling drugs kept me fed and kept me from falling into the seductive tales of American *success*. For queers, people of color, and the poor, success under these terms means serving in the army of assimilation commanded by the white middle and ruling class.

Drug dealing is, essentially, like all other work, an exchange of goods or labor for money, which strengthens capitalism and its structures of power. Yet I use this story with the hope of evoking a hybrid place of creation/destruction, resistance, and revolution—all means necessary and necessarily imagined must be deployed.

BIOS

Ralowe T. Ampu, MD, is a black asshole who writes occasionally but mostly makes very pretentious and self-indulgent rap music. If you have access to a computer that can do the whole internet thing okay, then check it all out for free at www.ralowesconfusedsuburbanlaughter.com. He's also an activist or something.

Charlie Anders is a giant peach in the chocolate factory. Her writing has appeared in *ZYZZYVA*, Salon.com, the *SF Bay Guardian* and dozens of magazines and anthologies. She's the publisher of *other* magazine at www.othermag.org.

Marlon M. Bailey is a PhD candidate in the African Diaspora Studies Program with a designated emphasis in Women, Gender, and Sexuality, in the African American Studies Department at the University of California, Berkeley. He is also an ABD Dissertation Fellow in the Black Studies Department at University of California, Santa Barbara. Marlon's dissertation work is on Ballroom, a Black gay subculture in the U.S., and is tentatively titled "Queering African Diaspora: Ballroom Performance and Kinship as Diaspora Practice." His most recent publication is entitled "Who's Doing it Now: Conversations with Brain Freeman on the Politics of Black Gay Performance," in *The Color of Theatre: Race, Ethnicity and Contemporary Performance*. Marlon earned a BA in Theatre/ Speech Education from Olivet College, an MFA in Theatre Performance from West Virginia University, and an MA in African American Studies from UC Berkeley.

Richard E. Bump, aka REB, has been called "the grand-daddy of the queer 'zine scene." He has been publishing his queer-punk-politic-porn 'zine, *Fanorama*, since 1992. He also runs Fanorama Society which distros 'zines created by inmates. He is a photographer, prison activist, and Super-

8 filmmaker who has appeared in *RFD*, *Afterwords: Real Sex from Gay Men's Diaries,* and *Out In All Directions: The Almanac of Gay and Lesbian America.*

Rocko Bulldagger is living the good life in Brooklyn alongside three seriously hot, polyamorous sex radicals. All she ever thinks about is dirty gay stuff, politics, and philosophy. She wants to write a book about love but just keeps writing 'zines instead. Dr. Laura originally appeared in one of her 'zines. Rocko's beloved affiliations include the House of Freak, Queer as Fuck, Busty Fetish Girls, and the Bent Stiletto Social Club.

Patrick Califia is the author of *Public Sex: The Culture of Radical Sex*; *Speaking Sex to Power: The Politics of Queer Sex*; and *Sex Changes: The Politics of Transgenderism.* He was cranky long before being diagnosed with fibromyalgia.

Clint Catalyst is the southern-fried, sissified author of *Cottonmouth Kisses* (Manic D), a tale of crystal methamphetamania, cracked club culture, and people doing things they think they need to do to get things they think they want (and then discovering it's not what they wanted after all). His writing has appeared in *Instinct, Hustler, LA Weekly,* the *SF Bay Guardian, Surface,* and *Permission* magazines, among others. With Michelle Tea, he co-edited the anthology *Pills, Thrills, Chills and Heartache: Adventures in the First Person.* He accepts suitors on-line at www.clintcatalyst.com.

Simone Chess is a graduate student in English at the University of California, Santa Barbara. Committed to activism in the academy, she looks forward to a lifetime of locating radical queer politics and identities in British Renaissance poetry.

Andrea Maybelline Danger is a radical artist living in the San Francisco Bay Area. She has illustrated *Sink or Swim: A History of Sausal Creek, Urban Wilds,* and *Go Fuck Yourself: A Guide to Do-It-Yourself Sex Toys.* She is forever in the process of drawing everything—from antiwar posters to do-it-yourself diagrams. Annie is presently in the process of compiling a book of personal stories about trans people's relations to touch. She likes "banging on buckets."

Gina de Vries, age twenty, is a queer femme pervy activist from San Francisco. She is the coeditor of the forthcoming queer youth anthology *Becoming: Young Ideas on Gender, Sexuality, and Identity.* Her writings have appeared in *Curve* and *On Our Backs* magazines and in the anthology *Revolutionary Voices.* Gina is a founding member of Come in Peace, a radical collective of artists and activists that aims to create feminist, antiracist, antipoverty, queer-positive, trans-positive, sex-positive, and antiwar media and protest. She goes to school on the East Coast, where she spends her time reading postmodern theory, dying her hair purple, drinking too much coffee, watching Canadian teen television, and missing the Bay Area.

Jennifer Flynn is a community organizer with the NYC AIDS Housing Network, a membership-led, community organizing and advocacy group committed to fighting for the rights of homeless people living with HIV/AIDS. She lives in Brooklyn, NY.

Jesse Heiwa is a queer social justice organizer. S/he also is a cofounder of OutFM, a multicultural, progressive queer radio program which airs on WBAI, listener-sponsored radio in NYC (www.outfm.org), and is an editor/photographer for *Color Life: Queer People Of Color* magazine. S/he was on the board of the Audre Lorde Project, a queer people of color organizing center, and in ACT UP NY. S/he is a co-founder of QFREJ—to be on its listserve, send an e-mail to: QueersForRacialAndEconomicJustice-subscribe@yahoogroups.com. S/he was one of the organizers of Queeruption in NYC and a participant in PRISM: Queer People Of Color organizing conference, among other things. E-mail hir at monacong@yahoo.com.

Jim Hubbard has been making films since 1974. Among his nineteen films are *Elegy in the Streets* (1989), *Two Marches* (1991), *The Dance* (1992), and *Memento Mori* (1995). His film *Memento Mori* won the Ursula for Best Short Film at the Hamburg Lesbian & Gay Film Festival in 1995. He is a cofounder and president of MIX, the New York Lesbian and Gay Experimental Film/Video Festival. Under the auspices of the Estate Project for Artists with AIDS, he created the Royal S. Marks AIDS Activist Video Collection at the New York Public Library. He curated the series *Fever in the Archive: AIDS Activist Videotapes from the Royal S. Marks Collection* for the

Guggenheim Museum in New York. He lives with Nelson Gonzalez, his lover of twenty-one year, in New York.

Priyank Jindal is a transgendered desi doing community-based organizing with youth of color in South Philly around issues of immigrants rights.

Stephen Kent Jusick has been curating experimental film since 1989 and making films since 1992. His ongoing and varied relationship with the MIX Festival began in 1989. In 1995, he founded Fever Films to distribute experimental film and video for public exhibition. Jusick has curated programs and exhibited at numerous venues, including Anthology Film Archives, the Baltimore Museum of Art, Princeton University, the Blinding Light!, MIX, the SF Lesbian & Gay Film Festival, I.C. Guys, dumba, and Queeruption. Since January 2001, his weekly CineSalon in New York City has attracted a hard-core audience of artists, dropouts, activists, drag queens, sex workers, radicals, and the occasional celebrity.

Alison Kafer is a restroom revolutionary, queer disability activist, and writer based in Southern California. Her previous work on bathroom politics has appeared in *That Takes Ovaries* and several feminist and queer 'zines. She is a PhD candidate in Women's Studies and Religion at Claremont Graduate University.

Priya Kandaswamy is a PhD candidate in Ethnic Studies at the University of California, Berkeley. She is currently working on her dissertation, which examines the intersections of race and gender in the U.S. welfare state's efforts to regulate sexuality, control labor, and police the boundaries of citizenship. Priya currently resides in Oakland, California, where she is exploring the radical possibilities of urban vegetable gardening.

josina manu maltzman, aka jo "the gross"ina voltina, lives in Philly. This essay is the result and continuance of many a kitchen table *shmues. dos gelekhter un der tselokhes iz bay mir der tokh in lebn . . . nu, un amol shnepsele trinkn mit fraynd. l'chaim intifada!*

Reginald Lamar is an artist, musician, writer, and performer living in San Francisco. In 2003, Lamar's rock band, Mutilated Mannequins, released the CD *Lordship and Bondage*, a glam industrial metal concept album exploring the life and death of a Negro dandy trying to live the unlivable life in America. Mutilated Mannequins' next disc, *Plantation Fantasy*, will be released in fall 2004 and goes to the deepest darkest places of sex and race in America. Lamar has stated that "it's an album about exploitation and dehumanization and the fucked up contracts and roles that people willingly step into. It's some really sexy shit."

Eli seMbessakwini used to be called Shorona. She's an Australian heaps-queer anarchist living in San Francisco (as best she can). She's made and is making videos (amongst other things), including "Intersex Exposition: Full Monty" and "Born Queer: Dear Doctors." Please see the website at www.geocities.com/greenpiratequeen, and contact her about these works at greenpiratequeen@yahoo.ca. Some of the kinds of resistance to capitalism she undertakes cannot be printed here (too naughty).

Tommi Avicolli Mecca is a longtime queer antiwar social justice activist and writer of Southern Italian American origin living in San Francisco. He is author of *Between Little Rock and a Hard Place* (1993) and *Hey Paesan: Writing by Italian American Lesbians and Gay Men* (1999).

Michelle O'Brien is a queer, genderqueer, and transsexual woman living in Philadelphia. As a writer, activist, and artist, she fights for social justice and health care with trans and genderqueer people. Coming out of anarchist political movements against imperialist war, capitalism, environmental decimation, and white supremacy, she tries to connect diverse issues and communities. She works as a social worker for trans people living with HIV. She welcomes contacts and can be reached by email at michelle@deadletter.org.uk.

OliveLucy is a writer, sex worker, sound artist, and phlebotomist/HIV counselor. Ze lives in Oakland, California.

Carol Queen got a PhD in sexology so she could say, "That's *Dr.* Queen, Mr. Helms." She's the author or editor of many books, including *The Leather Daddy and the Femme*, *Real Live Nude Girl: Stories of Sex-Positive Culture*, and (with Lawrence Schimel) *PoMoSexuals*. Visit her at www.carolqueen.com. By the way, her understanding of cultural politics is so determinedly nonbinary that she has a doctor of divinity in the Universal Life Church, and she recently (with her partner Robert) performed a queer marriage ceremony. Whatever makes you happy. Just think it through first, will you?

Jessi Quizar is a graduate student in Sociology at the University of California, Santa Barbara. Her areas of research are race, gender, and globalization, and her current project focuses on sex workers and activists in the Dominican Republic. She is a member of PISSAR and GenderQueerSB.

Rhani Remedes has been taking no shit since the day she learned how to hold a hot dog. She is the coauthor of the *S.C.U.B. (the Society for Cutting Up Boxes) Manifesto* and is published in *Breaking the Gender Mold* (Manic D Press). Her 'zine, *Wet Dreams on Fur Coats*, is hot and strange. She plays bass and vocal chords in the band Veronica Lipgloss and the Evil Eyes. Contact her at v_lipgloss@hotmail.com.

Mattie Udora Richardson is a writer and activist. Her work has appeared in a variety of anthologies, including *Every Woman I've Ever Loved: Lesbian Writers on Their Mothers*, *Does Your Mama Know: Black Lesbian Coming Out Stories*, *Sisterfire Black Womanist Fiction and Poetry,* and *This Is What Lesbian Looks Like: Dyke Activists Take on the 21st Century*. She is currently a PhD candidate at UC Berkeley in the African Diaspora Studies Program.

Justin Rosado is the Lead Organizer of FIERCE!, an NYC-based, revolutionary community organization dedicated to building power in communities of trans and queer youth of color. Justin is a long-time pier kid, a former member and outreach worker for the Neutral Zone, a drop-in center for lesbian, gay, bi, and transgender homeless and street youth in NYC. Justin was one of the initiators of one of FIERCE!'s first projects, the creation of the youth-produced documentary

Fenced Out. Fenced Out was created as a response to the displacement of LGBT youth of color in the West Village and the Christopher Street piers and a call to action to *save our space!*

SalMonella is a loosely defined anarchist who likes to drink tea from pink teacups. He also likes crusty boys in glitter pants, Oakland parks by moonlight, and garbage.

Stephanie Schroeder works as a publicist on Wall Street by day; by night, she hides away in Brooklyn, New York, to love and write with her lover and muse, Tina, and their two pooches, Bacchus and Meka. Stephanie has written for Technodyke.com, Proudparenting.com, PaintedLadyPress.com, was a reviewer for *Erotic New York: The Best Sex in the City*, and has published short fiction in *Hot & Bothered 3: Short, Short Fiction on Lesbian Desire*, as well as *Hot & Bothered 4*. Stephanie also has short fiction forthcoming in *Up All Night: Adventures in Lesbian Sex, Delicate Friction, Naughty Stories From A to Z: Volume 3*, and *Burned Into Memory: Stories of Lesbian Desire*.

Sarah Schulman was born in NYC in 1958. Novels: *Shimmer, Rat Bohemia, Empathy, People in Trouble, After Delores, Girls, Visions, and Everything,* and *The Sophie Horowitz Story.* Nonfiction: *My American History: Lesbian and Gay Life During the Reagan/Bush Years* and *Stagestruck: Theater AIDS and the Marketing of Gay America.* Plays: *Carson McCullers* (Playwrights Horizons) and *The Burning Deck* (La Jolla Playhouse). Citizenship: CARASA, ACT UP, Lesbian Avengers, Irish Lesbian and Gay Organization, Mix, and ACT UP Oral History Project. Awards: Guggenheim (playwrighting), Fullbright (Judaic Studies), Revson Fellow for the Future of New York, Stonewall Award for Improving the Lives of Lesbians and Gays in the United States, 2 NY Foundation for the Arts Fiction Awards, Two American Library Association Book Awards (fiction and nonfiction), Residencies at Yaddo and MacDowell, and Finalist for the Prix de Rome.

By day, **Benjamin Shepard** works in syringe exchange in the "Downtown Bronx," formerly known as the "South Bronx." By night, he is involved in campaigns to keep New York City from becoming a shopping mall. He is the author/coeditor of two books: *White Nights and Ascending Shadows: An Oral History of the San Francisco AIDS Epidemic* (Cassell, 1997) and *From ACT UP to the WTO:*

Urban Protest and Community Building in the Era of Globalization (Verso, 2002). His writing has appeared in several anthologies, including *The Encyclopedia of Social Movements* (Sharpe, 2004), *Democracy's Moment: Renewing Democracy for the 21st Century,* and *Teamsters and Turtles: Leftist Movements Today and Tomorrow* (both 2002, Roman and Littlefield).

Eustacia Smith is the Program Director for West Side Federation Senior and Supportive Housing's Ben Michalski Residence, a supportive housing residence for formerly homeless people living with AIDS. Staci is also a core member of Health GAP, which is fighting for access to life-saving medications in all countries. She lives in Brooklyn, NY.

Dean Spade is a trans attorney and activist, and founder of the Sylvia Rivera Law Project (srlp.org), a law collective serving low-income trans, intersex and gender variant people. Dean is also co-editor of the online journal www.makezine.org.

Eric Stanley is a high school dropout and Cultural Studies Ph.D. student at the University of California, Davis. Currently working with Gay Shame, he considers activism and vegan baking his most important work.

Cleo Woelfle-Erskine is the editor of *Urban Wilds: Gardeners' Stories of the Struggle for Land and Justice* (water/under/ground, 2003) and the forthcoming *Graywater Guerrillas' Guide to Water*. A cowboy naturalist and founding member of the infamous Pollinators crew and the Graywater Guerrillas, he hopes to build and inhabit a houseboat on Oakland's San Leandro Creek in the near future.

NOTES

QUEER PARENTS

1. Joan Nestle, *A Restricted Country* (Ithaca, New York: Firebrand Books, 1987).

SYLVIA AND SYLVIA'S CHILDREN

1. *Village Voice.* Summer Guide, May 14–20, 2003.
2. The phenomena is by no means unique to New York. An observer in San Francisco recently noted: "It is a bitter reality that the Castro's historic climate of political resistance has given way to a Homosexual Gentry who see homeless queer youth as an irritant on their way home from Pottery Barn" (see Read, 2003).
3. Lesbian Feminist Liberation (LFL) was formed in 1973 after seceding from the Gay Activist Alliance Lesbian Liberation Committee (Marotta, 1981: 10). For LFL, trans folks, "transvestites" as they were then referred, "were simply another breed of men determined to keep women down by telling them how they should look and act" (p.195).
4. Douglas Crimp (2002, p.15) notes that AIDS has been and continues to be used as justification as "previously abandoned or peripheral neighborhoods that were home to gay sexual culture were reappropriated and gentrified by the real estate industry, thus making them inhospitable to the uses we'd invented for them."
5. There is no evidence to confirm that HIV is transmitted any more frequently in public sex venues than at home between couples who forgo condom use (see Crimp, 2002).

CALLING ALL RESTROOM REVOLUTIONARIES!

1. We want to begin with an acknowledgment that we borrowed the idea for our name from PISSR (People in Search of Safe Restrooms), a San Francisco-based organization affiliated with the Transgender Law Center. The "A" in our name—for accessible—stems from our commitment to disability rights and access and our belief, which we detail below, that bathroom politics require coalition politics. As our name indicates, our work is very closely related to that of PISSR's, and we are deeply appreciative of their work in the Bay Area.

2. When we began explaining our work with PISSAR to new people, one of the most common concerns that we heard was about "safety." People worried about multistall bathrooms in particular, but in general they conjured images of (nondisabled male) lurkers in our radical restrooms, imagining homophobes, transphobes, and ableists waiting by the door for easy targets. Our challenge, then, is to acknowledge these fears, but pursue our project nonetheless. We know that no space can be guaranteed safe. Making a space gender-neutral doesn't completely remove the threat of violence. But we maintain that it also does not lead to new or greater threats than already exist. Instead, accessible, gender-neutral, well-marked restrooms are likely to increase one's comfort level. Safe and accessible bathrooms can reduce the "I don't belong here" factor. They allow for people to use the restroom easily, without discomfort or fear of being made into a spectacle. Safe and accessible restrooms probably also reduce the likelihood of individuals serving as gender police, harassing folks who they see as using the 'wrong' restroom.

3. For years, all the tampon/pad machines on campus had been stocked by a local vendor; when the vendor retired a few years ago, the campus administration neglected to replace them, leaving all the machines empty. Aunt Flo and the Plug Patrol decided to fill the gap, using volunteers to provide products for all the menstruating folks at UCSB. They supported PISSAR from the beginning, unanimously voting to give us the money we needed to purchase our bathroom monitoring tools: measuring tapes, gloves, uniforms, and so forth.

4. The harassment homeless folks often experience around bathroom use is a new area of concern for PISSAR. We began as a campus organization, a position that restricted our attention to campus bathrooms, which, at least at UCSB, do not see a lot of homeless activity. As we

grow, we hope to turn our focus to more community-wide bathroom issues, including the problems faced by many homeless folks.

5. There are some exceptions to this silence, perhaps most notably Laud Humphreys's scholarship on public sex. Laud Humphreys, *Tearoom Trade: Impersonal Sex in Public Places* (Chicago: Aldine, 1975). For a more recent examination of both Humphreys' work and the issue of public sex, see William L. Leap, ed., *Public Sex/Gay Space* (New York: Columbia University, 1999).

6. Many of us involved in work with PISSAR are also members of GenderQueerSB, a campus and community group of genderqueer and trans folk and their lovers and allies. In that forum, like many queer forums, we struggle to keep our conversations in our bodies. Mostly academics, we gravitate toward analytic comments about general trends and broad topics. We skirt specifics, talking about "sex," but not about the actual mechanics. We avoid risky danger zones like dealing with sexual violation and its toll on our flesh and minds—even in a group specifically designated as safe and open, in a group filled with people whose bodies are constantly in negotiation and scrutiny as they move through the world.

A TRAGIC LOVE STORY

1. *Low*, Kathy Acker and Nayland Blake.

THE POLLINATORS' TOOLBOX

1. Hard Hats (costumes)—to protect us from falling objects (like police batons) and surveillance cameras and to protect our messages from the public's ideas about what "Black-Clad Anarchists" do.

2. Megaphone (radio and printed media projects)—to break through the din of mass media voices and spread vital information across distance and social barriers.

3. Blueprints (freeschool)—to lay out the plans for new structures we have yet to build.

4. Ratchet (gender trainings)—to torque misguided cultural ideals into supportive, fluid guidelines geared toward community and self-expression.

5. Welding Torch (billboard alterations)—to cut into seemingly-impenetrable media and refashion it for subversive uses

6. Trowel (teaching in the straight world)—to transplant the skills and desires of our fertile sub-culture into the barren fields of the mainstream world.

7. Pipe Wrench (DIY eco-workshops)—to twist the flow of the waste stream away from destruction and towards sustainability.

8. Machine Shop (teaching youth)—to provide the means to negotiate all the projects, structures, and repairs we have yet to encounter.

9. Sawzall (transforming language)—to cut into social convention, however roughly, in order to make space for our kind when and where we need it.

10. Hammer (trainings and workshops within the community)—to build the basic structures which communities of resistance need to be able to survive the struggles they live out.

11. "To Those Born Later," *Poems,* Berthold Brecht, Edited by Willett, Manheim and Fried (Methuen 1979).

ACKNOWLEDGMENTS

Special thanks to the brilliant, beautiful, and bodacious Ralowe T. Ampu for giving so generously of her time, energy, and inspiration in order to help me finish this project.

For valuable editorial feedback and suggestions: Reginald Lamar, Kirk Read, and Eric Stanley.

To Steve Zeeland for encouraging me to do the first book—look at what's happened to me!

To Gay Shame for making San Francisco bearable.

To everyone who has helped shape, inspire, transform, and challenge my politics over the years—I wouldn't be alive without you.

To my family of choice—you know who you are.

Mattilda, a.k.a. Matt Bernstein Sycamore is a prancer, a romancer, and a fugitive. She's still look-ing for the answer. Mattilda is the author of a novel, *Pulling Taffy* (Suspect Thoughts, 2003) and the editor of *Dangerous Families: Queer Writing on Surviving* (Haworth, 2004) and *Tricks and Treats: Sex Workers Write About Their Clients* (Haworth, 2000). Mattilda is an instigator of Gay Shame: A Virus in the System, a radical queer activist group that fights the monster of assimilation. Visit www.mattbernsteinsycamore.com.